Negotiating Childhood

A Volume in the Series
CHILDHOODS: INTERDISCIPLINARY PERSPECTIVES ON
CHILDREN AND YOUTH

Edited by
Karen Sánchez-Eppler and Rachel Conrad

Negotiating Childhood

FRENCH COLONIALISM AND
AFRICAN CHILDREN IN
SENEGAL, 1848–1940

KELLY M. DUKE BRYANT

University of Massachusetts Press
AMHERST AND BOSTON

Copyright © 2026 by University of Massachusetts Press
All rights reserved
Printed in the United States of America

ISBN 978-1-62534-921-7 (paper); 922-4 (hardcover)

Designed by Deste Relyea
Set in Adobe Jenson Pro and Mr. Eaves
Printed and bound by Books International, Inc.

Cover design by adam b. bohannon
Cover cover photo by MD, An early twentieth-century postcard: *Scene from daily life in Dakar, Senegal, "Children on a holiday."* Via archives of senegal-online.com.

Library of Congress Cataloging-in-Publication Data
A catalog record for this book is available from the Library of Congress.

British Library Cataloguing-in-Publication Data
A catalog record for this book is available from the British Library.

Portions of chapter 1 were published in a previous form in "Changing Childhood: 'Liberated Minors,' Guardianship, and the Colonial State in Senegal, 1895–1911," *Journal of African History* 60, no. 2 (2019): 209–28.

Portions of chapter 1 were published in a previous form in "Runaways, Dutiful Daughters, and Brides: Family Strategies of Formerly Enslaved Girls in Senegal, 1895–1911," *Women, Gender, and Families of Color* 7, no. 1 (2019): 37–55.

The authorized representative in the EU for product safety and compliance is Mare-Nostrum Group.
Email: gpsr@mare-nostrum.co.uk
Physical address: Mare-Nostrum Group B.V., Mauritskade 21D,
1091 GC Amsterdam, The Netherlands

FOR MATTHEW, ISABEL, OWEN, AND AVA

Contents

List of Illustrations
ix

Acknowledgments
xi

INTRODUCTION
Childhood, Child "Protection," and the Colonial State in Senegal
1

CHAPTER 1
The Meeting Room
Guardianship and Childhood in Post-Emancipation Senegal
19

CHAPTER 2
The Reformatory
Penitentiaries for the Young and the Idea of Childhood in Senegal, 1888–1940
41

CHAPTER 3
The School
School Discipline and the Ideal African Child
70

CHAPTER 4
The Street
Public Spaces and Public Childhood
93

CHAPTER 5
The Body
Hygiene, Medicine, and Children's Health
117

CHAPTER 6
The Document
Chronological Age and African Childhood in Colonial Senegal
139

CONCLUSION
159

Select Bibliography of Archival Sources and Serial Publications
163

Notes
167

Index
207

Illustrations

Map of Colonial Senegal
17

TABLE 1. Liberated Minors in Saint-Louis, Senegal, 1895–1911
29

TABLE 2. Minor Detainees in Senegal's Reformatories, 1888–1938
50

TABLE 3. Ages of Detainees
51

TABLE 4. Sentence Lengths of Detainees
52

Acknowledgments

It seems fitting, in a book about the history of childhood, to begin by acknowledging the many ways my own three children have shaped, and have been shaped by, this book. My oldest child, now a teenager, was in preschool when I started working on this research in earnest, and it has been part of our family life for as far back as she and her younger siblings can remember. While it is true that being their mom has meant the book took longer to write than I had hoped, it is also true that experiencing the world through their eyes and talking to them about some of my sources shaped the kinds of historical questions I asked. Plus, time spent with these amazing kids and with my husband, Matthew Bryant, made the process much more fun!

Balancing an academic career with motherhood is not easy, and frankly it would not have been possible without help from many wonderful caregivers, teachers, relatives, and friends. I am especially grateful to my parents, Kerry and Becky Duke, and to my mother-in-law, Beth Bryant, who took turns helping with childcare so I could take research trips to Senegal or France or travel to conferences. I would also like to thank Marielle Salvatore, who provided excellent care in our home during the COVID-19 pandemic, when I was not yet ready to risk sending the kids to day- and afterschool care. And to everyone else who has loved my kids, taught them, cared for them, given them rides . . . thank you. You have made a bigger difference than you know.

Although my motherhood experiences in a way cemented my decision to write this book, my interest in the history of childhood in Senegal grew out of research I did for my first book, on the history of colonial schooling there. But it was, I think, my semester as a teaching assistant for a course on children and adversity in African history, taught by my late PhD advisor, Pier Larson, that first encouraged me to think in a sustained way about children as historical actors. And it was a conversation with Cati Coe at a conference way back in

2017 that gave me the push I needed to move things forward. When I told Cati about my sources and the various conference papers I had already written, she said, "Well, that's your next book, don't you think?" I received additional encouragement at an early stage from my Rowan colleague, Melissa Klapper, who shares an interest in the history of childhood, and from Corinne Field and LaKisha Michelle Simmons, who invited me first to participate in their incredibly productive workshop on the Global History of Black Girlhood and then to contribute to a special issue on a similar theme.

Like all works of history, this book could not have been written without the expertise and interest of numerous archivists and librarians. Thank you to the wonderful staff at the Archives Nationales du Sénégal in Dakar, where I have spent countless hours, for suggesting fruitful avenues of inquiry, bringing out the maximum number of files allowed each day, and generally creating a friendly and pleasant research environment. I am especially grateful for support from Fatoumata Cisse Diarra, former directrice of the archives, and from Sokhna Astou Seck Diouf, archive curator. This book also relies on material held at the Institut Fondamental d'Afrique Noire, and I am grateful for this institution and its excellent staff. In France, I benefited from the hard work and expertise of librarians and archivists at several institutions: the Bibliothèque Nationale de France (Paris), the Archives Nationales d'Outre-Mer (Aix-en-Provence), and the Archives Générales de la Congrégation du Saint-Esprit (Chevilly-Larue). The Congrégation du Saint-Esprit archive is a particularly lovely place to work, in no small part due to the interest, knowledge, and consideration of its archivists. Thanks to the late Père Gérard Vieira and to Martin Dejonge for making my research trips here so productive and pleasant.

Over the years, my book has benefited from the engagement of many colleagues who took time to read one or more chapters. Many thanks to Cheikh Babou, Owen White, and Matthew Swagler who each commented on a chapter, and to Corrie Decker and Sarah Duff who provided extensive feedback on the full manuscript. I am incredibly grateful to belong to a supportive department and college with a culture of sharing works in progress, and I want to acknowledge the generosity of Rowan colleagues who read and commented on early drafts of several chapters. These colleagues include Nawal Ammar, Corinne Blake, Emily Blanck, Bill Carrigan, Mikkel Dack, Josh Gedacht, Stephen Hague, Jim Heinzen, Jennifer Janofsky, Melissa Klapper, Janet Lindman, Jessica Mack, Jody Russell Manning, Lawrence Markowitz, Glenn McDorman, Scott

Morschauser, Chanelle Rose, Seran Schug, Debbie Sharnak, Q. Edward Wang, and Joy Wiltenburg. A special thank you to Zach Christman, who recruited one of his GIS students to make a map for the book, and thanks to Raven Vijayakumar for such a beautiful result.

Enriching conversations and encouragement from many fellow scholars also contributed to this book. These colleagues include Richard Roberts, Jessica Reuther, Elizabeth Foster, Rachel Petrocelli, Kalala Ngalamulume, Sarah Zimmerman, Dior Konaté, Emily Burrill, Abosede George, Emily Marker, Abigail Warchol, Anaïs Fuart, Gregory Valdespino, Ruth Ginio, and Martin Klein. I am forever grateful to Liz, Dior, Abbey, and Richard for generously sharing copies of key archival material that I would have otherwise been unable to access. I greatly appreciate Emily Marker, who invited me to share a paper, which became part of chapter 2, at the Rutgers University–Camden Lees Seminar, and I want to thank Cori Field and Nick Syrett, whose invitation to participate in their AHA seminar, "Chronological Age: Nation and Empire," gave me the opportunity to work through ideas that I took up in chapter 6. I have long recognized that choosing strong titles is perhaps my biggest challenge in writing, so I was particularly pleased to follow title suggestions made by Stephen Hague, Corrie Decker, and my wonderful editor, Matt Becker.

Matt and his team at the University of Massachusetts Press did much more than assist with titles, of course, and I am so grateful for all that they have done to make this a better book and to bring it to publication. I cannot imagine a smoother process or a more supportive team. External reviewers provided constructive feedback, thoughtful questions, and encouragement. And the production team has created a truly inviting book. Thank you.

I appreciate my institution, which has supported me in many ways, and which is a great place to work. Travel funding from Rowan University made it possible for me to present various stages of research at conferences and to return to the archives for brief periods. I could not have completed the book without the generous subvention and sabbatical leave I received in 2023–24.

Finally, I want to include a few personal notes of thanks. My long friendship with the Kandji family makes my time in Dakar so pleasant. To Mamadou Kandji and Fatou Diouf Kandji, thank you for providing such a wonderful home away from home. To Badou, Cheikh, Bass, Xuba, and Aïssatou, thanks for your friendship and support. In New Jersey, I appreciate the care and support I have received from dear friends Robbie and Julie Joseph and Jeff and Dawn Hiatt, and their children. Thanks for believing in me and for listening with so much patience as I talked (probably for far too long) about this project. And finally, though I began these acknowledgments with them, I would like to thank my children and my husband, who have dealt beautifully with my divided attention, long work hours, and occasional travel, and who make life so much better. This book is for them.

INTRODUCTION

Childhood, Child "Protection," and the Colonial State in Senegal

In 1931, Alioune Diop, a young teacher in Senegal, published an article entitled "History of a Black Pupil (by Himself)," in French West Africa's education newsletter. In his article, he sketched a childhood experience anchored in what we might call "traditional" practices but also profoundly shaped by the French colonial presence. Born in Saint-Louis, the colonial capital, in 1910 to Muslim Wolof parents, Diop, like other children, spent his early years in the care of his mother. Like other boys, he started at Qur'an school at age five, learning to recite the Qur'an under the strict supervision of a *marabout* (Islamic teacher). Although most boys stayed in Qur'an school until, by Diop's estimate, age eleven or twelve, Diop left at ten to attend the colonial regional school upriver in Dagana, where his uncle worked as director. A strong student, Diop was the only one from his school to qualify for continued study at the Lycée Faidherbe in Saint-Louis, where he began as a boarder in 1922 and eventually earned a certificate of secondary study, picking up some European habits along the way. Work for a commercial firm in Saint-Louis during school breaks beginning in 1926 kept him in touch with young people who did not attend school, though he admitted to feeling different from others in his society and not wanting to spend time with other employees outside of work. He credited schooling with expanding his worldview, noting that the final year's curriculum taught him to "love all men like brothers [and to] abandon the idea of tradition for that of progress." Because of his French schooling, he wrote, he "successively condemned slavery, *griots* [casted oral historians and praise singers], the uncleanliness of the home, beliefs that are contrary to hygiene, the method of instruction of the marabouts, etc."[1]

Diop's account could be taken as evidence of the impacts of colonial schooling on an individual African, of the cultural alienation or doubleness that schooling could produce, or of one young man's strategic efforts to navigate the changed circumstances and new opportunities of colonial Senegal. Indeed, the narrative undoubtedly bears the imprint of the *Bulletin de l'enseignement de l'Afrique Occidentale Française*, the publication founded in 1913 by Inspector of Education Georges Hardy to promote regular pedagogical discussions and share information among teachers in French colonial schools. Diop surely knew that his colleagues, some of whom were French nationals, and his superiors would read his account, and this may have led him to exaggerate praise of French education and his assessment of its impact on him.[2] But I would like to set aside the more obvious questions about the impacts of colonial schooling and to consider instead what this text might reveal about African childhood under French colonial rule. It is highly significant, I think, that Diop not only described his academic achievements but also stated unequivocally that he accepted French moral positions (for example, by critiquing slavery and *griots*), embraced French approaches to health and hygiene, and disliked certain aspects of Muslim education. These were all issues of concern to French officials, who had attempted—for decades by the time Diop was writing—to rework African childhood through child-focused institutions, policies, and interventions that came, by the 1920s, to be glossed under the rubric of "child protection" or child welfare. It is also significant that Diop made Wolof childhood legible to French readers by translating its stages and transition points into chronological ages. By mentioning his birthdate, notable since most African births went unrecorded at this time, he revealed an awareness of the growing importance of documented identities in the colonial context. Thus, stressing his adherence to French notions of discipline, morality, education, and hygiene, Diop highlighted his successes not only as a former pupil but also as a former "protected" child, and he acknowledged French goals of legibility by including ages and dates in his account.[3]

Child protection took on crucial importance in the rhetoric and ideology of French colonialism in West Africa during the 1920s and 1930s. It generated considerable correspondence, as authorities discussed how to combat infant and child mortality, increase school enrollment, regulate child labor, and handle court cases involving minors, or responded to interventions from the Colonial Ministry on these topics.[4] This preoccupation on the ground reflected increasing emphasis on social welfare in France and growing international concern with child welfare. Indeed, not long after Paris hosted a major international conference on child welfare in July 1933, the Colonial Ministry fielded an inquiry from the League of Nations Committee on Child Welfare about child-protection initiatives in the French Empire. It was in response to the ministry's request for a report on this subject that Governor General Jules Brévié offered a comprehensive overview of initiatives targeted at children in French West Africa, emphasizing the areas of health and hygiene, education and moral reform, other forms of assistance, and improved documentation—areas that correspond roughly to Alioune Diop's description of his changed worldview.[5] Even if investment of human and financial capital was uneven or, as Barbara Cooper has found for Niger and much of the Sahel, negligible, child-protection policies had a significant impact on some Africans' experiences of childhood in Senegal, and more broadly, they shaped ideas and norms associated with African childhood.[6]

Brévié's report also—and crucially—described the initiatives of the 1930s as the outgrowth of a long history of benevolent colonialism that, he asserted, had "always focused on protecting childhood" and improving people's lives.[7] Early on, military men and missionaries cared for African children by offering "medical care," supplying "provisions and medicines," vaccinating, and helping raise racially mixed (*métis*) children in group homes. Eventually, the administration took charge, scaling up health infrastructure and vaccinations, bringing health and hygiene measures into schools, and taking other actions to promote child welfare.[8] His was a narrative of progress viewed through rose-colored glasses, which left no space for Africans to challenge, negotiate, or even react. Yet Brévié's invocation of history invites us to consider the false starts and failures—in addition to what Brévié would have seen as successes—in the history of child welfare in French West Africa. This report's silence about African reactions and perspectives prompts us to ask how African children and their families responded to colonial concerns with their health, morality, and education, and to the interventions these concerns produced during the preceding decades. Together, Diop's personal narrative and Governor General Brévié's report raise important questions about the impact of French interventions on African childhood, the ways Africans shaped, challenged, or—as Diop appears to have done—accepted them, and what all this meant for the category of "child" itself.

These are the questions taken up in this book, which explores how colonial disciplinary initiatives and spaces, along with their associated recordkeeping, affected African childhood in Senegal from 1848 to 1940. As the oldest French colony in Africa and, from 1895, the capital of French West Africa, Senegal offers a particularly illuminating case study of French interventions into African childhood, since policies developed and tried here often served as models for policies implemented elsewhere in the federation. The chronology adopted in the book is also revealing because it highlights how experiences and understandings of childhood in the nineteenth century prepared the way for the more fully developed notions of child protection that emerged in the 1920s and 1930s.

Focusing on places where children encountered French discipline and surveillance—wardship courts, public streets, schools, juvenile reformatories, and medical spaces—and showing how officials worked to determine and document children's chronological ages, the book makes two linked arguments. First, colonial efforts to impose order on African childhoods had a significant and lasting impact but one that fell far short of French goals. Despite limits to budgets and personnel, French interventions ultimately had some success in mapping the category of "child" onto specific chronological ages, disciplining children's bodies with new ideas about hygiene and vaccinations, and using schools and other institutions to disseminate understandings of childhood marked by race, gender, and political status.[9] Officials implementing these interventions kept records—with varying frequency and levels of detail—simultaneously indexing *and* contributing to changing understandings of childhood. French habits of recordkeeping began to naturalize both the categories they tracked and the very notion that childhood should be documented. Second, the book argues that as the state developed policies for the "protection" of African children in the early twentieth century, designed, on the one hand, to ensure the future of colonialism in the region by training loyal and productive colonial subjects, and on the other, to portray colonialism as a "humanitarian" enterprise, state power came increasingly to depend on African children's cooperation. Yet cooperation was never guaranteed, and children sometimes foiled French plans. Overall, the book contends that children and the policies meant to "protect" them undergirded colonial power in Senegal and beyond; that colonial discipline and surveillance prompted new ways of thinking about, experiencing, and documenting childhood; and that African children contributed significantly to these processes, the legacies of which are still felt today.

(Re)Defining Childhood in Colonial Senegal

A central premise of this book is that French colonialism not only impacted the lives of the individual children who passed through its institutions by, for example, attending school, appearing before a court, or visiting a doctor, but that over the longue durée, it also prompted a reworking of childhood norms and of the very definitions of childhood. Scholars have long recognized that childhood is culturally constructed, that its meanings vary across time and place, and that states have taken an interest in establishing a clear line between childhood and adulthood.[10] Recently, historians of childhood in Africa have begun to pay particular attention to the ways childhood changed during the colonial period due in part to state intervention, though they also show that the idea of "childhood" remained fluid and variable despite state efforts to control it.[11] In this book, I move the scholarship forward by contributing a study of a French colony to a body of work that largely focuses on British colonial spaces, by showing how children themselves influenced state initiatives, and by offering a sustained analysis of colonial efforts to make African children more legible by ascribing and documenting chronological age. This case study brings to light how, compared to British colonial Africa, colonial childhood in Senegal developed over a much longer period, due at least in part to the particularities of the nineteenth-century French civilizing mission, which relied on colonial schooling to promote the dissemination of French language, culture, and morality.[12] Child-focused policies of the twentieth century built on, but also departed from, this earlier history, and my study historicizes this process.

Chronological age is, as historians Corinne T. Field and Nicholas L. Syrett contend, both a "vector of power" that modern states have used as an ostensibly neutral determinant of access to certain rights, benefits, and obligations, and a tool that could facilitate individuals' claims on the state, especially in the era before vital records were well maintained. Indeed, absent readily available identity documents and birthdates, chronological age was a matter of negotiation, and the processes by which it was determined, documented, and sometimes challenged are things we can study, asking ourselves, as Field and Syrett suggest, not "how old someone 'really' was, but who had the power to decide."[13] This is precisely the question I explore in the pages that follow (and especially in chapter 6), as I show how officials, interpreters, clerks, parents, and children themselves used, questioned, modified, and manipulated chronological age in various contexts and for different reasons. Indeed, the lack of birth registration—not even available to most Africans until after 1933—and the vast differences in how Senegalese and French people understood age meant that "childhood" status was neither self-evident nor precise. Yet over time, as the colonial state recorded ages for and information about increasing numbers of children, signaled the importance of age measured in years to access certain benefits and privileges, and established legal procedures for retroactively documenting birthdates or ages, chronological age took on meaning alongside existing social definitions.

Given my focus on the constructed and historically contingent notion of "childhood," I cannot provide a single definition or chronological age range that works across all sites and case studies considered in the book.[14] Instead, I take my cues from historical sources produced by various colonial interventions into African childhood as I trace how "childhood" changed in different contexts and at different times. French regulations and children's institutions always measured childhood with reference to chronological age, though the targeted ages sometimes varied. But marking off childhood, or some subset of childhood, in years proved difficult in Senegal not only because most births were not recorded by the state but also because this approach clashed with African understandings of age, and this opened up space for contestation and negotiation over *who* exactly counted as a child and *what* children were meant to do and experience.

Indeed, Senegal's various cultural and linguistic communities typically defined childhood with reference to capability, social relationships, and (sometimes) the completion of specific rituals. These assumptions were so fundamental to social life that they come through in the languages themselves. Wolof, for example, features a rich vocabulary of words related to childhood. The general term for "child," *xale*, encapsulates a range of ages and experiences, and can be modified to indicate whether the child is a boy (*xale bu góór*) or girl (*xale bu jigéén*). Additional terms, many of which appear in both historical and contemporary dictionaries, are much more precise, and significantly, they are defined by a child's skills and capacities or social relationships rather than their chronological age. Thus, *liir* means baby or nursling, *perlit* refers to a child who was recently weaned, *sepen* means a young child who has started to stand or walk but cannot yet speak, and *gune* (alt. *gone*) describes a bigger and more mature child who has begun to reason. Finally, *fero* applies to boys who have reached the age of reason but have not yet started puberty, and *aat* refers to an older boy who has not yet undertaken the circumcision ritual, which marks the end of boyhood.[15]

This rich vocabulary of childhood corresponded to actual practices as described in several autoethnographic essays written by African students at the William Ponty Normal School in the 1930s and 1940s. These essays are part of the "William Ponty Notebooks" collection, a set of several hundred summer assignments written by students from across French West Africa who attended the federation's most elite school. One writing prompt instructed students to "describe the system of traditional education of a society that you know well (education in the family, social rules concerning children and adolescents, stages of initiation and ceremonies that punctuate the child's phases of physical and mental development)," and several essays by Senegalese students address this question.[16] Even though their observations would have been circumscribed by this formulaic writing prompt and by their desire to meet their French teachers' expectations, the essays are still quite extraordinary documents, offering glimpses into how these students viewed their own societies and how they attempted at times to defend them to the French. Several Ponty students focused on the capacities and social relationships associated with each stage of childhood, though they also tended to attach chronological ages to their descriptions. Ibrahima Ben Mady Cissé's essay on Wolof children whose families had moved to Casamance offers a case in point. From birth to age three, Cissé wrote, children mastered physical skills like walking and talking. From age three to the time of circumcision, education inculcated values like politesse, discretion, and obedience, and included stories about the community and ancestors; beginning around age seven, parents would send children out into the community and to a Qur'an school. Following a boy's circumcision ritual, he received a condensed "apprenticeship" in the values, skills, and tasks of men.[17]

Texts by early observers—largely travelers, missionaries, and colonial officials—also emphasized the sociality and skills associated with various stages of childhood, even as they often tried to make the local terminology more legible to French readers by adding references to chronological age. Two ethnographies published near the turn of the twentieth century commented on the differences in clothing and hairstyles that marked different ages, in this way capturing cultural practices which Africans themselves used to signal different levels of capacity, maturity, and need for modesty. In general, the youngest children wore little or no clothing, adding a short cloth when they were a bit older (at perhaps six to eight years old, according to these writers). Children tended to have shaved heads, with or without tufts of hair, while older girls, women, and sometimes men wore more intricate hairstyles.[18] As officials in the early twentieth century collected information intended to support the ongoing project of codifying customary laws for each cultural group, they did not typically define childhood but instead focused on when it ended, since the age of majority affected the duration of parental rights and obligations, the ability to enter contracts, guardianship of orphans, and other matters related to family and civil law. Although officials often attempted to link "majority" to a specific chronological age, they also acknowledged the importance to Africans of other factors. In Thiès, for example, people reached majority by getting married, and this typically occurred around age twenty-five or thirty, according to a questionnaire completed by the local administrator in 1907. In response to the same questionnaire, the administrator of Bakel similarly understood that majority arrived with marriage, noting that boys often married at around age twenty, while girls married younger, perhaps at age fifteen.[19] A few decades later, an administrator working among Sereer-Ndut people suggested that civil "majority is determined by circumcision for boys, by puberty for girls."[20] In their clumsy efforts to clearly delineate childhood or its endpoint, these French writers mostly succeeded in showing just how fluid and contextually dependent it was.

Yet French understandings of both childhood and order hinged on knowledge of chronological age, and officials frequently expressed frustration that Africans did not keep civil registries and did not know their birthdates. Chronological age, in French thinking, was supposed to correspond to specific grades in school, and at several points, officials discussed and even imposed rules prohibiting young people older than sixteen from attending primary school. Age helped establish identity in an era before people carried identity documents, and as such that information appears after names of witnesses in court records, next to student names on class lists, in census records, alongside names of people liberated from slavery (though these spaces were sometimes left blank), and so on. Application of civil and penal law required knowledge of age, since guardians had to pay fines on behalf of legal minors when they were ticketed and since the penal code held that a child under age sixteen could be acquitted due to a lack of criminal capacity. And guardianship also depended on chronological age, since reaching the age of majority (as set down by French law) could remove a person from the guardianship system. Given that the image of France as a benevolent and humanitarian civilizing power depended heavily on imposing rational order and following a rule of law, French officials often proceeded as if chronological age were a fact or an attribute that they could discern simply by documenting it, but as they did so, they opened up spaces for Africans to maneuver. This mismatch between understandings of age and the negotiations—and even fictions—it produced are central to my exploration of the ways colonialism changed childhood.

Widespread racist beliefs that young Africans were sexually precocious or that they matured faster than white children undoubtedly led officials to artificially inflate estimates of Africans' ages. French officials, observers, and residents not only believed that Black African children grew up faster than French children but they also envisioned very different versions of childhood for these groups.

White children, many believed, should receive academic instruction on par with metropolitan schools and enjoy leisure time. Black children, on the other hand, were expected to work alongside their parents or in the colonial economy. They might attend school, but only for a few years, with the goal of learning French and a trade.[21] In addition, officials considered *métis* children (those who had both French and African—"mixed"—heritage) to be a group apart given their French "blood" and claims to status and citizenship. Although many of Senegal's deeply rooted *métis* families ensured bourgeois upbringings for their children and sent them to school alongside French children, officials were concerned when African mothers raised *métis* children without a French father's involvement. In these circumstances, officials sometimes sent these children to an orphanage, where they would receive a French upbringing and a local education.[22] The fact that the colonial state construed African and French childhood so differently in Senegal raises questions about the wider applicability of Abosede George's well-known claim that, in colonial Nigeria at least, the category of "the child" became the first "universal subject."[23] In colonial Senegal, French officials and residents viewed African children as potential reservoirs of disease, sources of moral or bodily contamination, and threats to public order and public space, even as officials also pinned their hopes for a productive and stable colonial future on trained, surveilled, vaccinated, and—if needed—rehabilitated former children. The Africans who accounted for the vast majority of Senegal's children, and who were viewed by officials as distinct from and inferior to French and *métis* children, are the focus of this book.

Accordingly, the book includes stories about children that demonstrate the contingent, evolving, and frankly messy notions of African childhood at work in Senegal from the mid-nineteenth century to the mid-twentieth. It focuses on, for example, a boy who, at an estimated age of ten, stood trial in a colonial court; a girl who, at around sixteen, became an adult by fleeing from her guardian and marrying a soldier; and a boy (young man?) who produced an alternative birth certificate to claim that he was sixteen, rather than twenty, in order to qualify for a grade-school scholarship for which eligibility ceased at nineteen. Their stories—and the stories of many others like them—show how young Africans shaped changing notions of childhood as they navigated and sometimes contested French efforts to impose specific visions of order and discipline on those officials identified as "children." They also demonstrate how gender, background, status, and specific circumstances could prompt young Africans to mobilize chronological age and the concept of childhood in different ways.[24]

Agency and Children's Actions

Questions about agency have shaped the field of children's history for a long time. Scholars have endeavored to demonstrate how children have acted in their own interests despite the marginality, dependency, and other constraints stemming from their young age and other aspects of their identities. Yet in their rush to portray children as significant historical actors, many scholars privileged certain kinds of actions, such as rebellions, riots, or political resistance, that grew out of moments of tension. This approach has produced a range of critiques, since, as Mary Jo Maynes notes, it leaves out *most* children, who were not involved in obvious resistance but instead, by choice or acquiescence, went along with what was expected of them. Mona Gleason takes Maynes's criticism further, arguing that establishing children's agency often becomes a "trap" that prevents scholars from investigating the impacts of children's actions and inaction. And Lynn M. Thomas has found that scholars of African history all too often offer up "agency as argument," which could be read as an attempt to "rescue" historical subjects by restoring them to history. These scholars and others urge us to move beyond simply concluding that children *had* agency, and instead to examine their motivations; the priorities, goals, or concerns they addressed; how they deployed agency; and its impacts. These writers also encourage us to rethink the meaning of agency itself, by considering what historical subjects themselves thought about it or by exploring the histories of children who went along, obeyed, or cooperated. Even when children did not act in ways they intended to be strategic or that were not openly rebellious, their actions and behaviors—taken in the aggregate—could affect the world around them.[25]

I build on this idea to explore the ways that African children in colonial Senegal contributed to the process of (re)defining childhood—in this sense, they were coproducers not only of the idea of childhood but also of certain state policies themselves, especially those that depended on children's cooperation. This book tells stories about children who resisted, strategically or not, French attempts to surveil, document, or impose discipline by, for example, running away from a reformatory or repeatedly misbehaving toward a guardian. But it also explores the experiences and contributions of children who accepted or even sought out French interventions, children who received awards for good behavior at school, who were content with their guardians, or who received the smallpox vaccine. This wide range of children's stories allows me to push back against Sarah Maza's provocative assertion that children's past perspectives and actions are inconsequential because they had little impact on the issues that historians have identified as central to "adult history."[26] By showing how the colonial state came to depend on African children in Senegal, and exploring how African children's actions shaped the policies the state could pursue, I challenge Maza's more limited outlook on the utility of children's history.

Along with agency, historians of childhood have often been preoccupied with questions about sources, including how we might work around the paucity of documentation and how we might read our sources, even those authored by adults, "against the grain" to understand children's perspectives and experiences. At the heart of the issue is often a concern with the extent to which children's voices are present in our sources. Scholars have been keen to demonstrate that we can reconstruct children's perspectives on the past from fragmentary evidence, to locate children in material culture, to use informed speculation to suggest what children might have thought, and to find other creative solutions when evidence is lacking or to compensate for the fact that child-produced texts were often written by elite boys.[27] This is important work, since we need to seek children's voices and perspectives in order be as true as possible to their experiences. But it also raises ethical questions about the extent to which our efforts to highlight children's voices, or to create new oral histories about childhood, might produce harm or evoke shame, especially when we explore what Nell Musgrove, Carla Pascoe Leahy, and Kristine Moruzi call "distressing histories of childhood" or sensitive topics. In addition, Marie Rodet and Elodie Razy note that by highlighting children's voices, especially the voices of contemporary children, scholars could put them at risk of condemnation or censure if the norms of their society do not permit children to speak out. These concerns urge us to understand the contexts (cultural, historical, social, religious) in which children share(d) their ideas and concerns or made demands, what they risked in doing so, and the (hoped for) impacts of their words.[28]

I have responded to the challenges of finding sources by or about African children by looking across a broad range of archival and published sources for evidence of their encounters with the state and their reactions to these encounters. I looked for children's "voices" in school assignments, including the William Ponty notebooks discussed above and a variety of others; in letters children wrote to teachers or officials; in their speech as reported in court transcripts, disciplinary proceedings in schools, police reports, reports from guardianship councils, and correspondence between adults; and in several published memoirs and personal narratives.[29] Some of these sources and many others—school inspection reports and teachers' quarterly reports, minutes of faculty meetings, accounts of vaccination campaigns, guardianship registers, sentencing orders for juvenile offenders, and correspondence about penitentiary-schools, to name a few—offer insight into children's actions and can form the basis for inferences about their perspectives and motivations. Numerous lists of children's names—students in various schools, detainees interned in a reformatory, minors liberated from slavery and placed with guardians, and many more—allow me not only to quantify certain kinds of encounters between African children and the state but to trace the state's efforts to document—and thus to make legible—the youngest members of the societies they administered. Colonial sources, especially reports and official correspondence, also shed light on the ways those in power were discussing African children, sharing and organizing information about them along the way.

Because my book explores colonial efforts to track and impose order on African children, and the negotiations around what it meant to be a child that these efforts produced, I take an expansive approach, including in my study all young people considered by representatives of the colonial state to be legal minors, those who claimed to fit into this category, and those who were students and prospective students in colonial day or boarding schools.[30] Yet at the same time, because most attempts at colonial discipline and reform focused on older children (those we might today consider "school-aged" and "adolescent"), and because I am interested in the responses and perspectives of children who had the capacity to act somewhat independently, I do not discuss the histories of babies or very young children in any sustained way. My book thus includes historical actors who might be glossed as "youth," but because they occupied colonial spaces intended for children, were treated as penal or legal minors, or were subject to a child surveillance regime, it makes sense to consider them together with their younger peers.[31]

Documentation, Legibility, and the Colonial State

As officials tracked and recorded information about African children and collected information provided by others (in correspondence, class lists, vaccination records, and the like), they made children more legible to the colonial state. The data the state amassed informed certain policy decisions, but just as importantly, it could be used to tout the impact of child-protection initiatives both in France and on an increasingly expectant global stage. Yet at the same time, some Africans began to recognize the importance of having their existence documented with the state, and they sought to shape what the state knew about them, or to obtain their own documents (of birth, age, vaccination, etc.). Eventually, this knowledge production and collection normalized the documentation of childhood, and this process is another important theme of my book.

The concept of legibility is most closely associated with the work of James C. Scott; it refers to processes by which states impose rational order, "simplification," and "standardization" on societies to facilitate tax collection, surveillance, administration, and other government functions.[32] The way I use it here draws on but also questions Michel Foucault's suggestion that the modern state derives power in part from creating methods of surveillance to produce knowledge about individuals, creating, as he put it, "a whole mass of documents that capture and fix them."[33] Some scholars have—rightly—questioned the utility of Foucault's theories for colonial history, suggesting, among other things, that colonial states often focused on knowledge not of individuals but of entire populations (cultural groups, residents of specific districts, or "tribes," for example).[34] But in Senegal, it seems that the state *did* require knowledge and documentation at the individual level, at least in certain contexts, even as it also associated people with groups. Officials needed to know people's identity and age in order to maintain the fiction of a republican and humanitarian state that functioned in accordance with the rule of law. The age of individual children mattered, since it could determine eligibility for school, whether a liberated minor had to remain under guardianship, or whether a minor detainee could be released from internment.

In this place where a significant majority of African births went unregistered until the late twentieth century, the state's efforts to record various aspects of certain children's life experiences—school enrollment, vaccinations, visits to the doctor, grades at school, arrests or fines, court appearances, and more—and to link them to chronological age began to introduce the idea that childhood *should* be documented, and that documented age and identity could form the basis for claims on the state.[35] Yet the state's lack of capacity, especially at the margins, offered opportunities for people to maneuver within the state's efforts to document them, obscuring legibility as they did so.[36] Despite the unevenness of colonial surveillance and recordkeeping, and limits to the number of children who were represented as individuals in any colonial record, these early initiatives helped prepare the way for the documented identities that became so crucially important to people's abilities to access rights, entitlements, mobility, and recognition as citizens over the course of the twentieth century. While much of the scholarship on identity documentation and civil registration in Africa focuses on the contemporary era or, if historically inclined, looks to colonial initiatives in the postwar period, I trace the emerging idea of the documented child much further back in time, to at least the mid-nineteenth century.[37] In addition, documentation was important not only because it reflected the state's bureaucratic capacity or contained glimpses of African efforts to negotiate the system but also because it moved people toward the notion that childhood should be legible to the state and that it should end at a specific chronological age.

Historical Context

The book begins in 1848, the year the French government decreed an end to legal slavery across the French Empire. This prompted concern in Senegal about newly emancipated children who lacked parents and who were leaving their former enslavers.[38] With financial and logistical support from the colonial administration, Catholic missionary orders already operated several public schools for boys and girls in Saint-Louis and Gorée, and a small number of enslaved children had attended these schools prior to 1848. But in the wake of emancipation, the chief concerns of both the administration and the notable residents of the towns centered on maintaining order and economic productivity and not necessarily maximizing academic instruction for formerly enslaved children. Thus, to address the perceived problem, Governor Auguste Baudin created in 1849 a system of guardianship to entrust formerly enslaved or orphaned children to local notables who were entitled to their labor in return for providing basic necessities and vocational training or education.[39] Until at least the early 1910s, guardianship, which I explore in chapter 1, structured daily life and social relationships for the thousands of children who fled slavery in the interior of Senegal and neighboring colonies, who were trafficked into an area under direct French control and then "redeemed" from slavery, or who were emancipated in 1849. Moreover, it imposed a specific French vision about how these children should live their lives. These ideas, animated by fear that children would not work and would threaten stability, reflected the labor demands and lingering stigmas of post-emancipation Senegal, but they also drew on metropolitan concerns about idleness, vagabondage, and—by the late nineteenth century—degeneracy, and the accompanying hope that hard work in agricultural penal colonies in rural France would produce reform in problematic French children.[40]

As France expanded its territorial control in Senegal in fits and starts from the 1850s, many officials viewed schooling as essential to the present and future of colonial rule. Young students, they thought, would not only encourage their families to accept the "benefits" of colonialism but would grow up to become loyal, French-speaking employees of the colonial state or contributors to the colonial economy, particularly important given ongoing needs for intermediaries and the limited reach of state power. Thus, French schools often appeared soon after conquest ended or protected status was arranged, such that seventeen schools existed in these newly acquired areas by 1895. Meanwhile, in a nod to the importance of Islam in the colony, Governor Louis Léon César Faidherbe created secular public schools beginning in 1856 and, in an attempt to cement alliances with traditional leaders in the wider region, established a boarding school in Saint-Louis for their sons and other male relatives in 1855, even as the administration continued to work with the Frères de l'Instruction Chrétienne (Ploërmel religious brothers) and Sœurs de Saint-Joseph de Cluny (religious sisters), who ran schools in several towns.[41] In contrast to the universal, free, and secular schooling implemented in France during the 1880s, schooling in Senegal was never intended to reach all African children, but even so, late nineteenth-century officials envisioned it as a vehicle not only for remaking African childhood but also for promoting French civilization and culture in African societies writ large.[42]

In this early period, most African children avoided the colonial state entirely, but some experienced its attempts to impose discipline and order by attending school or entering guardianship. Significantly, not only were the administration's emerging bureaucracy and most of its personnel concentrated in the capital, Saint-Louis, and on the island of Gorée, but these towns (with the addition of Dakar and Rufisque in the 1870s) had privileged status as communes under direct administration and their African residents, known as *originaires*, had certain citizenship rights. The state administered most of the rest of Senegal as protectorates, governed by custom, and considered residents to be French subjects, lacking voting and other rights. This distinction derived in part from Governor Faidherbe's decree of 14 November 1857, which, in a bid to avoid alienating African allies who were enslavers in surrounding areas, declared that the 1848 decree had no jurisdiction over territories annexed by France after its passage. This arrangement allowed slavery to continue outside the towns under direct French control and facilitated, under the guise of guardianship, illegal trafficking in enslaved children from these areas (and from farther away) into

Saint-Louis and Gorée, where these children could be redeemed and entrusted to guardians who wanted their labor.[43] It could be argued that this bifurcation in approach to administration also affected schooling, since schools and education personnel were disproportionately concentrated in the communes, and schools in these towns tended to offer a more rigorous, French-style curriculum.

Having more or less completed territorial expansion in Senegal by the 1890s, the administration shifted from military to civilian rule and its emphasis changed from conquest to *mise en valeur*, or development, an emphasis that extended across the new French West Africa Federation that was formed in 1895 to centralize administration of Senegal and several other French colonies in the region. Amid some international and domestic concern about issues like slavery and forced labor, French officials set about trying to pursue "development" in a way that would ensure profitability for France but also promote certain improvements in Africans' lives. The passage of a law in 1905 in France to mandate the separation of church and state reduced the state's ability to rely on Catholic missionaries to provide public services like schools and orphanages in Senegal.[44] In this context, the government general of the still-new French West Africa federation issued several decrees outlining uniform organization of systems of education, courts, and "native" healthcare; reforming guardianship; and ceasing recognition of the legal status of slavery. These decrees, issued from 1903 to 1906, significantly impacted African children in Senegal and the wider region by changing school curricula and calling for expansion of schooling, attempting to eliminate abuses of guardianship, establishing a smallpox vaccination requirement, and more.[45] These signaled a shift away from fear of disorderly African children toward the idea that even as they required discipline, at least some deserved French assistance and even pity. This sentiment likely picked up on changes in France, where an 1889 law allowing the state to end paternal rights in cases of "moral abandonment" and other changes had begun to recast problematic children as victims and the state as the protector of all children.[46]

Although they could be glossed as organizational changes, these decrees created real infrastructure—schools, medical dispensaries, clinics, free medical care, a court system—that became the foundation of the so-called child-protection programs of the 1920s and 1930s. Yet even as the state discussed and, at least in a limited way, implemented these reforms, it also demanded unpaid communal labor, promoted cash crop production, and imposed high levels of taxation on the populace. Combined with the economic impacts of the Great Depression, these policies made life difficult for children and their families.[47] Education

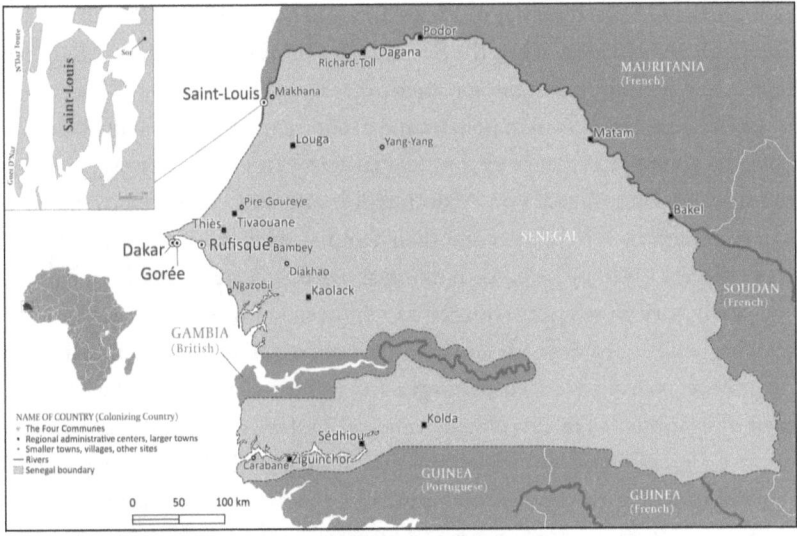

Senegal during French colonial rule, showing the towns and administrative posts mentioned in the text. Map created by Raven Vijayakumar.

reforms pursued in 1924 and again in the early 1930s introduced changes to school curricula that were intended to lead children to work in agriculture and manual trades; to teach some French, hygiene, arithmetic, and a few other subjects; and to ensure that people remained rooted in rural areas. Also in the 1930s, the government undertook initiatives intended to tackle infant and child mortality, as social welfare became central to the metropolitan government in the context of the Great Depression and increasing international concern with the issue. And in the mid-1930s, attempting to advance the progressive image of the Popular Front government, Governor General Marcel de Coppet took on some social, political, and labor concerns, issuing, among others, a 1936 reform that protected women and children who performed paid work. Suggesting an abiding interest in social issues, De Coppet in 1937 dispatched Denise Savineau, who had taken up a post in Dakar as an education advisor following the death of her administrator husband, on a seven-month tour of French West Africa, during which she was to collect information on women and families and compile an extensive report.[48] While the Popular Front fell before her field notes and final report, completed in 1938, could make much impact, the documents offer historians incredible insight into family life in the late 1930s, and they show that metropolitan preoccupations with children's vulnerability and need for protection had made their way to West Africa, though with very different goals.[49] The book ends in 1940, when the Second World War and its aftermath drove France to significantly shift the approach to social welfare in French West Africa.

The various child-focused policies and programs pursued from 1848 to 1940 not only served as evidence of the colonial state's intention, however limited, to impose a kind of order on African childhood and eventually to improve living conditions for children and their families during this period, but they also reflected (shifting) official thinking about two central questions, namely, (1) which African subjects counted as "children," that is, how was the category of "child" to be defined? and (2) what sort of childhood should Africans experience? What were their privileges and rights as children, and what were their obligations as French colonial subjects? Lest we overestimate the French state's progressiveness or commitment to "humanitarian" empire, we should remember that with their vision occluded by racism and a sense of cultural superiority, educators, supervisors of reformatories, police commissioners, and a range of other French officials consistently marked Black children as separate from and inferior to their white and *métis* counterparts, and as such planned different pathways for them to move through childhood—schools with heavy emphasis on agriculture and vocational training, mass vaccination campaigns and school-based medical care, interventions into their use of public spaces, lengthy periods of internment for even very minor crimes or misdemeanors. As I explore in the pages that follow, these pathways corresponded to a vision of colonial African childhood but one that children themselves contested, negotiated, and ultimately reshaped.

CHAPTER 1

The Meeting Room

GUARDIANSHIP AND CHILDHOOD IN POST-EMANCIPATION SENEGAL

In June 1849, the guardianship council of Saint-Louis responded to a request from resident Binta Sar, who sought guardianship over two boys, "Couly and Bacari," both around thirteen years old. These boys, likely beneficiaries of the French emancipation law of 1848, were "living as vagabonds," acting out residents' and officials' worst fears about the behavior of formerly enslaved people in the aftermath of emancipation. Significantly, these boys were not sleeping on the streets—each had a place to stay in a private home—but they had apparently taken advantage of their new freedom to decide not to work. Although the council did not deem Binta Sar an appropriate guardian, choosing instead to place each boy in an apprenticeship with a different master artisan, its swift decision to act in these cases and in many others like them sent a clear message that the state expected formerly enslaved and other marginalized children to work in support of the colonial economy.[1] As suggested by this example, the state used guardianship not only to make sure that formerly enslaved children had their basic needs met and stayed off the streets but also to promote the idea that marginalized African children should conform to French expectations of order and economic productivity.

The creator of guardianship (*tutelle*), Governor Auguste Baudin, offered it in 1849 to a concerned public as an antidote to the new French emancipation law, which, he claimed, had allowed children in Gorée and Saint-Louis to leave their former enslavers, "desert workshops," and reject apprenticeships in favor of "the disorder of a life of idleness and vagabondage." Baudin's decree assigned "paternal authority" to the state, allowing it or its representatives to appoint local notables as guardians of formerly enslaved children who lacked parental supervision. In return for agreeing to provide basic care, moral upbringing, and vocational training, guardians gained the right to their wards' labor. After mediating guardianship for the unaccompanied minors freed when emancipation went into effect in August 1848, the system continued to function as officials dealt with complaints about wards' behavior, handled requests to end guardianship or apprenticeships, found guardians for orphans, and most significantly responded to waves of children arriving in Saint-Louis, Gorée, and (later) administrative posts where the emancipation law applied from surrounding areas where slavery remained legal.

These later waves consisted of minors who had fled slavery and those who had been purchased, trafficked into Saint-Louis or another town, declared "free," and entrusted to people who wanted their labor.[2] No longer as necessary once the French finally decided to mount a real challenge to slavery across the region, eliminating legal recognition of slave status in 1903 and banning enslavement and transfer of ownership rights in persons in 1905, and no longer practical once thousands of enslaved people began leaving their enslavers at around the same time, guardianship fell into desuetude sometime around 1911. While significant gaps in the archival record prevent a full assessment of its magnitude, the available data indicates that guardianship affected at least three thousand children, and probably many more, in its six decades.[3]

This chapter explores how the state used guardianship to impose a particular model of colonial childhood on formerly enslaved children, considers guardianship as an early step toward documented childhood, and asks how children responded to French efforts to offer care but also control. Designed to force children like Couly and Bacari out of perceived idleness, to make them economically productive in a way that was legible to the state, and to subject them to French discipline, guardianship made clear that, for marginalized Africans in French-controlled areas, childhood was to be defined by certain types of work even as children's actions sometimes called this definition into question. This situation remained true even amid early twentieth-century efforts to reimagine the history of guardianship as one of humanitarianism—Lieutenant Governor Camille Guy in 1903 claimed that it had been envisioned in the 1850s as a "measure of protection and humanity"—and to enact reforms that required regular surveillance and better recordkeeping to reassert state control and end some of the abuses that had come to light. Despite the reforms and professed commitment to "humanity," guardianship continued to highlight tensions within state policies between protection and control.[4] Ensuring a supply of dependent labor in the aftermath of emancipation was always the focal point of guardianship, and although many liberated minors did not challenge this expectation, I contend, others pushed against it by running away, misbehaving, or otherwise rejecting it.

As officials recorded details of encounters between liberated minors and representatives of the state, they not only collected knowledge about individual children but also began to trace the contours of a distinctly colonial childhood, using French assumptions about chronological age to determine its endpoint and to make decisions about which young people were in fact minors over whom the state should have special protective authority.[5] This was not the first time French officials had created records listing (formerly) enslaved children. They had, for example, taken censuses, albeit sporadically, in Saint-Louis and Gorée since the eighteenth century, listing the free and enslaved people, including children, who lived in each household surveyed. Administrations across the French Empire generated inventories of enslaved people by the mid-nineteenth century, allowing them to provide enslavers with compensation following the 1848 abolition of slavery. And, from 1857 to 1903, officials in Saint-Louis entered names and other information of more than 28,900 Africans, including children, who had fled slavery in the region; the unaccompanied children among them entered guardianship and had their information recorded yet again.[6] Despite the existence of other records, I suggest that the registers of liberated minors and other unaccompanied children had a unique impact on understandings of childhood in early colonial Senegal. As recordkeepers ascribed chronological age, used it to determine who required a guardian (only those under the age of majority), updated records for certain children following additional encounters, and stressed the importance of these records to children's lives, they not only normalized documentation but in effect produced a new category of the (marginalized) colonial African child that differed profoundly from ideas about childhood as a reflection of capacity and social recognition with which children would have been familiar.

Several scholars have written about the history of guardianship in Senegal and in other parts of colonial Africa, often focusing on links between guardianship and the power of the post-emancipation colonial state. Martin Klein and

Trevor R. Getz, for example, are mostly interested in the intended functions of guardianship, its use as a cover for an illegal trade in enslaved children, and the quantitative data it left behind, which they use to shed light on slavery in the region in the second half of the nineteenth century. In a 2011 study, Bernard Moitt offers a more detailed sketch of guardianship's institutional history, positioning it as a structure that maintained the appearance that the state provided for liberated minors while allowing labor exploitation and a trade in enslaved children to continue. Moitt's 2024 book elaborates on these themes and also provides an overview of the types of labor guardians required, the exploitation or abuse that was part of this system, wards' occasional resistance, and their experiences of life events like sickness or marriage.[7] Senegalese scholars Ibrahima Thioub and Ousseynou Faye, on the other hand, approach guardianship as a window into the colonial state's efforts to control marginalized children amid rising concerns about unruly behavior and juvenile delinquency.[8] While I build on the descriptions of institutions, state power, and children's experiences found in these studies, I adopt a very different approach, using what Mona Gleason calls "empathic inference" to think through children's motivations and priorities, and exploring how their actions reflected back on state policy and contributed to changing ideas about African childhood.[9]

Furthermore, I rely on archival sources others have not used, most importantly a large trove of guardianship registers and inventories containing names, personal and demographic information, and updates on the well-being of hundreds of liberated minors. Produced as a result of the 1903 and 1904 reforms to guardianship, these documents shed new light on its impacts from about 1895 to 1911 and, more generally, on the ideas about childhood circulating at that time. Using these records and others, I built a database on guardianship at the turn of the twentieth century that includes information about more than 1,600 liberated minors, and I rely on it here to identify demographic trends and draw new conclusions based on quantitative analysis. Because there are more records for the years after 1895, and because many of them lend themselves to quantitative analysis, my exploration of guardianship in this period is richer, more detailed, and more data-driven than my discussion of the earlier period. In addition, the existence of so many more records for the period after 1895 exemplifies the state's efforts to turn marginalized children into traceable and legible recipients of state care, especially important as officials worked to convince others that French colonialism took a humane approach to development. Overall, I make the case that even if many liberated minors acquiesced to the idea that those from marginalized backgrounds should experience a childhood dominated by menial labor, gender constraints, and rigid expectations for behavior, others challenged this notion of childhood. Through their actions and reactions, children shaped what officials knew—or thought they knew—about marginalized African children, knowledge that in turn informed state action and that, once recorded, contributed to documentary childhood.

Guardianship in the Nineteenth Century

When Governor Baudin rolled out guardianship in 1849, he turned supervision of the program over to newly created guardianship councils (*conseils de tutelle*), one for Saint-Louis and one for Gorée, led by the assistant mayor of each town and made up of prominent residents and workshop supervisors. Tasked with selecting guardians, entrusting liberated minors and orphans, approving apprenticeships, handling discipline issues, maintaining records, and submitting annual reports, among other things, the guardianship councils almost immediately began fielding claims from residents who wanted guardianship over a particular formerly enslaved child or orphan and from master artisans who wanted to take on a boy as an apprentice.[10] During the first year or so, many prospective guardians had been enslavers prior to emancipation, and some—like Hélène Renaud, who wanted her "former captive, named Dorine, Bambara, age 12" to remain with her as her ward—sought guardianship over the very children they had once enslaved.[11] Even when notables requested guardianship over children in whom they had not previously had rights, they tended to come before the council with specific requests, as when a Monsieur and Madame Caminade sought "to bring up a boy and a girl, age 12 to 15 years." Sometime in 1850, the guardianship council's work shifted to focus primarily on finding guardians for children lacking parents who came to their attention, and on making new arrangements in cases of repeated rebellious behavior; guardianship requests became less common. In addition, numerous people claiming to be family members of formerly enslaved children sought the council's assistance in gaining guardianship over their young relatives.[12]

A reform to procedures for slave liberations, undertaken in 1857 by Governor Louis Faidherbe, required the chief of the judicial service to record details of each liberation in standard form. Those whose emancipation he recorded were to receive liberty certificates. Faidherbe's initiatives also prompted the creation of a new guardianship register, regular publication of names of liberated minors and guardians in the colony's official newspaper, and additional reporting, significantly increasing the state's documentation not just of adult's claims and requests for children but of certain details about liberated minors themselves. Although liberated minors would not have been able to read these documents, they must have known that they held a certain power—recording aspects of their individual identity and attesting to their status as liberated minors. Guardianship continued to attract Faidherbe's attention, leading him in 1858 to issue a set of expectations for master artisans with apprentices and for guardians, and in 1862 to eliminate guardianship councils and to give responsibility for the system to the colony's head prosecutor (*procureur général*).[13] Frédéric Carrère, head of the judicial service until 1866, implemented these changes in recordkeeping, launching a guardianship register (updated, irregularly, by others until 1874) that provides a lot less information about prospective guardians and their claims but somewhat more insight into the demographics and work experiences of minors themselves.

From its origins, officials intended guardianship to respond to concerns about idle children and the colony's ongoing labor needs by placing children with guardians who would, one way or another, ensure that they were economically productive and that they received the training they would one day rely on as adult workers. Baudin's 1849 decree creating guardianship indicated that the guardianship councils were to ask children what sort of work they preferred and, based on each response, find a guardian who would train them in "a trade, an industry or a profession." Astonishingly, the council at least occasionally followed Baudin's instructions, though their sense of obligation must have declined when their president argued that the colony's economic needs far outweighed children's preferences. The guardianship council should, he stated, "distribute" these children in "an appropriate manner" among the "manual trades [that are] most useful here," and should ensure that some took on the "indispensable" job of domestic service. Beyond its role entrusting minors to guardians and securing apprenticeships, the guardianship council also highlighted the importance of labor to childhood by imposing discipline on those who misbehaved or resisted work, removing children from guardians who seemed unable or unwilling to extract appropriate labor, and so on.[14] Although gaps and inconsistent use of terminology in the records make it impossible to provide a full accounting of guardianship in this early period, the inclusion of at least 549 names shows that many dozens of young people became wards between 1849 and 1874, encountering French expectations of childhood productivity and training as a result.[15]

Regarding labor expectations, then, guardianship had much in common with the urban domestic slavery it had replaced. Prior to emancipation in 1848, enslaved girls and women had worked primarily as *pileuses* (millet pounders), laundresses, and in other aspects of domestic service, and similar occupations predominated among female liberated minors. Indeed, the few entries that provide details about girls' labor from 1849 to 1874 make clear that they washed and ironed, sewed, did general housework and domestic service, and occasionally cooked. And much like the enslaved boys and men before them who had worked as day laborers, fishermen, domestics, and in certain specialized trades, liberated minor boys worked in a variety of manual trades and as domestic servants or cooks. In addition, in response to the need for trained artisans in the colony, the guardianship council entrusted many boys to master artisans from whom they were to learn to work as skilled joiners, carpenters, masons, tailors, and other tradesmen. In some cases, liberated minors entered official apprenticeships, usually lasting three to six years, with the artisans who provided training, while in other cases the relationship was less formally and contractually defined. The context of this work was different from that performed under slavery or by children of free status within their communities in that it featured the colonial state in a supervisory role. Thus, those who did not work diligently, who appeared idle while in public spaces, or who otherwise did not comply with labor demands might find themselves imprisoned for several days as punishment for vagabondage, as the young "orphan" Bilale experienced in December 1849.[16] Orderly provision of labor for the colonial economy was the most significant expectation placed on liberated minors, and its recurrent appearance even in these early incomplete records underscores the extent to which it was at the center of the state's efforts to remake African childhood and to make marginalized children more legible.

Yet despite their focus on what guardians, other claimants, and the colonial state wanted from these children, these records do offer glimpses into children's efforts to influence their own circumstances. They bear traces of complaints about living conditions from minors like Koli and Voltaire, apprentice masons whose tales in 1850 of poor clothing and food led the guardianship council to summon their master mason and demand improvements.[17] They hint at children's efforts to pursue their own plans or to reject the constraints of guardianship or apprenticeship, as when in 1861 Yoro, around sixteen years old, behaved so objectionably that the master artisan with whom he worked ended his apprenticeship nearly two years early, or when young Abile's behavior so challenged her guardians that she was reassigned twice during her first three years as a ward (1863–66).[18] They suggest that some of the children in whom the guardianship councils took an interest wanted to avoid the system altogether by leaving town or running away from a guardian. Minutes from the guardianship council meetings in 1849 and 1850 contain multiple references to liberated minors or other potential wards who could not be found or who were known to have traveled. In response to one woman's June 1849 claim, for example, members of the council could not track down one of the five minors over whom she requested guardianship and learned that two others—one of them enslaved by the claimant before emancipation—had left Saint-Louis. And in 1878, young Penda Tall ran away from her guardian of seven years, saying she wanted to live instead with a woman she claimed was her sister, though officials quickly returned her to the guardian.[19] These examples and a few others that made it into the archives, of course, account for only a fraction of the activity in which marginalized children engaged. They suggest not only that marginalized children at least sometimes pursued their own goals in the decades after emancipation but also that their actions could shape, and even challenge, the state's expectations for African childhood and their legibility.

Guardianship and Reform at the Turn of the Twentieth Century

Guardianship had been rife with abuse since its earliest days, and by the early twentieth century, this was becoming less tenable. Officially, guardians had to provide their wards with shelter, food, and clothing; tend to them when ill; and ensure that they acquired skills or a trade that would prepare them to make a living after they reached majority. They were strictly prohibited from selling liberated minors (slavery remained legal outside the towns of Saint-Louis, Dakar, Gorée, and Rufisque, and in other areas under direct French control), had to notify the administration of plans to relocate, and could only arrange marriages for liberated minors when granted official permission to do so. In practice, guardianship disguised an illegal trade in enslaved children, and even those guardians who had not knowingly participated in this trade generally expected liberated minors to perform work associated with slavery. Additionally, guardians frequently retained liberated minors well past their majority, spent bridewealth even though they were supposed to retain it, claimed rights in children born to their wards, and failed to notify the administration when they moved or traveled. The state made little or no effort to check back with wards after they entered guardianship, and as a result, intervened only in cases involving the worst physical abuse or when children misbehaved so often that guardians complained.[20]

By the early twentieth century, public opinion in France and in other imperialist countries had become increasingly concerned about slavery and its vestiges around the world. Prodded by the Colonial Ministry in Paris, Governor General Ernest Roume twice reformed guardianship, reflecting the changing sensibilities that produced a ban on enslavement and slave-trading across French West Africa in 1905. To address concerns about guardians' inappropriately benefiting from liberated minors' labor, Roume's 24 November 1903 decree indicated that, going forward, liberated minors should ordinarily be placed in institutional settings rather than with individuals. The hundreds of liberated minors already under guardianship would remain in private homes—the colony's vocational schools had limited capacity, and the public orphanage for boys would not open for another year—but they were not untouched by the reform. Indeed, in response to Roume's instructions, the lieutenant governor of Senegal, Camille Guy, quickly created "commissions charged with the surveillance and the protection of liberated minors" to attend to these children. Consisting of one or two colonial officials, the presiding judge of the local court, a "European or assimilated merchant or colonist," and two notables, the commissions were to proceed immediately with a "census" of all liberated minors in the registers to determine whether they remained with their guardians.[21]

Given the new focus on recordkeeping, Guy and Roume were alarmed when the Saint-Louis commission confirmed that the head of the judicial service had not adequately supervised or documented guardianship for decades. This realization prompted Roume's second reform, which in October 1904 put the secretary general in charge of the system, making him responsible for entrusting liberated minors to institutions or individuals, addressing discipline problems that guardians could not handle, coordinating with police to conduct investigations related to guardianship, and—assisted by the new surveillance commissions—maintaining up-to-date records.[22] These commissions, with a mandate to regularly "inspect" liberated minors after completing their initial census, played a critical role in the recordkeeping functions of the reformed system, first in Saint-Louis and a few years later in Dakar and other towns. Enlisting the police to deliver summonses to guardians' homes, commissioners convened at the courthouse to assess the health, "moral and material situation," and approximate age of the liberated minors who appeared before them. Over the years, commissioners saw many of these children multiple times, and eventually some guardians and a few wards began to complain about the frequency of the intrusion.[23]

The initiative produced documentation for some 1,620 liberated minors who entered guardianship during or after 1895 and recorded one or more subsequent encounters between a member of the administration or guardianship committee and at least 375 of these children, increasing their legibility to the state, normalizing documentation of childhood, and—it must be said—allowing me to use quantitative methods to gain a fuller picture of the lived experiences of marginalized children in early twentieth-century Senegal. As I discuss at length below, these records contain dozens of examples of liberated minors running away; achieving emancipation from guardianship by aging out, marrying, or having a baby; and transferring to a new guardian. They also offer occasional brief glimpses into children's assessments—positive and negative—of the conditions of their guardianship. They do not reveal whether exploitation decreased or material conditions improved, but the level of surveillance reflected in the records suggests that circumstances invited such changes. As the reformed guardianship system multiplied points of contact—many of them taking place in the courthouse—between liberated minors and representatives of the colonial state, it created space in which officials, guardians, and minors could work through expectations for the labor and conduct of formerly enslaved children in Senegal's towns, producing knowledge about these children all the while. In collecting and recording information about liberated minors and responding to children's actions, officials continued to define colonial childhood.

Liberated Minors and Labor after 1895

Preparing children to become productive workers took on new importance at the turn of the twentieth century, as officials touted economic development and social progress. Subject to state intervention and carrying the stigma of slave descent, liberated minors were part of this calculation.[24] Liberated minors in this period tended to be female (62.2%) and young but old enough to perform many household tasks and other labor, with 53.4 percent of them falling between the ages of six and ten, as shown in table 1. Despite the likelihood of error in these ascribed ages, an issue I explore at length in chapter 6, the fact that recorded ages were concentrated in this range suggests an intent to benefit from children's labor for years, since they would remain under guardianship until found to have reached majority at age eighteen. Ascribed and documented age thus had an important impact on liberated minors' lives, since it informed the state's decisions about their status. Information collected about liberated minors' origins reflects patterns of instability and warfare in the region during the late nineteenth century and shows that these children came to Saint-Louis from across the region but most frequently from hinterlands to the east, with recorded birthplaces referencing various sites within the Soudan (24.1% of the 806 entries that include birthplace information) or origins "among the Bambaras" (28.0%).[25] As they charted a path to at least give the appearance that guardianship was distinct from child slavery, officials and guardians continued to develop specific, and often gendered, expectations for the work performed by liberated minors in Senegal's towns. At the same time, some liberated minors envisioned childhood differently, rejecting overly taxing workloads and communicating their own ideas about how guardians should treat them.

TABLE 1. Liberated Minors in Saint-Louis, Senegal, 1895–1911, Ascribed Age When Entering Guardianship

AGE	NUMBER	PERCENTAGE
Under 5 years	48	3.63
5	100	7.55
6	155	11.71
7	158	11.93
8	146	11.03
9	107	8.08
10	142	10.73
11	73	5.51
12	112	8.46
13	85	6.42
14	82	6.19
15	52	3.93
16–19	41	3.10
Unknown/illegible	23	1.74
Total	1,324	100.01

Source: Liberated Minors Database.

Official rhetoric about guardianship had always emphasized training for liberated boys, deeming their labor essential to the economy, and this preoccupation continued into the twentieth century. Indeed, Roume's 1903 reform called on the administration to send newly liberated minors to public "institutions for aid or apprenticeship" or, under certain circumstances, to "private workshops."[26] Yet in practice, very few held formal apprenticeships or attended colonial vocational schools, as indicated by a 1904 study that found only seventeen boys learning trades like woodworking, carpentry, bread-baking, and bookbinding from master artisans in Saint-Louis. The colony's trade schools incorporated even fewer of these children, at least in the years before and immediately after Roume's reforms. Asked in 1904 to submit a list of liberated minor boys equipped to attend the Pinet-Laprade vocational school in Dakar, the guardianship commissions in Saint-Louis and Dakar came up with only a handful of names. Their counterparts elsewhere proposed none at all.[27]

In contrast, it seems likely that many liberated minors learned a trade by assisting their guardians with their work.[28] Of the 1,324 children who entered guardianship in Saint-Louis after 1895, for example, at least 299 of them were placed with Africans who worked as *pileuses* (millet pounders), laundresses, fishermen, traders, sellers, and cloth-dyers. Significantly, *pileuses*, laundresses, and cloth-dyers, all of them women, almost always took in female wards, while men who fished or engaged in trade predominantly served as guardians for boys.[29] These trends likely resulted from the gender preferences of guardians, who could make specific requests, and they might also suggest that the liberated minors learned these gendered professions from their guardians.

While some liberated minors specialized in specific trades, many—girls and boys—performed domestic service in private homes or in commercial settings. This was likely the experience of most of the over 175 liberated minors entrusted to colonial officials, interpreters, railway workers, soldiers, representatives of commercial firms, lawyers, and others in professions directly tied to the colonial administration or economy. And many of the 27 liberated minors entrusted to "property-owners" and the 232 placed with women listed as "housewives" or "wives," or as having no profession, probably worked in domestic service as well.[30] Indeed, European and *métis* guardians almost uniformly used their wards in this capacity, and the association between liberated minors and domestic service became so commonplace that some used the terms interchangeably.[31]

Yet although both girls and boys provided domestic service, gender shaped the nature of work performed. White or *métis* guardians who ran French-oriented households expected girls to do laundry, iron, clean, care for children, cook, and run errands. Hence, in a 1906 letter complaining about the attitude of his ward of ten years, Alexis Béziat referred to her as his "maid" (*ma bonne*). The following year, Dakar entrepreneur V. Peignet asked the government to make him the guardian of "2 young girls of 12 to 15 years for the service of my house." They would run errands in town, "wash dishes and help cook for me," he wrote, adding that he would treat them like they were his own children.[32] And in 1909, the administrator of Tivaouane, P. Godel, noted that Aïssatou had settled in to her relatively new role providing childcare in his own home.[33] These examples make clear that guardians in such households viewed liberated minor girls primarily as maids and child-minders. The nature of the work performed by liberated minor girls in homes following African customs is harder to discern from the archival record, but information compiled by the Rufisque guardianship commission in March 1906 provides some insight. The commission indicated that all seven female wards in African households did "housekeeping" (*ménage*) or worked in the "interior" of the house, in most cases living with the family or with other domestics.[34]

Liberated minor boys filled a wider variety of roles as domestics, serving as valets, butlers, and livestock attendants in addition to cooking, cleaning, and running errands. They performed these tasks almost exclusively for French officials and for those directly associated with the colonial administration or French economy.[35] J.-J. Crespin, an official in the secretary general's office, for example, had Balla Fall run errands and perform other household tasks. Mme. H. Bancal envisioned even more distinctly gendered roles for her wards when in 1908 she asked the secretary general to send her "two orphaned minors." Specifically, she requested a "young man, age 12 to 14, who will serve me by tending the small herd of animals that I keep in Guéoul," and a "little girl between 8 and 12 years, who I will teach to serve me and to work."[36] Other boys served as domestics in commercial enterprises or offices, jobs that girls do not seem to have performed.[37]

As they attempted to distance guardianship from exploitation, officials discussed the benefits of paying the oldest liberated minors, yet they do not appear to have questioned the assumption that formerly enslaved and other marginalized children should spend their childhood as manual or domestic laborers. This position certainly stemmed from concern about the viability of African economies as slavery declined, but it also reflected assumptions about class and social status originating in both France and West Africa. Indeed, metropolitan stereotypes linked idleness to vice in the working class, and in the region (former) slave status remained stigmatized and associated with particular types of labor.[38] Thus, although a 1911 manual for administrators indicated that liberated minors should attend the French school "whenever possible," and although officials often fretted about low enrollment at colonial schools, guardianship continued to emphasize work as the defining feature of childhood for formerly enslaved children in post-emancipation Senegal. This contrasted with metropolitan France, where the Jules Ferry laws of 1881 and 1882, making primary schooling free, secular, and mandatory, turned education into a formative experience for children of all classes.[39]

Although guardianship often successfully managed children's labor, unreasonable labor demands, criticism of work performance, and punishment sometimes prompted challenges to or ruptures in the system. By complaining to the authorities or running away, some liberated minors expressed dissatisfaction with their working conditions. These behaviors triggered inquiries and—at least occasionally—material changes in minors' circumstances. Although such challenges to guardianship were recorded relatively infrequently, the colonial archive contains enough of them to suggest that liberated minors both had their own sense of what constituted acceptable treatment and when their experiences fell short, they employed a variety of strategies to rectify the situation. In a few other cases, in contrast, liberated minors spoke or acted in ways that signaled acceptance of their circumstances. In these varied responses, and likely in others not captured by the colonial archive, liberated minors weighed in on what childhood might mean for those who had been liberated from slavery in post-emancipation Senegal. The reforms of 1903 and 1904 increased the likelihood that they would be heard.

Liberated minors sometimes complained to authorities about their guardians' impossibly high standards or disparaging remarks, a step that must have required considerable courage given their marginalized status. In December 1905, for example, Awa Siga told a police interpreter that she no longer wanted to stay with a Madame Lefranc because the woman frequently beat her. When a police officer inquired, Lefranc admitted to striking Awa with a shirt in a spat over laundry but maintained that she had not hurt the girl, a contention with which the officer agreed. Awa had done a poor job, Lefranc said, and had been "insolent" in response to criticism. She conjectured that Awa, who had recently accompanied her on a seven-month stay in France, begrudged having to return to a more constrained and difficult environment in Saint-Louis.[40] Whether or not this was true, it is certainly possible that Awa's experiences in France empowered her to pursue her own interests in Senegal. Bigué N'Diaye also expressed frustration with her guardian's criticism of her work, though she went about it in a different way. Appearing before the October 1906 meeting of the Saint-Louis guardianship commission, Bigué told commissioners that she wanted a new guardian, since Mme. A. Patterson was "never satisfied with her services" and was "continually reproaching her." Although guardians normally accompanied their wards to these meetings, Patterson had left the task to someone else on that date, and it is likely that her absence allowed Bigué to air her grievances more freely.[41] In turning authorities' attention to their complaints, these girls not only contested the stigma that allowed guardians to mistreat them but also attempted to use colonial structures to their advantage.

Liberated minors likewise sometimes ran away in order to escape harsh treatment or work demands that they found overly burdensome. And though liberated minors pursued such extreme actions relatively rarely—I have found only forty-one cases for Saint-Louis between 1895 and 1911—they tended to attract significant attention from the administration.[42] In March 1905, for example, Balla Fall ran away from J.-J. Crespin, an action that resulted in a three-day prison sentence aimed at disciplining him. Not yet fully recovered from an injury that had given him a reprieve from domestic service, Balla had packed his clothes and fled when asked to run an errand. Ultimately, fed up with this and other incidents of "misconduct," Crespin relinquished guardianship over the nineteen-year-old, and Balla was sent to the orphanage in Sor.[43] Similarly, in October 1906, Niélé Diara ran away from a Madame Vigier, who had been her guardian since 1898, the year of her emancipation at the age of seven. When the police found her, Niélé told them she had fled because Vigier had asked her to continue performing housework despite having a sore finger. Although the police commissioner doubted this explanation, noting that Niélé's finger wound appeared small, it is certainly possible that Vigier's demands seemed unreasonable to the girl.[44] Balla and Niélé thus seem to have rejected the expectation that they work while injured.

Other liberated minors fled guardians who beat them or failed to adequately provide for them. In 1906, for example, Sokhna Trawalé began repeatedly running away from her guardians. When the police asked why, she told them that Madame Gaillard frequently beat her without warning or reason. In February 1911, the police learned that a child named Bayérika had run away from Abou Diop because "she was not well cared for." Similarly, when the police located him in Goundou village in April 1906, fifteen days after he fled the Saint-Louis home of his guardian, young Abdoulaye explained that he was frequently beaten.

He also complained about missing out on schooling, noting that Baca Sar (N'Diaye), his guardian, did not send him to any school, French or Qur'an, suggesting that he wanted childhood to consist of more than just labor. Baca Sar vehemently denied these accusations, mustered witnesses to attest that Abdoulaye's misbehavior sometimes required physical "correction," and expressed sadness at the prospect of losing the boy he had raised for seven years, since around the age of four. In the end, Abdoulaye returned to his guardian, only to flee again a little over a year later, after which he disappeared from the archive.[45]

Although flight was usually precipitated by extreme dissatisfaction or mistreatment, it is significant that liberated minors often fled *to* a specific person—a friend, a protector, or even a lover.[46] Indeed, when police found Noumbé Daffa in the home of Hamet Guèye in November 1906, some five months after a scolding from her guardian led her to run away, they noted that she had a young child. Police provided no details about Guèye, but the situation suggests that he and Daffa had some sort of relationship. And in October 1907, a month after she ran away from her guardian at the approximate age of twenty-one, Soukeyna Diagne not only explained that she had fled due to mistreatment but also expressed her wish to remain with Katy N'Diaye, the woman with whom she had taken refuge.[47] The destination and new social relationships it allowed, it seems, could be just as important as negative experiences with guardians in motivating flight. Furthermore, at least twenty-seven of forty-one Saint-Louis runaways, including several of those discussed above, were thirteen or older, and perhaps nine of these had reached the age of majority but remained in guardianship. The decision to run away thus may also have reflected a desire for greater autonomy as they neared an age at which many married or struck out on their own.

Although disagreement regarding labor expectations and treatment was one of the most common sources of conflict between guardians and liberated minors, most liberated minors did not openly criticize their guardians or complain to the guardianship commissions. This lack of evidence almost certainly stems in part from colonial hierarchies that silenced many marginalized people, from gaps in the records maintained by commissions inclined to indicate that all liberated minors appeared "well," and from the fact that hundreds of liberated minors escaped commission surveillance entirely.[48] Yet it may also be the case that many children did not wish to complain. Perhaps, for some, guardianship offered stability or seemed less exploitative than slavery. Abibou M'Baye raised this possibility when he apparently told the commission in 1905 that he was "well cared for" and "content." There is some evidence suggesting that children developed emotional bonds with their guardians, and this too may have led to acceptance of or even appreciation for their situation.[49] Furthermore, some chose to remain with their guardians as paid workers after they reached majority. In 1906, for example, Yacine Diouf, age twenty-two, continued to perform domestic service for her guardian, a Monsieur Deproge of Thiès, after being removed from guardianship, though she now received a wage. These examples suggest that even as some liberated minors challenged stigma and mistreatment, labor, sometimes performed for guardians under altered conditions, remained an important economic strategy and childhood experience.[50]

By mediating guardians' access to labor and children's work experiences in colonial towns, guardianship provided an opportunity for those involved with it to shape trajectories of childhood for the formerly enslaved in post-emancipation Senegal. Neither officials, committed to economic growth and vocational training, nor town notables, guided by longstanding prejudices, questioned the assumption that work should define childhood for liberated minors, Roume's reforms notwithstanding. For their part, liberated minors generally accepted the idea that they should work—indeed, African adults also demanded labor from children of free status—but some of them challenged guardianship when the workload was too heavy or treatment too harsh. Through such actions, these liberated minors made clear that in an era of reform and antislavery rhetoric, post-emancipation childhood would need to be negotiated and not simply imposed.

Morality and (Mis)Behavior

Guardianship also structured debates about the behaviors deemed acceptable for formerly enslaved children and served, in a way, as an institution of moral reform. Indeed, liberated minors' behavior and morality worried officials, commissioners, and guardians alike. Guardians complained when wards acted out, asked the secretary general to help with discipline, and even sent unruly wards away. At the same time, guardianship commissions collected information about minors' "material and moral" status, asking questions of young people and their guardians to elicit this information.[51] By probing, evaluating, documenting, complaining about, and disciplining the conduct of liberated minors, officials and guardians sent a message to these children about the kinds of behaviors they considered unacceptable. Yet conversely, liberated minors may have deployed so-called misbehavior strategically, to register discontent with their circumstances or claim greater autonomy. The behavior of liberated minors became a significant point of contention, and the discourses surrounding it raised questions about how formerly enslaved children might contribute to and belong in Senegal's towns.

Guardians frequently complained that liberated minors refused to obey, failed to respond with appropriate respect, or habitually misbehaved. Indeed, guardians often cited "insolence," "disobedience," or "misconduct" as grounds for terminating guardianship, and in a few cases they accused liberated minors of theft. In November 1904, for example, sales representative Edouard Duprat sent minor Tiephi Samba away, explaining to the secretary general he could not "make use of [him] at all, due to the disobedience and ill will of this child." In late 1907, Edouard d'Erneville returned Alcagny to the administration, citing his "deplorable conduct." And in September 1909 the widow of Paul Deproge notified the official that she had recently turned her ward, Gaston Fall, over to the police since he had stolen from her over a long period. Unable to "correct" his errant behavior, she wanted to give up guardianship.[52] The secretary general typically accepted these sorts of complaints and worked to find new placements for the liberated minors in question, turning to the hospital, prison, or orphanage to take them in when private individuals did not come forward. Thus, through guardianship, guardians and officials worked together to enforce standards for liberated minors' behavior. They envisioned a childhood for these low-status minors that consisted of orderly service, respectful interactions with their guardians, and quiet obedience to French law.

Liberated minors, of course, did not uniformly accept these expectations. While many apparently complied, a small number acted out in ways that had disproportionate impact since they captured the time and attention of guardians, officials, and sometimes police. Their disobedience, disrespect, theft, and other undesirable actions can be read as what James C. Scott described as "everyday forms of resistance."[53] And, since complaints of misconduct sometimes resulted in a change in guardianship, such actions could have material impact on liberated minors' circumstances. In August 1906, for example, liberated minor Cécilé began refusing to complete her household work and started responding to her guardian with what Madame Le Franc called "extreme insolence." Furthermore, on two occasions, she fled to a Monsieur and Madame Roumégaux, who lived in the city of Saint-Louis, some distance away from the Le Franc home. Unable to tolerate this misbehavior, Le Franc sent the girl back to the administration, and the secretary general promptly made Madame Roumégaux her guardian.

Yet she remained uncooperative, and within days Henri Roumégaux notified the secretary general that they would not keep her since she was "lazy," "licentious," and always seeking to "escape." After a third woman agreed to take Cécilé but abruptly changed her mind when she learned about the girl's reputation, the secretary general decided to send Cécilé, who was about twelve, to the Catholic girls' workhouse. Although we cannot discern Cécilé's intent, it is notable that her disagreeable behavior ended her relationship with a series of guardians, ultimately bringing her to the Sisters of Saint-Joseph of Cluny.[54]

The outcome of habitual misbehavior was perhaps happier for Saïdane, a liberated minor who lived in Tivaouane and who found himself emancipated from guardianship at around age fifteen. Because he had run away several times from both local chief Maissa M'Baye and trader Amadou M'Boup, and because he had earned a reputation for a difficult and "demanding" temperament, no one wanted to take him in. In November 1909, the secretary general decided that Saïdane did not need yet another guardian but was old enough to support and take care of himself.[55] As in Cécilé's case, Saïdane's misconduct prompted discussion and then intervention from the colonial state, though with a different end. In refusing to obey and otherwise misbehaving, these liberated minors upset lingering social norms associated with slavery and made clear they wanted to belong in the community on their own terms.

Even as guardians and officials attempted to enforce specific expectations for the comportment of all liberated minors, they paid additional attention to girls, policing their mobility and their sexuality.[56] Guardianship commissions and police officers sent to investigate guardianship-related matters might have asked questions about sexual liaisons, and they took note of female minors' pregnancies, children, and marriages. More significantly, numerous guardians complained that older female wards committed sexual improprieties or went out at night without permission, and when they asked to terminate guardianship on these grounds, the secretary general obliged.

Hence, in September 1906, a Monsieur Fréau sent back a fourteen-year-old liberated minor after only ten days, describing her as "licentious (*vicieuse*) and lying." The girl, Sokhna Trawaré, did "not want to stay in my home unless I give her the freedom to run around where she wants at night," Fréau claimed, and would "not stay anywhere" unless permitted these liberties. Similarly, in January 1907, Charles Pellegrin planned to end his guardianship over Niellé, a girl of about fifteen who had come to his home a few months before. This liberated minor had "intolerable conduct," he claimed, continuing to "spend her nights outside" despite his efforts to correct her behavior.⁵⁷ In attempting to constrain the mobility and presumed sexual activity of their female wards, these guardians, one French, the other *métis*, positioned chastity as central to the girlhood available to liberated minors, yet they also reinforced slave-era norms giving enslavers control over the sexuality of the people they enslaved.⁵⁸

Fears that officials would judge them harshly for failing to instill bourgeois French morality in their female wards, that liberated minors would turn to prostitution, or that they could be accused of prostituting their charges likely played a role in leading these French and *métis* guardians to send problematic girls away.⁵⁹ Yet even as some guardians viewed the street as a space of sexual immorality, others created sexual danger inside their own homes, exploiting the vulnerability of their young wards. Indeed, liberated minors in Senegal were sometimes targets of sexual advances, including rape, from their guardians and employers, a problem exacerbated by the widespread stigma linking slave status or descent to sexual licentiousness.⁶⁰ In August 1906, for example, a liberated minor named Awa fled the sexual abuse she suffered in the home of her guardian, Marième Sow of Saint-Louis. When the police tracked her down to nearby N'Dar Toute, where she was staying with a Monsieur Bara N'Dao, they found the twenty-year-old in an advanced stage of pregnancy. She had run away, she explained, because her guardian's husband had fathered the child, and the family had started treating her poorly after they learned of her pregnancy. Given this, the police commissioner called on the secretary general to house Awa in the civil hospital instead of returning her to her guardian. The police commissioner's willingness to put aside his usual skepticism at liberated minors' complaints suggests that this sort of exploitation may have been common.⁶¹

Sexual encounters, whether consensual or forced, could directly impact girls' status as wards, especially if they produced children. Officials, commissioners, and some guardians promoted sexual restraint among liberated minor girls, yet the state also recognized childbearing and marriage as indicators of majority that could emancipate girls from guardianship. This was the experience of some, though certainly not all, of the 83 young women who had one or more children and the 132 young women who married between 1895 and 1911 while still under guardianship in Saint-Louis.⁶² Although these numbers surely include some exploitative sexual encounters and may reflect guardians' desire to receive bridewealth in arranging marriages for female wards, it is also possible that some liberated minor girls pursued sexual relationships strategically. Indeed, not only could marriage or childbirth lead the state to remove a young woman from guardianship but to the extent that liberated minors decided about sex for themselves, they made a powerful statement about personhood, pushing back against the idea that guardians, like enslavers of the past, should control dependents' sexuality. In disobeying, disrespecting, running away, and having sex, liberated minors challenged assumptions about how dependent and formerly enslaved children should behave. After Roume's reforms, the increasingly frequent surveillance and tracking of liberated minors highlighted the ways the state had fallen short of its aims of protection and forced officials to adopt a more expansive understanding of colonial childhood.

Conclusion

For over sixty years, guardianship influenced debates about how post-emancipation society would function and how childhood might be defined for the formerly enslaved. The specifics of the debates are harder to discern for the period before 1895, since there are long gaps in the sources and the extant records focus mostly on the identities and claims of those who wanted to be guardians. Even so, we can catch glimpses of negotiations over the terms of post-emancipation childhood when wards requested certain types of apprenticeships, sought changes in guardianship, or attempted to opt out of the system entirely. Such actions sent the message that minors did not want to unthinkingly accept colonial expectations. With increased emphasis on monitoring and recordkeeping after 1903, guardianship took on new importance as the colonial state began to more aggressively undermine slavery in the region, develop new bureaucratic structures, pursue secularization, and promote economic development. Yet despite efforts to portray guardianship as a project of "humanity," the state continued to expect liberated minors to accept an idea of childhood defined by domestic or manual labor; by deference to guardians, local notables, officials, and others with status; and by acceptance of French moral standards.

Liberated minors, on the other hand, at least occasionally challenged dominant expectations, linked to slavery, about their work lives, interactions with guardians, and sexuality. Most often, however, they seem to have found a way to move through guardianship without overtly challenging it, a position reflected in the fact that most guardianship commission records indicated only that one or more members had "seen" the child in question, often adding that he or she was "well" or "well-treated," or much more rarely noting that the minor was "happy" or "content."[63] The children who challenged guardianship and those who accepted it alike contributed to French understandings of African childhood. As they surveilled and documented as many liberated minors as possible—including those who reported contentment, those who ran away, and those in between—officials not only gathered information that could help inform policy but also began to construct the architecture of documenting childhood, architecture they could elaborate on in other contexts.

Children's actions and perspectives are important in their own right, and insofar as records offer glimpses, they not only allow us to better understand the experiences of formerly enslaved children and young people but also reveal that such actions had a significant impact on post-emancipation Senegal as children used the state's emerging concern with child protection to challenge extreme mistreatment and combat certain kinds of stigma, or signaled that their situation was acceptable. Through this push and pull between challenge and acceptance, liberated minors themselves helped to define childhood for marginalized Africans in post-emancipation Senegal.

CHAPTER 2

The Reformatory

PENITENTIARIES FOR THE YOUNG AND THE IDEA OF CHILDHOOD IN SENEGAL, 1888–1940

On 14 February 1892, while traveling by train to the penitentiary-school in Thiès, young Moussa was briefly separated from Amady Bakily, the police officer tasked with overseeing the boy's transfer there. Questioned after the fact, Moussa maintained that the incident had been entirely accidental, telling investigators that he had received permission to use the restroom while the train was stopped in Kébémer and that, with Officer Bakily still on board, the train began to pull out of the station before Moussa's return. The police officer, on the other hand, claimed that the boy had jumped from the moving train and run away. The boy and the police officer agreed that Bakily had quickly exited the train to pursue Moussa, leaving behind in his haste the boy's few possessions and his own change of clothes, the pocket of which contained a cache of important documents pertaining to Moussa's detention as an "insubordinate" liberated minor.

Bakily soon located Moussa, and the following day the reunited pair made their way to Thiès, where for nearly eight years, young Moussa would live, work, and receive moral and academic instruction at the hands of Spiritan Fathers who received state funding to operate this reformatory alongside their Catholic mission station and school.[1] Although the police officer found Moussa relatively easily, he did not manage to recover the items left behind on the train, and subsequent searches for the documents came up short. The incident triggered two police inquiries, one focused on how the boy and his chaperone became separated and a second dedicated to the missing documents themselves. On 5 March, the interior director finally requested new copies of Moussa's change of guardianship certificate and court order, and the director of the penitentiary-school received them on 8 March.[2]

Moussa was one of dozens of African children to spend time—usually many years—in a juvenile reformatory in colonial Senegal. Most fell into the legal category of "minor detainees," children determined by a colonial court to have committed a crime or misdemeanor but to have done so "without discernment," or without criminal understanding, by virtue of their young age. A few ended up at the reformatory through other processes, with the most common pathway the one experienced by Moussa—a transfer of guardianship from an individual to the penitentiary-school "for reasons of discipline."[3] Moussa's story not only sheds light on specific techniques of discipline the French state applied to African children deemed insubordinate or criminal, but it also points to the centrality of documentation to colonial discipline and moral reform. Indeed, additional details of the incident, such as the interior director's desire to understand how Officer Bakily had managed to lose track of documents "entrusted to him personally," or the involvement of four officials in a weeks-long and ultimately fruitless recovery effort, might prompt us to ask why the colonial state valued documents pertaining to seemingly marginal children.[4] And furthermore, questions about Moussa's conduct—was he really left behind or was he trying to escape?—turn our attention to some of the ways that children themselves shaped the state's disciplinary approaches and apparatus.

These issues animate this chapter, which explores the history of Senegal's juvenile reformatories and the children, all boys, who lived, worked, and received training within. From 1888, when the French entered into an agreement with the Spiritans to run a penitentiary-school at their mission in Thiès, to 1927, when the administration tried yet another approach to juvenile reform, the state established a series of four such institutions, each of which had an impact that extended far beyond the relatively small numbers of boys interned. While these reformatories shared certain characteristics—all were in remote locations, promoted reform through agricultural and manual labor, and aimed to mold unruly boys into productive young men and docile colonial subjects—the goals of reform shifted over time, reflecting evolution in French ideas and practices as well as local priorities. When it came to girls, on the other hand, officials were at a loss. Lacking separate institutions for girls and concerned about the moral implications of interning them in the same reformatories as boys, when courts ordered girls to spend time in a "house of correction," the state ended up confining them to women's sections of adult prisons, if they detained them at all.

The chapter is particularly concerned with child detainees' experiences of internment, arguing that while carceral spaces marked them—and brought them into the documentary record—children did not simply accept this imprint. While some children generally cooperated with expectations, others pushed back against French demands that they obey institutional rules and personnel, follow arbitrary timetables, or perform specific types of work. Such continued unruliness could necessitate changes in disciplinary approach or call the entire enterprise into question. Even as it emphasizes the limitations of juvenile reform, however, the chapter also explores its impacts. Reformatories were intended to enact a specific vision of colonial boyhood, a vision that must have affected detainees, their families, and at least some subset of the larger community, though this is difficult to measure. The extremely limited sources related to girls in women's prisons raise questions about whether officials believed that African girls deserved a girlhood at all. Equally significant, the documentary apparatus the state relied on to track detainees and justify interning children contributed to the emergence of documented childhood, creating certain categories of childhood that were of interest to the state and normalizing the idea that aspects of children's lives should be recorded. As in the case of liberated minors discussed in chapter 1 but unlike the schoolchildren I discuss in chapter 3, this documentary intervention targeted marginalized children.

Responses to juvenile delinquency among colonial administrations in Africa have drawn considerable scholarly interest over the last couple of decades, not least because children who posed problems for the state are overrepresented in colonial archives. Much of this work focuses on male youth in urban centers in British colonies like Nigeria, South Africa, or Tanganyika during the interwar or postwar periods, and highlights colonial efforts to remove delinquents and vagabonds from the city's public spaces by sending them back to the rural areas from which they most often had come, entrusting them to community or family members, or interning them in a juvenile facility. Abosede A. George's excellent study of girlhood in colonial Nigeria is a partial exception, in that it focuses primarily on reform efforts targeting girl hawkers in Lagos, though one of her chapters offers a history of a reform school for boys.[5] The handful of studies that explore the history of reformatories in Senegal—which notably extends much farther into the past than in British colonial Africa—typically interpret them as indicators of the power of the colonial state and its limitations. In his foundational essays on this topic, Ibrahima Thioub situates Senegal's reformatories within a longer history of French efforts to impose discipline on marginal children and maintain order in the colonial city. And Ousseynou Faye examines the tensions and shifting balance between the state's impetus to protect and to punish African children.[6]

In this chapter, I offer a new reading of the dynamics between the interests of the colonial state in Senegal and those of the juvenile detainees in its care by centering detainees' experiences and their broader implications. I describe the carceral spaces in which they lived; their daily routines and isolation; and their strategies of cooperation, resilience, or resistance as they encountered French efforts to remake African boyhood, and I argue that as the state sought to impose new behavioral norms through the reformatory, detainees' reactions underscored the limitations of the state and its disciplinary regime, which could neither fully protect nor fully control the young people under state care. I also find that in Senegal, despite the fact that officials looked to metropolitan practice for inspiration, reformatories imposed a particular vision of boyhood that was colonial, racialized, and clearly differentiated from French boyhood, while the internment of girls in women's sections of prisons had the effect of depriving them of girlhood altogether. Hence, juvenile reform in Senegal did not construe African children as "universal subjects" as George finds for her Nigerian case. Finally, this chapter traces French efforts to maintain accurate reformatory records, suggesting that by extending the practice of documentation to detainees, many of whom came from marginalized families that might otherwise have largely escaped state intervention, especially in this early period, the reformatory regime may have had its widest-reaching impact.

Institutions, Rules, and Unruly Children

Although the first juvenile reformatory in Senegal opened in 1888, this institution was not the administration's first attempt to reform and discipline unruly children. Officials developed the guardianship system, explored in chapter 1, to respond to concerns that newly freed children might challenge colonial stability. Colonial courts put children on trial when they were charged with crimes, and they could sentence children to time in an adult prison when found guilty or when acquitted due to a lack of criminal understanding. Prisons sometimes had "youth" sections, but in practice there was not much separation between young people and adults within these carceral spaces. In addition, the state sometimes entrusted young offenders to prominent residents as apprentices, and—if they were deemed to lack criminal understanding—sometimes returned them to their families for rehabilitation.[7] By the late 1880s, officials had become increasingly concerned that adult inmates negatively impacted the morality and impeded the rehabilitation of young offenders interned in colonial prisons, and they began to consider alternatives. These concerns led to creation of the first juvenile reformatory in Senegal, the Thiès penitentiary-school, which beginning in 1888 the Spiritan Mission operated with support and funding from the administration.[8]

Discipline, order, and training were central to the earliest vision of child reform, and these goals continued to drive each of the institutions that followed. The 13 August 1888 decree establishing the penitentiary-school noted that inmates would be "raised together (*élevés en commun*), under strict discipline," while performing agricultural and other work and receiving "elementary instruction," and the October 1888 contract between the administration and the mission added that detainees had to undergo "training" (*formation*) and laid out a payment agreement.[9] A new nine-year contract, signed in January 1894, decreased funding and made some other changes but retained the emphasis on discipline and instruction, noting that the "moral and professional education" and "elementary instruction" provided should reflect detainee "aptitudes."[10] Although this institution shared elements of its approach with the "agricultural penitentiary colonies" that had reformed child offenders in France since the mid-nineteenth century, intended outcomes differed in important ways. While French institutions aimed to use the natural environment to redeem children who would become citizens and to showcase the French state's ability to provide for its citizenry, the Thiès penitentiary-school was to provide moral reform and training deemed appropriate for African detainees in a French colony.[11] Missionaries touted as success stories detainees who seemed "resigned" to their detention, who accepted baptism or took an interest in the church, or who worked productively for the colonial economy—as a cook or a server in a European home, for example—after release.[12] This ideal of boyhood (and male youth)—accepting of French culture and Catholicism, obedient to missionaries and French officials, and employed in subservient roles within a largely European economy—differed profoundly from what boys encountered in their own communities, where they were expected to obey their fathers or uncles, demonstrate honor and fortitude, study the Qur'an and practice regular prayer (in Muslim areas), and learn the trades of their fathers or other men in the community.[13]

No juvenile reformatory functioned in Senegal for much of the early 1900s—the Thiès penitentiary-school closed in late 1902 when high costs, low numbers, and increasing emphasis on secularization made it impossible to renew the contract—resulting in a return to older methods for addressing juvenile crime, including interning children in adult prisons or tasking families with rehabilitation.[14] By 1911 and 1912, however, officials had begun planning to intern minors at the agricultural station in Richard-Toll, one of several such stations in the colony where French agricultural specialists, aided by African laborers, conducted research on the economic viability of various crops and growing methods. At Richard-Toll, located about one hundred kilometers inland from Saint-Louis along the Senegal River, researchers were particularly focused on developing better irrigation techniques. The decision to send detainees here signaled a subtle shift in the aims of juvenile reform, which now privileged agricultural labor above all else in a setting more akin to a labor camp than a school. Planning emphasized practical matters like rations and budgets, along with, as the lieutenant governor put it in November 1911, the "disciplinary regime under which the young detainees sent to Richard-Toll would be constrained."[15]

It was not until March 1912 that the Richard-Toll agricultural station received formal recognition of its role in providing training for the colony's marginalized children. Yet Lieutenant Governor Henri Cor's ordinance said nothing about detainees, instead creating an "agricultural orphanage" to receive "abandoned children and children whose parents would like to have them pursue an agricultural apprenticeship." For the first few months, the facility functioned as outlined in the ordinance, and twelve young "pupils" had arrived by November, some of them sent by their parents and others identified as "orphans." But in December 1912, two "detainees" arrived, having been ordered by one of Senegal's courts to spent time in a "house of correction," indicating an expansion of the institution's functions.[16] The decision to incorporate more categories of marginalized children likely stemmed from budgetary concerns, but it may also have reflected new thinking about juvenile reform in France, where psychological studies linking the emerging construct of "adolescence" with rebellion had informed a 1912 law that created separate juvenile courts and deemphasized institutionalization. Although this law did not go into effect in Senegal, it is possible that the thinking behind it encouraged officials to try a new approach to juvenile reform in the colony, allowing detainees to mix with orphans and "pupils" so as not to isolate them in penal institutions, despite long concerns about the moral implications of doing so. This is consistent with the views espoused in a 1913 article, aimed at teachers in colonial schools, on the "benefits" of French rule, which included the "agricultural orphanage of Richard-Toll" as an example of colonial "childhood protection" initiatives.[17]

Yet this arrangement did not last long. The lieutenant governor issued an order in February 1916 to establish an "agricultural penitentiary" for minor detainees in Bambey, a village in Senegal's peanut basin, and officials stopped sending detainees to Richard-Toll; the orphanage likewise moved to Makhana the following year. The daily routine at Bambey did not seem substantially different, though it probably placed an even greater emphasis on agricultural production for the colonial export market. Research at the Bambey agricultural station, to which the reformatory was attached, focused on all aspects of peanut cultivation, Senegal's main cash crop, though the station also produced a variety of food crops and raised livestock.[18] Instead of producing to support their families and local communities, as boys outside the spheres of French influence would have learned to do, detainees in Bambey likely heard the message that African boys of marginal backgrounds, whether they came from towns or the countryside, should aspire to produce peanuts for the export economy while accepting French notions of proper conduct and discipline.

Yet despite the recognized importance of discipline, officials soon realized that the agricultural station at Bambey was not up to the task of reforming errant children. The station director, for one, wrote in 1922 that he wanted the penitentiary to "disappear" from the facility, citing the poor quality of detainees' labor, their disorderly behavior—which ranged from petty theft to flight—and the cost. Furthermore, he pointed out, his employees devoted themselves fully to scientific work and had no desire to be prison guards.[19] In 1925, asked to comment on an inquiry from the lieutenant governor of French Soudan about the feasibility of sending young offenders to Senegal, the administrator responsible for Bambey agreed to the plan but expressed doubts about the efficacy of juvenile reform. "Moral results" had been "rather problematic," he noted, and the penitentiary's greatest success had been protecting people from minors' "misdeeds for a rather long time." Such reservations must have been widespread, since a 1938 report on Bambey's successor institution recollected that Bambey's operations "were not satisfactory."[20]

By 1927, the administration had begun to explore relocating the penitentiary, and in a 20 September decree, the lieutenant governor ordered the creation of a new facility for the internment of minor detainees. Situated in Carabane, a remote village on an island in the Casamance River of southern Senegal, the

École Professionnelle Spéciale (Special Professional School), as it was known, began receiving detainees in December of that year. The reformatory in Carabane differed from its predecessors in several ways, perhaps most notably, as Ibrahima Thioub has pointed out, in its administration and funding. While earlier institutions supported agricultural research or other activities, Carabane was solely dedicated to rehabilitating minor detainees and was categorized as an institution of "Public Instruction" for the purposes of budget and oversight. Connected to both changes, it emphasized education and training over work requirements, though it continued to impose strict discipline and to function as a carceral space. This was especially evident in the envisioned separation of the facility into two distinct areas, the "penitentiary" section for minors found to have lacked discernment or those convicted of crimes but given short sentences (under two years), and the "correctional" section for convicted minors sentenced to more than two years. Those in the "correctional" section were to be kept separate from others as much as possible and were subject to a higher level of supervision, but rations, rules, and daily routine—six hours of manual training and work, two hours of academic instruction—were consistent across the sections.[21] This change tracks with a metropolitan reform law of December 1927 that turned state juvenile facilities into "houses for supervised education" (*maisons d'éducation surveillée*) in response to public demand for youth centers focusing on rehabilitation and job training rather than punishment.[22]

Reforms in 1927 in both Senegal and France, then, echoed the new focus, widespread in Europe, North America, and elsewhere, on saving, rehabilitating, and protecting marginalized children—indeed the Carabane facility was, to one official in 1936, a "school for the reeducation of perfectible subjects." Yet the imagined outcomes differed strikingly from metropole to colony. Whereas in France, social workers and others wanted to reform juvenile delinquents so they, as citizens, could help build a nation plagued with low birth rates and so-called degeneracy, the Special Professional School in Senegal reflected the ongoing commitment to reforming boys into disciplined subjects who would follow colonial laws and build the colonial economy. Although the approach to reform had shifted to once again incorporate some academic study along with training in a variety of skilled trades and manual labor, young detainees continued to be groomed to fill subaltern roles that met French needs, a colonial vision of boyhood that differed significantly from the ideals espoused in African communities, where boys had to labor for their fathers or uncles while showing them respect and obedience.[23] These trends continued into the mid-1930s, as the Popular Front's emphasis on social welfare infused colonial governance and encouraged the development of new child "protection" policies. Even as officials began in 1937 to limit *who* could be detained as they discussed a major overhaul of the juvenile justice system, and despite some differences in approach and focus, the core characteristics desired of a rehabilitated African boy remained remarkably consistent.[24]

Overview of Detainee Populations

These reformatories never interned large numbers of children, and they did not entirely shield minors from adult prisons, but their prominence in official thinking about African children suggests that they had an outsized impact on ideas about boyhood in colonial Senegal. Nearly all minor detainees had spent at least a few weeks in an adult prison while awaiting trial, and some unknown number of minors served their entire sentence in adult prisons, despite eligibility for internment in a juvenile facility. This was the case for all young female offenders, given the lack of reformatories for girls and the state's prohibition—for moral reasons—on interning girls and boys in the same juvenile institutions.[25] Available records suggest that the detainee population at the penitentiary-school in Thiès peaked in 1892 at twenty-nine. The agricultural penitentiary/orphanage at Richard-Toll housed fifteen minors in 1913, and the population at its successor institution in Bambey seems to have interned fifteen to twenty-six, depending on the year. Numbers climbed during the Great Depression, with the Special Professional School in Carabane interning forty detainees in 1929 and fifty the following year. By 1938, however, the number had declined to twenty-four. The statistics given in the preceding discussion and presented in table 2 below appear in the archival record as aggregates, that is, they are statistics included in reports, budgets, and correspondence.

For the entire period (1888–1938), I have located the names of 175 detainees, and I have been able to learn at least a little more about most of them. There is only one girl on my list, Léonie Guèye, though neither Léonie nor the handful of other girls tried for criminal activity during this period spent time in the reformatories.[26] Available documentation provides ages for 102 of these children at the time of their arrest or trial, and these appear in table 3 below. Nearly always the result of officials' approximations or negotiation between detainees and the police officer, court clerk, magistrate, or other official who produced paperwork, rather than an accurate measurement of detainees' chronological age, these

TABLE 2. Minor Detainees in Senegal's Reformatories, 1888–1938

DATE OF STATISTIC	REFORMATORY	NUMBER OF BOYS
July 1888	Thiès	5 detainees
April 1889	Thiès	12 detainees (plus 10 orphans and 10 day students)
November 1889	Thiès	17 detainees (plus unknown number of orphans and day students)
December 1889	Thiès	19 detainees
December 1892	Thiès	29 detainees (plus 20 orphans)
September 1899	Thiès	9 detainees, 2 liberated minors
January 1900	Thiès	9 detainees
April 1901	Thiès	10 detainees
1913	Richard-Toll	15 orphans
May 1921	Bambey	26 detainees
July 1922	Bambey	15 detainees
January–February 1926	Bambey	23 detainees
1929–1930	Carabane	40 detainees
1930–1931	Carabane	50 detainees
1936	Carabane	36 detainees
February 1938	Carabane	24 detainees

Sources of data: Thiès Journaux, 1886–1900, Senegal 3i2.17, AGCSE; Sénégal et Dépendances, *Conseil Général, session ordinaire de 1889* (Saint-Louis, Senegal: Imprimerie du Gouvernement, 1889), 337; *Rapport du Comité de Surveillance du Pénitencier du Thiès, 1893* (Saint-Louis, Senegal: Imprimerie du Gouvernement, 1893), Senegal 3i1.22a3, AGCSE; État nominatif, 8 September 1899, 3F26, ANS; Directeur du Pénitentiaire to Secrétaire Général, 39 April 1901, F26, ANS; Gouvernement général de l'Afrique Occidentale Française, *L'Afrique Occidentale Française en 1913: Rapport d'ensemble annuel* (1913), 260; Directeur de la Station Expérimentale de l'Arachide to Inspecteur Général de l'Agriculture, de l'Élevage et des Forêts, 8 July 1922, 3F27, ANS; Administrateur Baol to Gouverneur, telegram-letter, 2 February 1926, 3F27, ANS; Gouvernement General de l'Afrique Occidentale Française, *Budget de la Colonie du Sénégal, exercise 1930* (Saint-Louis, Senegal: Imprimerie du Gouvernement, 1929), 165; Gouvernement General de l'Afrique Occidentale Française, *Budget de la Colonie du Sénégal, exercise 1931* (Saint-Louis, Senegal: Imprimerie du Gouvernement, 1930), 165; Instituer Supérieur (for Chef du Service de l'enseignement primaire) to Lieutenant Gouverneur Sénégal, 31 August 1936, H284, ANS; Administrateur Supérieur Casamance (E. Némos) to Gouverneur Sénégal, 25 February 1938, H284, ANS.

numbers offer insight into French assumptions about African children and age. Furthermore, the act of recording them contributed to the rising importance of identity documentation, as I discuss in chapter 6.

TABLE 3. Ages of Detainees

ESTIMATED AGE	NUMBER OF DETAINEES
9 years	3
10 years	9
11 years	5
12 years	5
13 years	14
13 or 14 years	2
14 years	22
15 years	18
16 years	18
17 years	3
18 years and older*	3
Unknown	73

*These students, all of them sent to Carabane from the neighboring French colony of Soudan in 1929, were too old to be detained in a juvenile facility. It is unclear why (and if) they were allowed to remain there.

Source: Minor Detainees Database.

Notably, eighty were thirteen or older, suggesting that the administration was most concerned about the disorderly activities of older children and more willing to remove these minors from their families and communities for rehabilitation. Discussions about potential reform led the head of the judicial service in 1938 to order courts to cease sending children under thirteen to a reformatory, further emphasizing the importance of this age. Many detainees came from Senegal's cities and towns, especially Saint-Louis, Dakar, and Rufisque, but others were from rural areas; in the mid-1920s, the neighboring French colony of Soudan began paying Senegal to take in a small number of detainees. A significant majority of the forty cases where the crime is known involved nonviolent offenses like theft (twenty-two cases) or vagabondage (four cases), but in a few cases courts determined that minors committed violent crimes including murder (one case), homicide (two cases), rape (*viol*, one case), and attempted train derailment (one case).[27]

Yet, irrespective of the offense, most sentences were long, ranging from a few months to eleven years, with five years being most common, as indicated in table 4 below. Courts tended to require internment for the maximum length of time allowed by law (73 of the 114 cases in my database with known sentences), so younger children could receive substantially longer sentences than their older peers for similar misconduct. Indeed, children's sentences to "houses of correction" were typically much longer than prison sentences for adults convicted of comparable crimes. A 1911 court case involving three members of a family from Guet N'Dar, a fishing village outside Saint-Louis, offers a particularly compelling example. Convinced that Niégui Fall and her two sons, ages eleven and (probably) nine, had attacked a man with a knife, the court convicted the mother of assault and battery and sentenced her to forty-five days in prison. Although it acquitted the boys, who were too young to be held responsible, the court required that they serve time in a "house of correction," the older boy until age eighteen and the younger one until age sixteen—seven years, compared to their mother's forty-five days![28]

TABLE 4.   Sentence Lengths of Detainees

SENTENCE LENGTH	NUMBER OF DETAINEES
<1 year	3
1 year	3
2 years	7
3 years	12
4 years	17
4.5 years	1
5 years	29
6 years	17
7 years	13
8 years	5
9 years	1
10 years	5
11 years	1
Unknown	61

Source: Minor Detainees Database.

Paradoxically, perhaps, these disproportionate sentence lengths reflected French belief that children held potential for the future and could be reformed, while African adults required punishment and might never achieve rehabilitation.[29] Reformatories were thus mechanisms for remaking African boyhood to support French goals, though African boys' actions had a significant limiting effect. Even so, the more time boys spent living in a reformatory, the greater the potential impact of French discipline, order, training, and efforts to turn boys into productive workers for the colonial economy.

In some cases, the reach of reformatories extended beyond the colonial court system to include boys whose guardians or parents were fed up with their rebellious behavior, suggesting that these institutions—and perhaps the vision of reformed boyhood they offered—had begun to impact the broader society. In the late nineteenth century, for example, the Thiès penitentiary-school received several "insubordinate" liberated minors like Moussa, with whom this chapter began, who had repeatedly butted heads with their guardians, run away, or been in trouble with police. In these cases, in response to guardians' complaints or decisions to terminate their role, the state transferred guardianship to the institution and required liberated minors to remain there until majority. In an even more striking example from 1927, a Dakar restauranteur and father, Bilaly Kamara, turned to the reformatory as a tool in disciplining his own son, who had not responded to other methods. At a loss for what to do to correct the behavior of his sixteen-year-old who kept stealing money, Kamara petitioned the court to send the boy to the Agricultural Penitentiary in Bambey for as many as six months, at Kamara's expense. In signing off on the request, the head prosecutor and lieutenant governor mimicked the nineteenth-century French practice of paternal correction, which gave fathers the authority to obtain short-term disciplinary imprisonment of their wayward—but not necessarily criminal—children.[30] I find this incident especially compelling because it not only suggests that the reformatory was positioned to apply French ideas of disciplined African boyhood beyond the population of juvenile offenders to other children but that it had begun to shape ideas about boys' discipline and education circulating in the larger African community (though its impact is difficult to quantify).

Thus, despite shifts in the location and internal organization of reformatories and despite some changes to the ideologies animating them, the boys who spent time within encountered relatively consistent core ideas about colonial African boyhood. Like liberated minors, who had similarly marginalized backgrounds and low status in colonial society, reformed detainees were supposed to accept boyhood defined by compliance with French rules and "discipline," "modern" (French) agricultural labor, manual work on French infrastructure, and notions of French morality, leading them to accept their subject status and to work in support of colonial economic priorities, rather than prioritizing respect for their fathers and labor for their communities. Unlike most liberated minors, however, detainees encountered these ideals in carceral spaces, where they were subject to much more constant and rigorous surveillance. Meanwhile, girls caught up in the colonial legal system did not receive comparable messages about girlhood from a state that seemed preoccupied with protecting (or regulating) their sexuality more than anything else. Given the longevity of these French disciplinary techniques, the decision to situate reformatories in four different sites, and the public nature of sentencing decisions (which regularly appeared in the official newspaper), it seems likely that Africans became increasingly aware of the existence and practices of these institutions. Detainees themselves were of course most affected by their experiences in French carceral spaces, and while some appear to have largely gone along with French expectations, others pushed back against this disciplinary regime.

Carceral Spaces, Child Reform, and Detainee Experience

All four of the reformatories were located in remote areas, reflecting the belief that isolation, a rural milieu, and work—often agricultural labor—could contribute to reform.[31] In addition to its utility in providing opportunities for farm work and removing young offenders from the temptations of the city (where many of them had been arrested and tried), the remote location enforced separation between detainees and their families, often presumed to be inadequate parents or guardians. In 1899, for example, even as members of the surveillance commission called on magistrates to view the juvenile penitentiary as a punishment of last resort, and to use it only when thorough inquiry found a minor's family unsuitable, they also disparaged African families for their supposed inattention to their children. While in general even "the best organized penitentiary" lacked the "moralizing power of the family," they wrote in their report, in Senegal one frequently had to "count on the indifference of the natives, unaware or pretending to be unaware of the fate of their children." Such circumstances, they continued, made it incredibly difficult for "magistrates to know the degree of morality of the families to whom children could be returned." Members thought that parents or other relatives probably could have assumed responsibility for at least some of the minors interned in Thiès, but given French critiques of African families, they understood why magistrates had placed them in an institution.[32] Indeed, before the head of the judicial service issued new instructions in 1938, the assumption that parents were incapable of properly supervising their children's moral development led magistrates to sentence African minors to time in a reformatory in almost every case, even though the penal code and the 1924 French West Africa justice decree allowed courts to release minors to their families. This practice continued in Senegal long after metropolitan reforms had encouraged courts to keep young offenders out of institutions whenever possible.[33]

By the late 1930s, as officials placed increasing emphasis on childhood protection and child welfare in French West Africa, some had begun to question the wisdom of such extreme isolation—Carabane was particularly difficult to access since it was not only remote but also an island. Hence, during her visit to Carabane, Denise Savineau, technical advisor for education, spoke with twelve of the detainees about their families, learning that none were in touch with their parents and that only six of the twelve corresponded with any relative. If the Special Professional School were situated elsewhere, "less distant from their families," she wondered, "would the children perhaps be less forgotten, and would the directors, surveilled from close by, commit fewer abuses?" At around the same time, in a report on the Special Professional School, an administrator, E. Némos, worried that children from rural areas had missed opportunities to learn local agricultural techniques from their families, and that all detainees "will have also lost all contact with family life and native society and I do not see how they will re-adapt."[34] As I explore below, other evidence suggests that detainees worked hard to maintain social and emotional connections, so the situation may not have been as dire as Savineau and Némos feared. Regardless, the colonial state maintained the reformatory in Carabane until the early 1950s, when a facility in Mbour took its place, though after 1938 courts were encouraged to entrust children to family or community members when possible. By removing children from their families—or, later, inserting a court representative into family relationships—the state positioned itself to make an outsized impact on their lives.

In addition to the realities of confinement and forced separation from family and community, minor detainees lived under "strict discipline," which personnel maintained in various ways. Some observers noted the "penal quality" of the institutional spaces like dormitories and eating areas, and at least in the Carabane period, a European gendarme served as the director and warden, and two "gardes de cercle" supervised the young detainees, the shift to an education model notwithstanding. Despite occasional criticisms of personnel, especially missionaries, for their leniency, in practice detainees suffered severe punishment when they broke rules, resisted, or otherwise misbehaved. Early on, methods included corporal punishment, restraint in irons and chains, and imprisonment in a cell, usually for a period of a few days. Although the Thiès penitentiary-school lacked cells onsite during the early years, rebellious detainees could undergo punishment in a cell or metal restraint at the nearest administrative post. By 1893, the facility had several cells and the director was seeking funding for more; the facility continued to rely on corporal punishment as well. Despite some notable differences in regulations by the Carabane period, which encouraged rewards for good behavior, banned all forms of corporal punishment, and listed punishments ranging from reprimands to time in a cell or transfer to the correctional section, detainee treatment may not have changed significantly in practice. Although the cells were empty and the harshest approaches were not in use when Savineau visited Carabane in 1937, she learned that some recent directors had punished detainees by striking them or forcing them to eat hot peppers. These methods must have predated the director in charge of the Special Professional School in 1933, who touted the successes of his "firm" discipline but claimed to maintain it through "remonstrances" and verbal interventions. Rations, funded through the colony's budget for prisons and comparable to what adult prisoners received, also contributed to the penal atmosphere. Even as surveillance committees and reformatory personnel claimed that the food was adequate, detainees complained about the quantity.[35] These disciplinary practices show how protection blurred with control as French officials attempted to ensure that detainees complied with their rules.

Reformatories were built on a belief in children's capacity for redemption, and accordingly their chartering documents laid out plans for reeducation and training for productive adulthood. In practice, these activities occupied significant time in detainees' daily routine, though time allocated to them shifted amid debates about how best to approach juvenile reform. In the early 1890s, detainees at the Thiès penitentiary-school spent three or more hours each day in class, two hours in manual labor training, and two hours gardening or washing. They were expected to speak French at all times and could incur punishment for using their own languages. In 1892, the appointed reformatory surveillance commission alleged that the mission had improperly benefited from detainees' agricultural labor while failing to rehabilitate them, and other critics took the mission to task for prioritizing detainee labor over instruction and training. But the apostolic prefect (a Monseigneur Barthet) claimed that the purpose of the penitentiary-school was "to reform (*moraliser*) the children in her care through the habit of work," doubling down on the centrality of outdoor labor to juvenile reform. Seven years later, a differently constituted surveillance commission appreciated the mission's efforts to cultivate a "taste for work" among detainees, yet it encouraged the Spiritans to emphasize trades like masonry or metalwork rather than teaching gardening to so many (at the time, eleven of twelve were learning gardening). Their report also indicated that formal instruction focused on religion and morality, and missionary records make clear that at least some detainees aided in the religious activities of the mission and received instruction to prepare them to receive the sacraments.[36] Through this mix of activities, despite shifts in allocation, missionaries aimed to turn detainees into hard-working, moral, French-speaking, and—they hoped—Christian African boys who would one day become productive adult colonial subjects.

At Richard-Toll and Bambey, where penitentiaries were connected to agricultural stations, the emphasis on farming was likely much greater, but a lack of evidence prevents me from saying much about the balance between labor and other activities. The 1913 annual report for French West Africa, for example, noted that the "agricultural orphanage" attached to the Richard-Toll station housed fifteen children who were "employed in the various agricultural tasks of the station, in caring for animals, etc.," and also learning elements of beekeeping.[37] For the purpose of administration, funding, and reporting, the administration categorized these reformatories as agricultural facilities, not schools or prisons, doubling down on the importance of manual labor. Christian instruction, of course, no longer applied in the fully secular institutions that succeeded the Thiès penitentiary-school and came after the laicization laws in France.

The expectation that detainees contribute to the work of the agricultural station continued when the agricultural penitentiary moved to Bambey, and reports from 1922 and 1923 indicate that detainees tended livestock, fetched water, worked in the plant nursery, threshed peanuts and millet, sorted peanut seeds, and cleared an unwanted hedge during these years. Agricultural labor thus clearly remained central to the approach to rehabilitation, notwithstanding the Bambey agricultural station director's complaints about its inefficiencies. The penitentiary's budget, he argued in 1922, would be better spent on ten adult laborers who "would do three or four times more work than all the detainees together."³⁸ Although none of the extant documentation suggests that detainees received formal education in the agricultural reformatories at Richard-Toll and Bambey, it shows that they experienced discipline, order, and agricultural labor using European methods. These institutions presented these qualities as the crucial characteristics of a reformed African boy and future contributor to the colonial economy.

At the Special Professional School at Carabane, detainees spent much more time in academic and vocational training, but labor remained the primary focus and the essence of the approach to reform. Each day, detainees attended two hour-long classes, offered by the director of the local public school, covering "spoken French, reading, writing, [and] arithmetic," and they were supposed to learn trades like masonry or carpentry from a master artisan, following a training program developed by the Public Works Department. In practice, only some detainees pursued apprenticeships with artisans—formal training in skilled trades consistently fell below expectations—while others worked in the facility's garden, maintained or improved its buildings and fences, constructed terraces, or worked to build up or maintain the island's shoreline, roads, and wharf, tasks typically associated with corvée labor. During the 1930s, at least, Carabane's approach also featured regular instruction in morality coupled with "firm" discipline, and the director evaluated detainees' moral improvement, publicly acknowledging those who made the most progress.³⁹

By the mid-1930s, some officials had begun to raise questions about the quality of instruction and training offered at Carabane and about the goals of the institution, and their critiques shed further light on detainee experiences. In 1936, for example, an official with the teaching service worried about the prestige that he feared certain "fundamentally bad" detainees might derive from their schooling after their release, and he advocated offering academic instruction only to children identified as truly reformable. It does not appear that officials implemented this change, despite the secretary general's receptiveness, but even so the discussion suggests that questions circulated about whether a singular vision of colonial African boyhood could apply to all Africans.

In 1938, Administrator Némos took a very different tack, focusing on shortcomings in instruction and training that failed to ensure "moral improvement" and left detainees unprepared to pursue a trade at the time of their release. The artisans in charge of training, he wrote, lacked skill and a logical "method," and the teacher had the impossible task of teaching pupils who varied widely in age ("from 10 to 18 years"), region of origin, ethnicity, and previous school experience.

To his mind, the reformatory had become a "simple house of detention" that succeeded only in preventing young offenders from doing additional harm and not at rehabilitation. Denise Savineau, who visited Carabane at around the same time, agreed with some of these critiques but worried more about the challenges young people would face after their release than about the depth of their rehabilitation. True, their academics were "mediocre," but at least they could speak and understand some French, she noted. And even though they had only "rudimentary tools" for use in manual trades, they could carry out tasks "properly," if very slowly. The school could do right by its inmates, she argued, with reforms to the vocational program, directors who continued to treat the children as "schoolboys" rather than criminals, and a program to provide former detainees with housing and a job.[40] These critiques suggest that despite the uneven quality of instruction and varying degrees of harsh discipline and punishment, Carabane encouraged detainees to accept a version of colonial boyhood that, as before, emphasized compliance with French rules and labor for the colonial economy but that included new elements like exposure to basic academic subjects and a wider range of trades, reflecting shifts in French thinking about juvenile reform and child protection.

By structuring time, requiring labor, and imposing academic instruction and vocational training, the disciplinary and rehabilitative strategies envisioned for the reformatories contributed to the emerging notion of the African boy in colonial Senegal. To the extent that reformatories implemented these strategies, they helped to impose new ideas about order and discipline into certain African boys' daily lives, though this was limited by insufficient funding and, as discussed below, detainees' responses and resistance. Furthermore, if officials hoped that agricultural and manual labor, along with some formal instruction, would restore the morality of wayward children, they perhaps also envisioned it as a formative and even protective experience for any African boy, especially for those of humble backgrounds. Indeed, the goal of turning boys—delinquent or not—into economically productive adults who would embrace the many social, cultural, economic, and political changes brought by colonial rule connected discourses about juvenile delinquency to larger discussions of the nature of African childhood. Former detainees formed a bridge between the juvenile carceral spaces in which French ideas took precedence to local communities where French influence was often much weaker.[41]

Girls, notably, remained outside this vision, and this can only partly be attributed to the fact that they accounted for just a small (but currently unknown) percentage of children who were arrested, tried, and remanded to correctional facilities. Indeed, as scholarship on other parts of colonial Africa makes clear, colonial states most commonly associated juvenile crime with boys and therefore targeted efforts to address it at male youth. Furthermore, colonialists gendered as male the category of "youth" itself.[42] Yet girls did come before colonial courts, and courts did, after acquitting them due to their young age and lack of criminal understanding, order girls interned in a "house of correction" for an extended period. Required to act on these orders, officials ended up sending girls to women's sections of adult prisons, since the colony had no specialized facilities for girls. In doing so, they sent the message that unlike boys, African girls were not redeemable (or not worthy of the investment such redemption would require), raising questions about whether under the colonial regime girlhood existed at all for marginalized African girls.

These issues come to light in one of the best documented juvenile cases involving a young girl who passed through colonial courts before their reform in the late 1930s. When she was arrested for theft in July 1922, her third arrest for the same offense, the Saint-Louis court determined that thirteen-year-old Léonie Gueye could not be released to her family again but should be interned until she reached majority. Yet officials soon learned that the juvenile reformatory in Bambey could not fully separate her from the male detainees, prompting a decision to keep her in the women's section of the prison in Saint-Louis, where she had been taken upon her arrest, in the interest of morality. When Léonie's stepfather sought clemency on her behalf in 1924, the head prosecutor examined her case and raised several ethical concerns: Léonie would end up staying in an adult prison for around eight years—much longer than the sentences adults received for similar crimes—despite the fact that the court had acquitted her of criminal responsibility. He also worried about her exposure to other female inmates, imprisoned following criminal convictions. In short, Léonie's imprisonment failed to meet the court's intent: to have her perform labor, to ensure "her moral preservation," and to protect the "future of the society" through her reform in a house of correction. Despite the judicial official's strong support for transferring the girl to Bambey, the lieutenant governor refused on moral grounds and also pointed out that colonial prisons served a much wider variety of functions than did their metropolitan counterparts.[43] In making this decision, the lieutenant governor chose to see Léonie Gueye as a young woman whose sexuality the state needed to protect (or regulate) rather than as a girl—a child—in need of instruction, training, and reform. His actions suggest that even as the state sought to limit and constrain the boyhood available to marginalized African boys, it used courts and prisons, much like it used guardianship, to minimize—and even deny—the existence of African girlhood altogether.

Detainees in the Reformatory: Resistance and (Re-)Connection

The process of reimagining colonial childhood in the reformatory was not the preserve of French officials and personnel alone, of course, but a negotiated process involving the African children interned inside. Although the archival record contains very little evidence of detainees' words, perspectives, or voices, it does shed light on their actions. Records show, for example, that while some detainees complied with rules, others rebelled; while some stayed put until their release, others ran away; while some participated in the project of reform, others resisted French efforts. I suggest that we might read these actions as a commentary on the reformatory and on tensions between the vision of childhood it promoted and the local childhoods with which detainees would have been most familiar, which allowed children considerable autonomy and responsibility as long as they demonstrated respect and fulfilled labor obligations to their fathers or uncles.

French observers and reformatory personnel sometimes reported that detainees were satisfied, even "enchanted with their lot," but descriptions of their actions show that at least some pushed back against a disciplinary regime designed to promote what the French understood as order and appropriate training, and rejected French efforts to isolate them from the families and communities deemed problematic.[44] The voluminous records of the Thiès penitentiary-school contain many references to escapes and work avoidance, and sources related to the agricultural penitentiary at Bambey and the Special Professional School at Carabane suggest that detainees continued to resist in this way in the 1920s and 1930s. And, at least in the early period (for which many more sources are available), detainees countered efforts to cut them off from their families with efforts to remain connected, often running away *to* places of community and returning to a family member or community of origin upon release, in patterns consistent with children fleeing guardianship.

In correspondence and reports, officials involved with the various reformatories notified Senegal's administration of misbehavior, suggesting that French efforts to inculcate detainees with specific ideas about boyhood did not go uncontested. Despite an effort to minimize negativity, necessary since continued funding depended on success, even missionary correspondence and internal records contain many descriptions of the ways detainees challenged the disciplinary regime. The penitentiary-school director, for example, noted with some satisfaction in a March 1897 mission journal entry that the head prosecutor had "spoken severely" to the children locked in cells when he visited. The director could keep them in cells for as long as he wished, the official explained, and he could "call on the gendarmes, put them in irons. The penitentiary," he continued, "is the prison for young people, who must be in cells as soon as they behave badly."[45] This record, meant for internal mission use, hints at the widespread problem of misbehavior and at missionaries' frustration with it.

In later institutions, personnel were much more direct in their complaints. In his 1922 report, for example, the director of the Bambey agricultural station lamented the fact that detainees stole "fruits, vegetables, peanuts, millet, tools as soon as they thought themselves out of sight," and had the audacity to take items and money from station employees' residences. Additionally, there were "work stoppages, mass protests, even rebellions against the guards, and frequent escapes."[46] And in 1938, Denise Savineau wrote that the detainees at Carabane had exhibited "sneaky" and "rebellious" behavior under previous directors, stealing from the village and school at every opportunity. Even a cell hardly "managed to contain them," she claimed. The new director's efforts to provide good nutrition, firm but kind discipline, and engaging activities had produced positive changes in the children, she noted, acknowledging, perhaps unintentionally, the utility of rebellion in producing improved living conditions.[47] Indeed, it seems likely that detainee resistance in Richard-Toll and Bambey, and perhaps also in Thiès, contributed to French decisions to close these reformatories and try a (slightly) different approach somewhere else. In this way, children's actions could draw attention to the limitations of colonial interventions into childhood, which required the cooperation of children, their families, and their communities to succeed.

Of all misbehaviors, attempted and actual escapes generated the most angst (and correspondence) from reformatory personnel, often prompted a police response, and occupied the attention of some officials. Documentation is richest during the Thiès period, allowing for some analysis of detainees' strategies and informed speculation about their motivations. For this period (1888–1903), fifteen of the forty-three detainees in my database (34.9%) escaped from the Thiès penitentiary-school, and a few more mounted unsuccessful attempts. Although I have uncovered information about only two individual detainees who fled a penitentiary during the period after 1903, the 1922 report about Bambey quoted above hints at the director's frustration with escapes, and historian Ibrahima Thioub suggests that many detainees ran away from Bambey. As Dior Konaté notes, many prisoners escaped from adult prisons in the colony; it thus seems likely that young people ran away from all four of colonial Senegal's juvenile institutions.[48] Facilitated by minimal security—lacking personnel and resources, for example, the Spiritans had abdicated responsibility for runaways in their 1888 contract with the administration—and often animated by detainees' desires to return to familiar people and places, escapes represented the firmest resistance to French approaches to disciplining and reforming African boys.[49]

Detainees took advantage of lax security and moments of decreased supervision to make their escapes, while personnel attempted to disrupt their plans. Upon his rearrest in September 1892, for example, Ibrahima Dialo explained that he had run away from the group as they went on a stroll, having noted the lapse in supervision. In April 1893, a liberated minor named Mamadou ran away during an afternoon eclipse. In October 1894, Sadio Dialo and Mamadou Samba waited until evening, received permission to use the toilets, and then ran away under the cover of darkness. And in February 1901, Ibra Poye escaped in the predawn hours, as detainees left their dormitory to prepare for the day.[50] Escapes like these prompted the director of the Thiès penitentiary-school to ask in 1895 for much more rapid and thorough responses from the police, who assisted penitentiary personnel in their efforts to locate escapees. Help from the police was crucial, he pointed out, since "it is only the fear of being retaken by the police that can keep certain lazy, naughty, and hypocritical characters here and force them to work." Missionary records suggest that they tried to maintain security, imposing restrictions and punishments when they thought it necessary. To that end, someone entered this note into the mission's journal in October 1895: "Three children from the penitentiary (Demba, Amadou Sèye, Boulanger), incited, are thinking of leaving. They are put into cells." The procureur general, for his part, thought the mission needed to improve its supervision of the young detainees.[51] Irrespective of their long-term success, these attempts to flee the reformatory called into question many of the basic premises of its disciplinary regime and, by extension, the norms of boyhood it was meant to enact.

At least some escapees planned their destinations strategically, attempting to rejoin a family member or other social connection, or heading for British Gambia, where they could evade French authority. Missionaries were aware of both trends and mentioned them in correspondence. Indeed, in January 1896, following a string of escapes from the institution, the director of the penitentiary-school, Père A. Sébire, commented on the attraction of "finding themselves in security in English territory," and noted that this possibility "troubles these unruly young minds and leads them to escape." During his predecessor's tenure, several detainees had fled to Gambia, and knowledge of that fact apparently enticed young people to attempt to follow their example. "Hatred of work and love of liberty," Sébire concluded, "is very strong among them."[52]

Some detainees chose to run *to* family members or other people they had known prior to their internment, suggesting that despite French efforts to isolate them from their families and communities, detainees worked to maintain these social connections.[53] In September 1892, for example, Ibrahima Dialo (recorded age ten) ran away a mere two weeks after his arrival at the penitentiary-school. The procureur general questioned him several days later, after police had located him, and learned that he wanted to "go find a relative of his former master so he could get him to Saint-Louis."[54] This incident shows that detainees could attempt to strategize around existing relationships, even relationships of dependence and slavery. Ibra Poye's flight, mentioned above, provides even stronger evidence of the continued power of social connection. In February 1901, after less than a month at the institution, Ibra ran away, surprising the director, who noted that the boy had not given any indication of his plans. But despite this surprise, the director knew where to focus his search, noting that the boy had likely headed for Yène, the village near Rufisque where his family resided. A few days later, Ibra returned to the institution, having been located at his parents' home. The director learned that Ibra had only wanted to "see his father, who he hadn't seen in four years," and that another detainee had encouraged him to escape. In his final report on the matter, the director noted that Ibra had resumed his work following punishment, and sought to explain the large number of escape attempts that, he thought, resulted more from "childishness and a need for liberty than from malice."[55] African children, he insinuated, did not take to the French institution and its project of reform, and running away was a clear way they demonstrated this.

Although evidence is sparse, these trends seem to have continued after the closure of the Thiès penitentiary-school. Most compelling is the case of a young detainee at the agricultural orphanage at Richard-Toll, Abdoulaye Konaté, who ran away at around 7 p.m. on the evening of 14 July 1915 (had staffers let their guard down as they celebrated France's national independence holiday that evening?). In a letter written about the incident the next day, the head of the agricultural service encouraged the lieutenant governor to monitor river traffic around Saint-Louis, young Abdoulaye's presumed destination, in case the boy had stowed away on a ship. He was a relatively new arrival at the orphanage, having been sent there from Saint-Louis following a court decision ordering him to spend three years in a house of correction, and according to the agricultural station head, he was "well known to the Police" in that city. Like his predecessors in Thiès, then, this official in charge at Richard-Toll assumed the runaway had headed home where he likely had not only a history of encounters with the police but also a family or other social network.[56]

A rare letter written by a minor detainee during the Bambey period hints at some of the other ways young people might have attempted to shape their circumstances and remain connected to the social networks that were important to them. On 10 September 1925, the Correctional Tribunal found that Fara Diallo, "age 16," had lacked criminal capacity in committing theft and fraud and ordered his transfer from the civil prison in Saint-Louis, where he had been interned since his arrest a month earlier, to Bambey, where he was to remain until reaching majority. Shortly after that decision, young Fara wrote to the lieutenant governor seeking to avoid moving away from the town where he had social connections—he had been working there as a "boy" (household servant) at the time of his arrest, though he had been born in Kaédi—and out of the prison where he had begun to work as a cook's aid. Expressing remorse and a commitment to self-improvement, he urged the official not to send him to Bambey, where he might not be as useful and where he would be "far from those who will be able to take care of me." Despite the warden's positive assessment of his conduct and work ethic, however, the administration ordered his transfer in November.[57] It is significant, I think, that Fara wanted to remain in prison in a town where he knew people. This may be evidence of the existence of social networks involving people inside and outside penal institutions, as Konaté describes, or it may suggest that he had formed strong bonds with adults inside the Saint-Louis prison.[58] Regardless, even if ultimately unsuccessful, he pushed back against French efforts to remove him from the community he had built, emphasizing connection amid isolation.

This evidence, though fragmentary, offers glimpses into some of the ways detainees could shape perceptions and assumptions about marginal African children in colonial Senegal. At least some detainees proved adept at evading carceral spaces, and some pushed back against the rehabilitation agenda in other ways. Others did not overtly resist, but I have not found evidence to shed light on their motivations or their perceptions of the reformatory. Reformatories were designed to enforce specific ideas about time, work, behavior, and childhood norms. Even if reformatories did not produce the model colonial subjects French planners envisioned, it is improbable that young detainees remained unaffected by their experiences inside.

Discipline and Documentation in Juvenile Reform

One of the most impactful practices of the reformatories over the long term may have been the documentary regime they helped elaborate. Officials relied heavily on various sorts of records to legitimize reformatories, justify their legal right to intern minors, keep track of minors' conduct and release dates, and locate minors who managed to escape. Along with the records generated on a child's arrest and in trial, these records made visible and knowable dozens of boys *and* girls who otherwise might have remained on the margins. Prison wardens kept registers (*registres d'écrou*) that documented all people—adults and children—in the prison's custody for any length of time. At a minimum, each of these entries consisted of a name, an age or birthdate (often an estimate) and birthplace, parents' names, the prisoner's profession, date of entry, date and nature of the court's decision, and sentence length. To initiate a transfer from the adult prison to a juvenile reformatory after trial, lieutenant governors required copies of sentencing documents and relevant information from the prison register, retaining some copies in the archives and sending others to the reformatory. Like prison wardens, reformatory directors maintained prison registers, and these records along with their official correspondence contributed to the process of documenting marginal children. The 1927 ordinance that created the Special Professional School listed no fewer than ten types of registers the school's director would need to maintain, at least six of them recording information about individual detainees! Further, identification documents produced for at least some detainees beginning in the 1920s collected physical descriptions (including height, skin tone, facial shape, scars or other markings, etc.), past arrests, and other details in addition to other standard information. At around the same time, increased focus on sanitation and hygiene in French institutions meant that local health officials had to maintain individual medical records for all detainees.[59]

The crucial importance of documentation to French interventions became clear in lapses, at moments when colleagues did not provide appropriate information or when penitentiary registers and other records were not properly kept. In 1899, for example, members of the surveillance commission reported that the Thiès penitentiary-school did not possess copies of judgments or sentencing orders, resulting in an incomplete prison register and potentially challenging the legitimacy of internment. Furthermore, they continued, officials had sent minor detainees to Thiès without identifying documents, making it nearly impossible to locate escapees who could simply "change their names according to the needs of the moment." Gaps in the record raised questions again in 1926, when the commandant of Baol learned from the newly appointed police commissioner that the "prison register of the young detainees" at the Bambey reformatory "had been kept in a most superficial fashion," lacking details about arrival dates, sentence lengths, and more. Bambey was in Baol, and thus the reformatory was ultimately the commandant's responsibility, so he pledged to rectify the situation immediately, even as he blamed the previous police commissioner for the shortcomings.[60]

These official documents, used to establish legality and detail custody, were created by the colonial state's administrative and judicial structures at specific transition points. But reformatory directors also tracked mundane information related to daily operations, and they made observations about detainees in this context. In 1897, seeking to formalize the collection of other kinds of information about detainees, the director of the penitentiary-school received approval to issue individual notebooks (*carnets*) in which teachers could record detainees' grades for academic work, vocational training, and conduct. The surveillance commission had suggested that such booklets might help former detainees obtain jobs.[61] Although sources do not reveal whether this plan ever moved beyond the prototype phase, the fact that it was discussed and approved suggests that officials viewed reformatories as an opportunity not only to reform problematic children and make them more legible while doing so but also to continue to exert influence—through the lingering effects of documentation—on these children long after they left the reformatories. In addition to its practical function, then, individualized paperwork held significant power in the eyes of the colonial state, and this perhaps explains why officials were so concerned about Officer Bakily's loss of Moussa's paperwork long after the escaped detainee was recaptured. While detainees and their families could limit the effects of this documentary regime in their own lives by, for example, using aliases or providing false information, they could not reign in the growing importance of documentation to African childhood on a broader scale.

Conclusion

Given the small number of children directly touched by these reformatories from 1888 to 1940, we might ask about the extent of their impact on children more broadly, and on ideas about children and childhood that circulated among representatives of the colonial state and ordinary Africans alike. I cannot make conclusive pronouncements on this question given the limitations of available sources, but many officials' continued commitment to and engagement with these institutions suggest that they shaped French thinking about how to reform African childhood, and public knowledge of these reformatories suggests that their impact on African communities reached much farther than the children they detained. Many officials continued to support the idea of the reformatory, despite the fact that some reports questioned their value and even proposed closing them in favor of other approaches to juvenile reform. In the midst of the Great Depression, faced with a still small but growing population of juvenile detainees, the administration proposed and the Colonial Council supported increasing funding for the reformatory in Carabane.[62] And finally, administration and judicial officials, wardens, reformatory directors, and others produced reams of correspondence related to these institutions as they sought to ensure they functioned well. Taken together, this longstanding—if sometimes conflicted—support and voluminous documentation suggest that the administration's stake in these institutions was much greater than the small population of detainees might imply.

Although the impact of reformatories on African communities is harder to gauge, some evidence suggests that its significance extended beyond the institutions themselves. Dior Konaté points out that colonial prisons inscribed French power onto Senegal's landscape, contributing to "crime-control by enhancing the visibility of imprisonment," and it seems likely that reformatories had a similar effect.[63] In addition to their physical presence, reformatories occupied space in print media, since for much of this period the colony's weekly official newspaper printed information from internment orders, including detainees' names, their parents' names, their places of birth, and their sentence lengths. Despite limited literacy rates, this practice probably disseminated knowledge of French interventions vis-à-vis African children among the broader public.[64] Knowledge about the institutions also spread firsthand, through encounters between detainees and nearby communities. Food may have brought together residents of the Richard-Toll community with the children of the agricultural station, since in 1913 the director proposed purchasing local produce and meats to supplement their rations of rice and dried fish. It is unclear whether this went forward, however, and in 1915 the French administrator in the region claimed that the Africans of Richard-Toll could not "get along with the European agriculturalists who live in the official Station." He did not mention detainees or orphans, but his comment suggests there were certain tensions with the local community.[65] Tensions were likely present in Bambey and Carabane, where sometimes detainees stole from nearby homes, prompting the director of the Bambey agricultural station to advise moving the penitentiary far away from residential areas.[66] On the other hand, in her 1938 report on the reformatory at Carabane, Denise Savineau noted that detainees liked to fish, and that they sold some of their catch "very cheaply to the residents of the island." They would have been able to interact with people on the outside through their leisure activities, and Savineau even attended a soccer match, refereed by the reformatory's director, between "pupils at the Special school, and children of the village."[67] By the late 1930s, then, the reformatory at Carabane seemed to cast a wide shadow into the surrounding community and perhaps farther beyond.

Reformatories did not bring about the full rehabilitation that French officials envisioned, due in no small part to detainee resistance but also to insufficient resources, staffing, and other issues, but they did shape childhood experiences in the colony. Given their focus on boys from the margins, reformatories reached at least some children who did not attend colonial schools, extending the state's influence to additional populations. As institutions that were—in practice if not by decree—segregated by race and sex, reformatories imposed specific ideas about what African boyhood should look like. Required to participate in vocational training and rudimentary academic instruction deemed appropriate for their station in life, boys would have learned about the economic roles officials expected them to fulfill as adults. Girls, in contrast, experienced prison life as young women, since colonial officials did not envision girlhood for girls from the margins. Subjected to "strict discipline" of various sorts, detainees would have understood that the state demanded obedience from African children, even as some of them rejected this demand by running away. Perhaps most significantly, reformatories helped naturalize the role of identification and other documents in children's lives by fixing their names, ages, and identities, recording their (mis) behaviors, and introducing them to the technologies of reading and writing.

CHAPTER 3

The School

SCHOOL DISCIPLINE AND THE IDEAL AFRICAN CHILD

In April 1914, Seydou N'Diaye faced likely expulsion from the médersa, the state-run Franco-Muslim school in Saint-Louis where he had held a scholarship. Described by school personnel as rude, noncompliant, unable to take criticism, slow to progress, and "the worst of all the second-year students," Seydou's most recent offense was challenging a Madame Calvayrac on a grade she had given him in spelling. Evidently trying to smooth things over and avoid expulsion, Seydou promised the director of the médersa in an apology letter that he would stop being "bad or insolent," and he also apologized in front of his classmates for his "indiscipline." Surprisingly, on the same day, Seydou sought permission from the head of the political bureau to withdraw from school. Had the apology not gone well? Or was he trying to develop a backup plan? Although it reflected significant knowledge of the education hierarchy and its priorities, Seydou's strategy to salvage his school attendance, or perhaps only his reputation, seems to have failed since the lieutenant governor drafted an order to cancel his scholarship for "general insufficiency in conduct and application."[1]

Seydou's alleged misconduct, the consequences he faced, and his efforts to avoid the most serious repercussions highlight a largely unexplored aspect of colonial schooling—the meaning and process of discipline in these colonial institutions aimed predominantly at African children. This incident, like many others, involved a white teacher (Madame Calvayrac) and a Black student, raising questions not only about how race and racism figured into punishment but also how race shaped the very definition of a "disciplined" schoolchild. And finally, the fact that what appears to be a straightforward school discipline issue required the lieutenant governor's attention similarly raises questions about the relationship among discipline in schools, student (mis)behavior, and the colonial state itself. This chapter explores these issues, asking how the colonial state in Senegal from the 1860s to the 1930s used school discipline as a mechanism for working out what the ideal colonial African schoolchild would be. These ideals overlapped with, but also departed from, the vision of childhood offered to liberated minors and minor detainees, since education involved even greater emphasis on French cultural values, along with academic and vocational training. At the same time, the chapter asks how African children's responses shaped French policy and discourses about childhood and class, and it considers how the effort to track and enforce discipline contributed to the documentation of African childhood.[2]

Considerable scholarship has established that colonial schooling reflected the goals of Christian mission and the colonial state, whether these goals were conversion to Christianity, cultural assimilation and "civilization," or creating an underclass of African workers and farmers trained in European methods. Studies have examined how school curricula, textbooks, and assignments affected students' worldviews or habits; how the status of "student" or "school leaver" shaped how others perceived them and how they perceived themselves; and how the culture of the colonial school—uniforms, schedules and time, eating at table, rules and punishment—reoriented students' daily lives, sometimes setting them at odds with their families.[3] "Discipline" pervaded nearly every aspect of a student's experiences in school, affecting pedagogy and classroom learning, reputation as a "good" or "problem" student, and expectations for comportment. But although many studies tell us that African students sometimes rebelled against school "discipline" when it became too harsh or unattainable, we have much to learn about what school discipline meant, how it affected childhood, and the extent to which it mattered to the colonial state. This chapter begins to address these gaps.

In colonial Senegal, school "discipline" had several distinct but related meanings. First, school inspectors and directors used the term when evaluating teachers' authority and effectiveness, glossing what we might think of today as classroom management. Discipline reigned in a classroom when the teacher had the authority to ensure that students stayed on task, remained quiet, paid attention, and conducted themselves in an orderly fashion. Second, and relatedly, teachers, school directors, inspectors, and other officials concerned themselves with students' conduct at school, expecting "disciplined" behavior, which, as I discuss at some length below, involved several key—and remarkably consistent—traits. When students repeatedly fell short of these behavioral expectations or rebelled against them, they had to undergo disciplinary proceedings of one sort or another. In this third use of the term, "discipline" implied the processes—reprimands, punishments, hearings, and so on—by which school authority figures attempted to correct students' misbehavior. This chapter focuses primarily on discipline as it related to students (i.e., the second and third definitions laid out above), since they best allow us to trace discourses about and experiences of childhood.

Schools were central to French plans for the "civilizing mission" of the nineteenth century, and they remained central as the emphasis shifted in the twentieth century to *mise en valeur*, social welfare and "humanitarian" colonial rule, and child protection. Officials valued schools because they not only taught specific skills and content but because they also socialized future workers into French cultural practices, behaviors, and perspectives, both through the curricula and through school rules, behavioral norms, and codes of conduct. Furthermore, schools offered unique opportunities to exercise significant influence on and surveillance of African children, and officials' intense interest in schools generated considerable knowledge and documentation (grades, reports, minutes of discipline hearings, etc.). Schools, of course, not only generated documents about children but also taught literacy and engaged students in the production of the written word, thereby playing a particularly important role in the normalization of documented childhood. By turning untutored and disorderly African children into disciplined, attentive, and documented students, officials and educators worked to create a childhood ideal that could spread widely as education expanded, contribute to the reform of African childhood, and produce literate auxiliaries and French-speaking peasants who would be loyal colonial subjects. These goals came into particular relief in the small number of schools, mostly in Saint-Louis and Dakar, with mixed African and French enrollment, where patterns of harsh punishment meted out to African students suggest that educators viewed certain cultural practices as discipline problems. African children, of course, shaped this reworking of childhood, meeting some French expectations while pushing—or writing—back against those that clashed too strongly with their cultures or that were too restrictive in other ways, thereby questioning the logic of a colonial project which had hung its future on the successful "civilization," socialization, and education of at least some African children.

Schools and Colonialism in Senegal's History

Colonial schools have a long history in Senegal, with the first boys' schools dating to 1816 and girls' schools to 1826. Limited to Saint-Louis and Gorée for the first few decades, both boys' and girls' schools faced obstacles, not the least of which was the fact that they competed with Qur'an schooling and with community-based socialization and training. In addition, boys' schools suffered from frequent turnover and periods without teachers, while the Sœurs de Saint-Joseph de Cluny, Catholic women religious who ran the girls' schools, found that Muslim families were extremely reluctant to send their daughters. Responding to numerous requests from Senegal's governor and the minister of the marine and colonies, the Frères de l'Instruction Chrétienne (Ploërmel) missionary order took the lead on primary schooling for boys after they arrived in the colony in 1841, offering a metropolitan-style education with emphasis on religious training, along with some vocational skills. In addition, missionary brothers from the Séminaire du Saint-Esprit (Spiritans) created Catholic boys' schools alongside many of their mission stations. In the mid-1850s, Governor Louis Faidherbe established a secular primary school in Saint-Louis, a model that was replicated in outposts along the Senegal River for a few years during the 1860s.[4] As territorial expansion and conquest intensified in the late 1880s and 1890s, colonial schools proliferated, touted by officials as essential to the civilizing mission. Girls' schools, which emphasized domestic skills and the French language, operated in the communes and at a few mission stations during the nineteenth century, and girls could attend some "mixed" schools in other French outposts.[5]

By the later nineteenth century, many officials worried that French schools might produce so-called *déracinés*, or culturally "uprooted" people, and they sought changes to eliminate this risk and ensure that former students would want to work in sectors, like agriculture, that would advance French economic goals.[6] These concerns shaped Governor General Ernest Roume's milestone November 1903 decree on education across French West Africa, which established a shared pedagogical vision and organizational structure with three types of primary schools at its base. At the primary level, village schools, which would open wherever there were enough school-aged children, were to provide rudimentary academic instruction and training in agriculture and skilled trades. Regional schools, to be established in larger population centers, would offer basic instruction to local children and more advanced, locally "adapted" instruction to select students from across the region. Urban schools would provide a metropolitan-style curriculum in population centers with significant numbers of European or "assimilated" residents. And a variety of specialized schools, including a normal school, would offer more advanced training to a small number of students.[7]

Although the basic structure outlined in 1903 remained in place for decades, subsequent reforms created new types of schools—a médersa (Franco-Muslim school) in 1909 and a secondary school in 1910, for example—and later placed even greater emphasis on practical and adapted education for Black students.[8] Although it ultimately had limited impact, Governor General Jules Carde's 1924 decree called for more village schools and a renewed focus on school gardens and agricultural education, and it excluded most Black students from classes offering metropolitan curricula. In the early 1930s, Governor General Jules Brévié and his education inspector, Albert Charton, pushed for further reforms designed to ensure that students would return to their rural lifestyles after leaving primary school. They required the renamed *rural* schools to devote most of the school day to lessons in agriculture, manual work, and French; mandated regional schools to include agricultural and vocational training and to admit fewer students in upper grades; and indicated that the school day should include significant time for students to practice manual labor.[9]

It was this reformed approach to education that Brévié and others put forward during the 1930s as evidence of "child-protection" efforts in the colony, as they responded to inquiries from the Colonial Ministry and the League of Nations and attempted to stress the "humanitarian" side of colonial rule. Indeed, in a March 1934 letter to the minister, Brévié claimed that schools were the best way to "improve the lot of native childhood." Most school leavers, he continued, ultimately returned to their communities of origin where they would "become farmers or village artisans." Others would attend a superior primary school, which would equip them to hold lower-level positions with the administration or be "commercial employees, shopkeepers, or specialized workers." A few top students could attend the William Ponty School, going on to become teachers or work for the colony's various services in positions requiring literacy. Brévié also touted efforts to increase school enrollment and attendance across the federation, noting that the Ponty School was busy training more African teachers to staff primary schools and that a recent loan of 8 million francs would fund construction of many new schools.[10] While Brévié did not make this point, any increase in attendance, of course, would bring more children into contact with an institution of the colonial state, the discipline it imposed, and the ideal African childhood that it worked to promote.

Yet despite Brévié's comments, which are part of a larger history of French rhetoric valuing mass education accompanied by generally insufficient investment in schooling, most school-aged African children did *not* attend a colonial school. In the 1934 letter quoted above, Brévié estimated that in Dakar in 1933, only about 50 percent (2,531) of the approximately 5,000 school-aged children were enrolled in a French public or private school. He did not give a comparable percentage for the rest of the Senegal colony, but it would have been much lower, since only 10,517 boys and 725 girls were enrolled across this much larger territory.[11] These numbers offer a snapshot of a longstanding trend in Senegal, where only a small percentage of school-aged children ever attended school, either because their families were not interested or could not do without their labor, or because classes were full or there was no school nearby. Yet despite these limitations, school discipline had a much wider impact on African childhood in colonial Senegal since it helped to define the behavioral norms expected of the schoolchild, an archetype the colonial state put forward as an ideal for African childhood. Furthermore, effective school discipline required records, leading teachers, school directors, and education inspectors to produce copious amounts and increasing people's familiarity with documenting childhood.

Class Rules, Teachers, and Defining the "Disciplined" African Child

To mold and control African students' behavior in the classroom, in the hallways and cafeterias, during recreation times, and, when applicable, in the dormitories, education personnel implemented rules, engaged in surveillance, and doled out rewards and punishments. Despite their efforts to "adapt" the curriculum to meet what they understood as local needs and capacities (by focusing on agricultural and vocational training), French educators unsurprisingly did not revise school rules to account for cultural differences but rather used school discipline to redress behaviors they found problematic regardless of whether they were part of local culture. French officials and educators continually pointed to schooling as a key feature of child welfare policy and assumed that French-educated school leavers would help sustain colonial rule, giving the ideal of the disciplined African schoolchild who embraced the French presence and understood their aims much wider relevance in French thinking and in the policies they targeted at children.[12] Experiencing strict rules, evaluation of their behavior, punishment of misconduct, and recognition of well-behaved students, African children developed intimate knowledge of the behaviors valued by the French.

The high-ranking colonial officials who enacted school discipline codes did not have a hand in their everyday implementation, of course, but delegated this responsibility to teachers, heads of school, and other education personnel. The effort to impose hegemony through school discipline relied most heavily on the cooperation of teachers and school monitors, 72 percent of whom were African in 1912.[13] Although children are the focus of this book, it is worth pausing for a moment to consider why African teachers might have agreed to uphold discipline, as defined by the colonial state, in their classrooms. African teachers had been through colonial schools themselves, and for some, acceptance of what they had learned led them to try to recreate the experience for their students. In addition, communities often respected teachers, and this may have encouraged some to use discipline to position themselves as true authority figures.[14] Others, in contrast, were less supportive of school rules but had to contend with school regulations governing personnel and with regular inspections during which an administrator, the head of the education service, or (later) a school inspector evaluated their teaching. Those who ran afoul of personnel codes or whose classroom "authority" was deemed insufficient could face disciplinary action including demotion or dismissal.[15] Given the stakes, it appears that most teachers—African and European alike—at least attempted to enforce school discipline.

Handbooks, faculty meeting minutes, administrative decisions, and other documents describe the punishments teachers were allowed to impose, offering insight into expectations for discipline and student behavior. In his 1911 employee handbook for the division of Native Affairs in Senegal, for example, Émile Roux explained that teachers and school directors could punish students who had failed to meet behavioral or academic expectations by deducting points from their grades, reprimanding them, withholding recess, imposing detention, or suspending them from school for up to three days (the last one likely required the director's involvement). Requests for longer suspensions had to be decided on and ordered by the lieutenant governor.[16] This approach to punishment in the classroom mostly held steady into the 1930s, despite a few additions and modifications. Under a 1925 ordinance, teachers could punish students by giving them "poor grades, lessons to relearn, assignments to redo, additional assignments, Thursday detention, [and] exclusion from class or study hall." After input from a school's disciplinary council, consisting of several teachers who convened to discuss student misconduct and to recommend punishments, the director could impose more serious consequences, such as "temporary suspension or expulsion from the course." In 1932, the director of the Dakar secondary course asked teachers to stop sending students out of class since this punishment allowed troublemakers to escape "surveillance" and potentially make additional mischief. The other punishments allowed by the 1925 ordinance remained available—the director favored detention since it would get parents more involved—and teachers in other schools likely continued to use exclusion from class as a disciplinary tool.[17]

Although school rules, handbooks, and education inspectors' reports made clear that students and classrooms should *be* disciplined, they did not usually define this term, perhaps because their authors assumed that teachers and other school officials knew discipline when they saw it. Such a belief would seem to be born out in the way that educators used the schools' disciplinary apparatus to discourage certain behaviors while rewarding others. The trends and patterns in the types of behaviors they found problematic versus those they highlighted as exemplary reveal that "discipline" was associated with a stable set of behaviors over a long period and across many different types of schools. From the 1880s through the 1930s, if not longer, teachers, educators, and officials consistently valued five attributes—obedience; respect; hard work; regular and timely attendance; and calm, quiet demeanor—in schoolchildren, no matter their race, gender, or political status, though racism led many to assume that African children would not display these behaviors without threat of punishment. Emphasis on these attributes ran through several versions of ideal childhood that functioned in this period, from loyal French subject or—for *originaires*—citizen and eager adopter of French "civilization" in the nineteenth century, to informed peasant and grateful recipient of French protection from the 1910s. Indeed, amid shifts in administrative priorities from the "civilizing mission" to *mise en valeur*, and finally to social welfare and child protection, officials consistently positioned schooling as crucial to the continued success of colonial rule, since schools offered an opportunity to combat disorder and indiscipline—characteristics racist observers associated with African children—in the next generation of colonialized workers. Schools, the discipline they imposed, the information they collected, and the documentation they produced, therefore, played a particularly central role in remaking *African* childhood.

In the 1930s, more than one hundred years after the first colonial schools opened their doors in Senegal, school "discipline" and teachers' authority continued to occupy the administration, and efforts to track the successes and failures of "discipline" shed light on how officials thought about the concept. Education inspectors often took note of student (mis)behavior as they evaluated teachers' preparation and classroom performance and assessed other aspects of each school. Accordingly, of nearly 140 school inspection reports from boys' and girls' schools across the colony during the 1930s, approximately 45 included one or more comments about specific student behaviors. The inspectors who produced these reports praised student behavior almost as often as they criticized it, and their most frequent positive observations about students emphasized their attentiveness in class (ten reports). Although only one report specifically noted that students were obedient, inspectors wrote more generally about good behavior or strong discipline—implying obedience—at least seven times. Other compliments noted students' diligence (five reports) and liveliness (four reports). The most common complaint, on the other hand, mentioned seventeen times, had to do with noise levels, with inspectors often specifying that the students talked at inappropriate times, talked too loudly, or chatted with each other instead of focusing on lessons. The inspectors expressed strong disapproval of students snapping their fingers during class in five additional comments, apparently unaware or unconcerned that this was an acceptable means of seeking attention in many of the region's cultures. Lateness, lack of sustained attention, and movement about the classroom also drew negative attention in multiple reports.[18] This set of school inspection reports, then, suggests that the education hierarchy in the 1930s expected obedience, respect, quiet, punctuality, and focus, without giving much thought to the values and cultural practices students brought with them.

Teachers, school directors, and administration officials had appreciated these traits for decades, and they periodically expressed satisfaction when students exhibited them or pointed to their absence as cause for concern. In the second half of the nineteenth century, when officials and teachers focused primarily on expanding schooling into newly acquired territories and improving disappointingly low enrollment and attendance, correspondence dealt with student discipline and conduct only occasionally. But when they did discuss discipline, they described it in terms consistent with those used in the 1930s. In 1865, for example, a teacher at the new school in Dagana, himself *métis* and from Senegal, wrote glowingly about his students, whom he described as obedient, good listeners, and regular attenders, before requesting that the administration send gifts to reward their good behavior and progress.[19] Similarly, a list of students who had enrolled at the secondary school in Saint-Louis between 1884 (when the school opened) and 1889 used the adjectives "hard-working," "quiet," "docile," and "obedient" numerous times to describe students whose conduct and discipline had met French expectations.[20]

School directors used comparable language in the education certificates they sometimes produced in support of specific students' applications for scholarships, school admission, or employment. In a 1904 education certificate submitted with a scholarship application, for example, the director of the Rufisque boys' school attested that Fara Diaw (who was Black and approximately thirteen years old) had behaved well during the 1903–4 school year and, using fairly typical complimentary language, described the boy as "hard-working, attentive, studious, polite, sweet, and obliging."[21] And in October 1920, the director of the Dakar boys' school (Rue de Thiong), a Monsieur Calvayrac, provided Amadou Sylla (Black and aged fifteen) with the school certificate he needed to complete his request for a scholarship for the médersa in Saint-Louis. Verifying that the boy had attended his school since November 1916 and had made some progress, Calvayrac praised him for "always showing himself to be hard-working and submissive," traits that indicated dedication and deference to French authority. In a letter supporting Amadou's application, the government's delegate in Dakar described the school certificate as "not bad" and urged the lieutenant governor to weigh it more heavily than the applicant's limited writing ability. In doing so, he suggested that obedience and dedication should outweigh academic achievement or ability in assessments of African students.[22]

School inspection reports, produced since the 1910s and with increasing regularity in the 1930s, highlighted similar attributes—obedience, deference, quiet demeanor—when explaining their positive assessments of the "discipline" in a particular class. The inspector of primary instruction for Senegal, for example, observed in 1933 that Mamadou Hadramé Ly's class at the regional school in Kaolack was "very lively, very active, disciplined, [and a class] where everything gives an impression of tidiness, of cleanliness, of order, and of labor and application at the same time." Two years later, he rated discipline as "satisfactory" in Tamsir Touré's class at the same school, explaining that Touré's students were "active without being noisy."[23] Similarly, in late 1934, the schools inspector expressed his appreciation of the "firm" discipline in Babacar N'Diaye's midlevel class at the Rufisque school and offered a rather precise description of what this looked like. The students, he wrote, were "clean and polite. They are attentive during lessons. Exits and returns take place in good order and without noise."[24] Thus, time and again, French teachers, school inspectors, and administration officials emphasized the importance of order, attentiveness, obedience, and quiet demeanor as characteristics of the disciplined schoolchild.

On the surface, these characteristics might seem innocuous and neutral, intended simply to create a classroom environment that was suitable for the pedagogies used at the time. But in fact, this sort of conduct in African students was remarkable to French authorities precisely because they interpreted it as evidence that school discipline had succeeded in leading Africans to overcome their supposed deficits of conduct, character, and attitude. These assumptions, which reflected widespread racist beliefs about Black people in Senegal, elsewhere in Africa, in the Americas, and beyond, led many educators and officials to impose stricter discipline and harsher punishments on African children, whose very Africanness they found problematic, and to allow them fewer opportunities for second chances than they afforded to European or so-called assimilated students. Racist tendencies to view cultural differences as behavioral problems to be remedied, then, were at the heart of the disciplinary apparatus of the colonial school and animated its role in remaking African childhood to fit French colonial ideals.

French authorities, officials, and colonialists generally accepted racist ideas about African inferiority and backwardness, and concerns about African students fit into this larger trend. In a 1908 report, for example, the director of the École de la Rue de Thiong boys' school in Dakar blamed the supposed indiscipline of African students on innate traits, claiming that "this languidness, this indifference is an obvious result of native character, always partial to the 'principle of the least action.'"[25] Similarly, a 1912 report on the Normal School included blanket criticism of Senegalese, and especially Wolof, students, claiming that despite their "intelligence," many of these students were "lazy, liars, vain, arrogant," and that as such, they accounted for a significant number of expulsions from the school. The report's author hedged these comments, however, noting that this criticism did not apply to all Wolof students, that some of the school's strongest students were Wolof, and that some Wolof graduates had become skilled teachers.[26] And an article printed in an official French West Africa newsletter in 1937 revealed that these stereotypes remained current at that time when it commented that many teachers believed that regardless of curriculum and pedagogical approach, "the Black is lazy, he will always be lazy because this is a defect of his race."[27]

Deficit thinking also shaped teachers' assumptions about African schoolgirls. Although the curriculum differed substantially from that of boys' schools, emphasizing domestic skills and downplaying academics, girls' schools—like boys'—promoted respect, quiet, obedience, and regular attendance, and added modesty to their vision of discipline. As they did with boys, teachers and officials not infrequently relied on racial stereotyping to explain why African girls fell short of their expectations. A complaint about irregular attendance lodged in 1906 by the director of the Dakar girls' school illustrates. "European pupils only really miss due to sickness," she wrote, "but Black children miss simply out of indifference and laziness." Her counterpart at the Saint-Louis girls' school issued a similar critique in 1911, noting that while European and "assimilated" girls, who were "supervised by their parent," had strong attendance, "native girls, left to themselves, miss class at the slightest excuse, [and] their attendance is very irregular." She observed further that in contrast to European and "assimilated" students, "conduct and manners among natives leave a lot to be desired."[28] A final example from a 1933 inspection of the Regional School in Kaolack reveals the longevity of these assumptions. Given what he knew about "the fanciful character of young native girls, their fundamental indiscipline, their lewd girlishness, their indifference regarding instruction," the inspector of primary schools in Senegal was "astonished" by the "keen desire to come to school" and devotion to their teacher among the Kaolack schoolgirls, and was pleased with their compliance with the school's hygiene initiatives.[29] This school, he suggested, had been particularly successful in helping African girls overcome their supposedly innate tendencies and to move closer to the French ideal of the colonial girl-child.

Praises and Punishments

Even though egregious and repeat offenses received more attention from teachers and officials, teachers often handled discipline issues quietly, and likely addressed the most minor ones through the easiest mechanism—grades. Students received grades on their conduct, allowing teachers to punish minor offenses by docking points and to reward cooperative, quiet, and obedient students with high marks and positive comments. In at least some schools, teachers adopted the metropolitan approach of regularly announcing student grades in academic subjects and possibly in conduct as well.[30] This practice gave teachers leverage in shaping students' behavior, since the public sharing of grades encouraged comparisons between students. Further, teachers regularly sent report cards home, giving parents insight into their children's performance at school. Even though illiteracy limited many African parents' ability to understand this information, regular grade reports had the added benefit, the director of the Dakar boys' school observed in 1915, of enlisting parents' support in addressing problems or encouraging students to stay the course.[31] Significantly, grades and other teacher feedback about student behavior communicated notions of the ideal child not only to students but to their parents as well.

Schools also used prizes and awards to encourage disciplined behavior and to disseminate colonial hopes for African childhood. At annual prize ceremonies, held before an audience of students, parents and other family members, teachers, African dignitaries, and—in towns and administrative centers—French officials, one or more students received awards for exemplary conduct after a prominent person gave a speech. Not only did awards for conduct allow schools to encourage certain behaviors but officials could use their speeches to paint a picture of an ideal, disciplined student. In the opening speech of an early twentieth-century prize ceremony, for example, a school official praised students for good behavior and obedience to the government general, and encouraged those who had not received awards to work harder in the future.[32] Accounts of prize ceremonies often appeared in the colony's official newspaper, allowing the text of each speech and information about awards conferred to reach people who had not attended, thereby further spreading ideas about school discipline. Around the turn of the twentieth century, in particular, teachers also distributed rewards less formally, recognizing good behavior, regular attendance, and academic progress with small gifts like sugar, soap, cloth or clothing, sweets, books, and even small amounts of money.[33] These rewards reinforced ideas about discipline and school behavior being taught and modeled in the classroom, and also promoted the school within the larger community.

Teachers and school directors periodically rewarded students for good behavior, strong academic performance, regular attendance, and the like, but the emphasis in the archival record, of course, is on responding to discipline problems. Indeed, when students got into trouble, the responses of their teacher, the school director, the disciplinary council, and/or other aspects of the school's disciplinary apparatus worked not only to reassert the authority of any educators who felt themselves challenged but also to reinforce the idea of the disciplined child. All students were supposed to comport themselves well and follow the rules, of course, but educators were particularly keen to identify and punish African students who fell short. Since schools were central to the colonial enterprise, indiscipline among African students could be construed as a challenge to the authority of the colonial state; conversely, punishment—even of offenses that seem minor by today's standards—was necessary both to eliminate that challenge and move African childhood incrementally closer to the colonial ideal.

Educators and officials consistently worried that misbehavior in schools could substantially challenge teachers' authority, whether the students in question intended their actions this way or not, and this concern came through in many examples of disciplinary actions taken against students at the turn of the twentieth century. In 1892, for example, a teacher at the School for Sons of Chiefs and Interpreters sent a Black student to the director's office after he disobeyed and responded rudely to a school monitor. In 1905 and 1906, the Rue de Lanneau boys' school in Saint-Louis suspended a Black student for stealing school supplies and a white student for "mistreating a much weaker pupil" and then disrespecting the teacher.[34] And several years later, the governor general portrayed two Black students as bad influences at the Normal School in a letter laying the groundwork for their expulsion. The students, one from Senegal and the other from Dahomey, had shown "laziness and indiscipline," character traits that were particularly worrisome in teacher candidates at a time (1912) when teachers in both Saint-Louis and Rufisque had recently rebelled against their superiors. It was especially important, the governor general thought, for future teachers to show "respect for authority" while also learning "love of their work."[35] These snapshots involving student misconduct and punishment in different schools over about twenty years suggest a certain consistency in how educators envisioned and implemented discipline to inculcate this respect for authority. And given that most of the disciplined students—in the cases summarized above as in the archive as a whole—were Black, they suggest not only that discipline was an important feature of African childhoods but also that race and racism shaped the very the meaning of "discipline."

As schooling in the colony underwent expansion, increasing bureaucratization, and reform during the 1920s and 1930s, these core ideas about indiscipline and unacceptable student behavior remained remarkably stable. In 1921, for example, the headmaster of the Lycée Faidherbe explained that he had needed to expel only one student during the year (Amadou Diouf, who was Black), and that he had done so as punishment for frequent absences and insufficient progress. The headmaster also mentioned the student's "insolent attitude toward one of his teachers and the indecent gesture of which he was guilty," though the official downplayed the importance of these factors in the expulsion decision.[36] And at the same school, the headmaster wrote in April 1922 about three Black students whose personalities were "too independent," at times making them "resistant to discipline and even disrespectful toward certain teachers," behaviors for which they had been punished. A few months later, he notified the lieutenant governor that he had suspended a different Black student for eight days because he had insulted his white or *métisse* teacher, a Madame Brian, in front of classmates when the student was supposed to be apologizing for previous displays of "very insolent" behavior toward her.[37] Because it called French authority into question (in addition to the fact that it was unacceptable for children to behave in this way), this sort of conduct was particularly objectionable when it came from African children.

An incident from the early 1930s in Dakar's Cours Secondaire shows how students' race could shape teachers' expectations for their behavior and decisions about appropriate punishment. Two years after the director of this secondary institution had beseeched his faculty to "be firm and to crack down on" any misbehavior amid rising "impertinence and insolence," the school's disciplinary council convened to deal with two cases, the first involving a student whose name suggests family origins outside Senegal, perhaps in North Africa, and the second involving a Black student from Senegal. The council first discussed young Alfred Jaouiche, who had appeared three times previously and who was described as suffering from a "mental illness." His "intolerable" conduct—including failure to complete schoolwork, repeated lateness, extreme distraction, and "brutal" behavior toward his classmates—led the council to recommend expulsion if his parents did not agree to withdraw him from school. In the second case, council members decided to suspend young François Sy for two days as punishment for impudence, having a "bad attitude in class," talking loudly out of turn, and having a "combative character." The council noted that they planned to expel him in response to any additional "misconduct."[38] Despite Alfred's repeated bad behavior, the discipline council showed him leniency and understanding in several ways, allowing him to appear before the council multiple times before seriously considering expulsion, explaining his conduct as a result of "mental illness," and giving his parents the opportunity to shield him from expulsion by choosing withdrawal. François, on the other hand, a Black student whose behavior posed a greater threat to French authority, received no such consideration. Instead, at what appears to have been his first hearing, the disciplinary council responded not with a second chance but with a significant punishment, and it did so in response to relatively mild misconduct. Rather than involving his family in the matter, the council simply resolved to expel him after his next misdeed.

Teachers, school directors, and administration officials, unsurprisingly, conceived of discipline and—especially—punishment differently depending on whether the behavioral problem came from a white, Black, or *métis* student. The resulting differential enforcement, and the assumptions of African deficiencies on which it was based, had important effects on African students, since it sent the message that successful students needed to conform to behavioral norms that indicated submission or subservience. Teachers also reinforced the importance of these behaviors by publicly rewarding students who exhibited them, giving them high grades (often read out in class), praise, and even prizes in end-of-year ceremonies. Through their own experiences or through those of their classmates, students learned that these behaviors were essential to the ideal of the African schoolchild promoted by the French, an ideal that had considerable symbolic importance given officials' emphasis on schooling as the key to a successful, productive, and stable colonial future. This schoolchild ideal, then, was not innocuous at all but carried significant political weight, as did the inability (or refusal?) of many students to achieve it.

African Students and the Disciplinary Apparatus

Confronted with these ideas about the ideal student and expectations for disciplined behavior, African children most often simply conformed to the expectations. By doing so, they might receive high marks for their conduct, have their names added to the honor roles, or garner recognition at prize ceremonies. They could at least sometimes count on positive reviews of their dedication and achievement on the school certificates they might need to apply for admission or scholarships in another school or to seek a job. More rarely, children pushed back against these French ideals, intentionally or not, by breaking rules or, more subtly, by refusing to engage with the disciplinary process, voting with their feet and leaving a school before punishment could occur, or refusing to accept a punishment assigned to them. Even though European and assimilated children also misbehaved, challenging individual teachers' authority or even undermining their schools' routine stability, African students' interactions with schools' disciplinary apparatus had higher stakes for the state, since they called into question the state's ability to mold Africans into ideal colonial children, to "protect" African childhood, and to ensure the colonial future. By complying with or evading French discipline, occasionally forcing officials to adjust rules and procedures, and influencing what educators documented—and therefore what was known—about African children, students helped produce colonial childhood in Senegal.

Motivated by intense concerns about African students who challenged school discipline, and keen to document disciplinary encounters, educators and officials produced abundant records regarding students they found problematic, leading to an overrepresentation of these students in the colonial archives. Indeed, despite the fact that—as indicated by the *absence* of documented concerns or misbehaviors—most African students at least appeared to accept French rules, it is difficult to find in the colonial archives much evidence about individual students who thrived under the disciplinary apparatus of French schools or children who appreciated the ways school discipline changed what it meant to be a child. Reports, statistics, and correspondence suggest that most students fell into this category, and as the employment and status advantages that could accrue to those who had attended school became clearer, many children and young people—and their families—would have been motivated to accept French rules so they could stay in school.

Narratives written by African students or former students, however, can offer insight into how they wrestled with and ultimately responded to the school environment and the rules that governed it. Perhaps the most useful examples come from ethnographic essays written by students at the William Ponty School in the late 1930s and 1940s, in which several student authors compared French schooling to local tradition. Serigne Fall Seck suggested that traditional education in Cayor and French education were "incompatible" in their approach to discipline and their content but portrayed himself as a supporter of French methods, suggesting that—at least in an essay he knew would be read by his French teachers—he could abide by and perhaps find value in French rules and expectations for behavior.[39] Moctar Bâ, writing about a Peulh village, and Souleyman Wane, writing about Toucouleur education, in contrast, thought that French discipline could build on the approaches to discipline and training used in their home communities. Thanks to the discipline they received at home, Bâ suggested, Peulh children would be more receptive to French schooling, while Toucouleur children, according to Wane, could use the leadership emphasized in traditional training to encourage others to accept French discipline at school.[40] Even if they came to different conclusions about how French discipline would interact with traditional practices in their communities, all three student authors suggested they had no problem accepting it for themselves.

Although most students likely did not rail against French rules, some did try to challenge them, and this pushback at least sometimes occurred in small, unplanned moments. Even so, such actions could present enough of a challenge to a school's rules or to the teachers' authority that teachers felt they had to respond. In June 1904, for example, Papa N'Diaye, a student at the Normal School in Saint-Louis, muttered "some words in Wolof" in response to his teacher's corrections. The teacher, a Monsieur Vernochet, was incensed that this "particularly lazy student" had spoken in this way. After another teacher revealed that the same student had behaved similarly toward him "several times," the teacher's council accepted Vernochet's suggestion that they impose a public reprimand.[41] French schools generally prohibited students from using Indigenous languages, and doing so could result in punishment. In this case, Papa N'Diaye likely spoke in Wolof strategically, so that he could express his true feelings aloud while hiding their full meaning from the teacher, a French man who likely understood Wolof imperfectly, if at all. Through actions as simple as speaking in their own languages as they negotiated the "tensions" of colonial rule, African students could call into question the state's ability to reshape childhood into something the French could easily control.[42]

In towns with more than one school, students went so far as to avoid punishment in one school by enrolling in another, to the great annoyance of the teachers and school directors who not only wanted to see penalties through but who also had to account for fluctuations in attendance. By choosing to continue receiving a French education in a new school while avoiding an unpleasant experience at their original one, these students sent the message that they rejected a particular effort to impose discipline and not schooling itself. In December 1903, for example, young Ibrahima N'Diaye submitted a complaint to the head of the education service, claiming that the director of his former school (the École Duval in Saint-Louis) had refused to give him the prizes he had earned months before because he had left Duval to attend the Ploërmel school. Calling out the director, Ibrahima wrote that since all government schools were under "a single chief," it was his understanding that a student could decide which one to attend, "that is to say, the one where he [would] learn the best."[43] To him and many others like him, French schooling could be part of African childhood, but families and children should retain a certain amount of control over the experience.

Asked to comment on the complaint, a Monsieur Garrigues, director of the École Duval, admitted that he had withheld Ibrahima's prizes but rejected the idea that this was because the student had switched schools. Instead, he explained, it was a punishment for the "insubordination" young Ibrahima had displayed when he insisted on skipping a grade and recruited classmates to join him in protest when he was told this was not possible. Unlike his classmates, who had relented and then received their prizes, Ibrahima had refused to back down, instead changing his enrollment to the Ploërmel school in Saint-Louis. Although the head of the education service ultimately dismissed Ibrahima's complaint due to this "indiscipline," he notified Garrigues that the student "had a right to his prizes." The archive is silent on whether they were ever returned.[44] These competing narratives are fascinating in their own right, and regardless of which you believe, they suggest significant tension in the relationship between Garrigues and Ibrahima N'Diaye. The incident also—crucially—highlights officials' and teachers' anxieties about student conduct that might detract from the perceived authority of the educational hierarchy. Indeed, even relatively mild "indiscipline" could give children a certain amount of leverage over their teachers, their schools, and the education they received.

Educators in Dakar had similar concerns about students abruptly changing schools to avoid disciplinary measures or to escape teachers they did not like. A 1907 incident in the Dakar boys' school (Rue de Thiong) offers a particularly compelling case. When a student misbehaved and then persuaded his classmates to side with him, their teacher, a Monsieur Niénat, asked the school director to impose punishment, arguing that this would protect his authority in the classroom. Yet the director, a man named Domenge, decided against significant punishment, and in response to Niénat's complaint, defended his use of "moderation," which, he claimed, had prevented numerous students from simply leaving the school. Some of the students bristled at Niénat's approach to discipline, Domenge noted, since they felt he had only "contempt" for some of them and suggested that this was because they were Black.[45] In other documents, Domenge proposed that Niénat's status as an *assimilé* created classroom management issues and faced accusations that he had offered special opportunities to the white students in the school he directed, suggesting that his own racism may have played a role in these students' actions.[46]

Domenge raised this issue again the following year, noting that students at the Rue de Thiong "are very independent and many would rather leave school temporarily than undergo a punishment." Abdoulaye M'Bengue, who taught at Rue de Thiong, offered more detail in his complaint about the same phenomenon, noting that it was facilitated by the "proximity" of his school to others.

"When the students are punished," he explained, "they leave the school that they first attended and go have themselves admitted to one of the two other schools." He called on the governor to do something to address this problem, which was "to the students' detriment" and which caused "trouble for the teachers."[47] This strategy to limit the impact of school-based discipline seems to have appealed to students whenever and wherever they could choose between schools, and it had staying power, even after the administration developed policies to stop it.[48] By escaping French discipline in this way, students limited its ability to constrain and redefine African childhood, at least for a time.

Changing schools was not the only approach to avoiding French colonial discipline, however. Indeed, by simply skipping school strategically, African students could shield themselves from unpleasant efforts to enforce discipline in schools. In 1907, for example, the director of the combined Normal School and School for Sons of Chiefs and Interpreters surmised that high absence rates on Saturdays might reflect students choosing not to endure a public reading of their grades.[49] Perhaps they were trying to send a message that they did not appreciate this aspect of their school experience. If significant numbers of students stayed away, the public reading of grades lost power, since its utility as a disciplinary tool relied on the pride or shame students could derive from others knowing their scores. Similarly, in the same year, a teacher at the girls' school in Dakar reflected on the obstacles the school faced in improving students' attendance, one of which stemmed from the school's expectations for good hygiene and cleanliness. Many girls, the teacher explained, struggled to keep their only dress clean enough to meet the standards, and at least one student had left the school to avoid being reprimanded for wearing a dirty dress.[50] In this instance, as in the one above, students engaged in a small action to send the message that they would not accept a particular disciplinary initiative of the colonial school.

Students also occasionally circumvented or rejected school discipline when it conflicted with the expectations of their families or communities. They might, for example, not report back to school on the designated restart date or miss multiple days at other times for reasons the French found illegitimate, frustrating, or "backward," as when in March 1904 only a few students returned to the Saint-Louis boys' school after the break for Tabaski (Eid al-Adha), having decided among themselves to take a few additional days.[51] Such absences could also be explained by students' needs to help their families with the harvest, contribute to the household economy in other ways, undergo the circumcision ritual, tend to dependent relatives (especially mothers and sisters) following the death of a household head, and fulfill other familial obligations. Despite the frequency with which this happened, student requests for permission to leave school to deal with a family issue could be contentious, as when education officials rejected Mamadou Djigo's efforts to unenroll from the médersa so he could care for his ailing mother and support his sister and two young brothers in Sedhiou. When he persisted with his request, the school director expelled him for "insubordination," a harsh response that suggests the director felt his authority threatened.[52] Indeed, absence from school—which many French educators viewed as a particularly irksome discipline issue—often reflected ongoing tensions between the demands and obligations of family life on one hand and French expectations that pupils in colonial schools always prioritize their schooling and respect colonial authority above all on the other. Yet no matter how much officials and teachers might claim to require enrolled students' presence in schools, students and their families ultimately had the upper hand, especially since French plans for schooling would fail if students chose to stop attending.

As these examples show, African students engaged with French hegemony in and through the mechanism of school discipline. Many wanted to be part of colonial schooling, realizing that job opportunities and status were at stake, and did what their teachers and school directors expected of them. Others embarked on a pathway through schooling but wanted to have some influence over the terms of their participation, and attempted to tread a line between recognizing certain aspects of French authority but not allowing that authority to fully redefine and control African childhood. When children challenged school discipline in significant ways, they sent educators and officials scrambling to reimpose it, underscoring the power they could wield. Their actions reminded French officials that in a colony which had staked its future on the "protection" of African children and the reform of African childhood, children themselves had to be consulted and convinced to buy into the process.

Conclusion: Documentation and Discipline in Colonial Schools

The history of colonial schooling is also a history of documentation of children, of the production of a certain kind of documented childhood. Indeed, African students—most of whom lacked birth certificates—had to make themselves legible to the state to enroll in and attend school. Their names, ages, birthplaces, and parents' names had to be collected and inscribed in a register or added to a list, documents that became part of the schools' archives and informed teachers' and school directors' reports to the state. Schools tracked children throughout their time in school, collecting and recording their grades, logging their attendance and classroom behavior, documenting awards and prizes, recording minutes in meetings where teachers discussed student issues or heard disciplinary proceedings, and more. These records not only created aggregate knowledge about African students that could inform school policies but also noted the achievements and failures of individual children, advancing the idea that children *should* be documented and surveilled by the state or its institutions. In addition, schools at least sometimes provided students or their families with documents that could support—or stymie—their efforts to obtain scholarships, admission to higher-level schools, or jobs. The certificates of attendance, school-leaving certificates, and reference letters that came from schools could have real impact on the opportunities students and school leavers were given or denied. In attaining literacy, schoolchildren themselves came to better understand and appreciate the power of the written word under colonial rule, as they used their newly acquired skills to take stock of the records others generated about them and, sometimes, to produce documents about themselves. The realization that they could benefit—personally and directly—from the educators' and officials' efforts to record details about their birth, school enrollment, performance, and achievements likely encouraged more Africans to accept these recordkeeping habits, further normalizing documented childhood.

This chapter has discussed some of the negotiations involving African students, teachers, school directors, and higher-ranking officials in the French administration over how an ideal colonial schoolchild could reasonably be expected to behave. By approving and implementing school rules, punishing misconduct, and rewarding desired behaviors, the education hierarchy attempted to impose a particular vision of order on African childhood. This vision, communicated at school, reached more young people as the colonial period wore on and as attendance gradually increased, to some 27 percent of school-aged children by the immediate postcolonial period.[53] Yet there were always some students who challenged French goals; indeed, while some students met expectations for behavior, others did not, and their misbehaviors presented a challenge to the state's authority, which depended in part on a commitment to the "civilizing mission" and later to child "protection." Because of its implications for the state's image, students' misbehavior—even when relatively mild—demanded attention and time from the colonial hierarchy and required teachers to reassert their authority through punishment, yet the impulse to punish was moderated by the need to prevent a proliferation of disaffected school leavers or expelled students who might become *déclassés* and further challenge the state. And though these are difficult to trace, recurrent or widespread indiscipline could also lead to policy changes, as when authorities made it more difficult to enroll in a different school following complaints that students were avoiding punishments by changing schools.

For their part, since schooling conferred status and employability in the colonial economy, students had an interest in *not* being expelled, and once the importance of documents became clear, in maintaining a clean record of conduct. Efforts to ensure and track discipline generated significant correspondence—including occasional letters from students—reflecting the importance of schools and children to the future of the colonial state and contributing to the development of documentary childhood. Yet the vision of a well-behaved, orderly, and legible child advanced in and through the school was in fact co-created by teachers, officials, and—to some extent—students themselves.

CHAPTER 4

The Street

PUBLIC SPACES AND PUBLIC CHILDHOOD

Throughout 1935, a particularly detail-oriented police commissioner in Kaolack, Senegal, kept careful records, producing one- to two-page reports each week that summarized the work of his officers. The forty-eight extant reports list arrests, minor offenses, and miscellaneous other police activities, and together they offer insight into French efforts to impose specific visions of order on the African public spaces they were trying to control.[1] Unsurprisingly, the reports show that police focused on crimes like theft (which accounted for 89 of 174 arrests, or 51.1%) or prison escapes (19 arrests, 10.9%), and responded to assault (resulting in 35 of 260 tickets) or physical fights (51 tickets). Perhaps more striking, and ultimately more significant for the story I tell in this chapter, was the attention police gave to other uses of public space that ran counter to French sensibilities of order and legibility, such as loitering, gambling, and being loud. This focus led police to make 46 arrests for vagabondage (26.4%) and to issue tickets for a wide variety of other behaviors, including hygiene infractions (21 cases), playing games of chance (also 21 cases), public urination (16 cases), and more.[2] Police, gendarmes, and hygiene agents in Kaolack and elsewhere helped the state to colonize public spaces and to bring them into line with French aesthetics, ideas about order, and approaches to sanitation. This stood to have a significant impact on how Africans—including children—moved through that space, conducted business, and went about their daily lives.

Although the documents available for Kaolack allow for unusually granular analysis, more fragmentary evidence from other towns and years displays similar patterns, suggesting broad continuities in policing, crime, and nuisance violations across the colony, patterns that must have had an impact on African children.[3] With this discussion of policing priorities as a backdrop, this chapter explores how African children experienced the state's efforts to control public spaces in colonial Senegal, how they encountered and responded to policing and surveillance of these spaces, and how these encounters impacted ideas about childhood in Senegal. It focuses in particular on how children experienced French policies on hygiene and sanitation, religious alms-seeking, and vagabondage—enforcement areas that corresponded to common childhood activities—and on how, by passing through to complete their chores, living and working in homes that opened up on these spaces, seeking training in the Qur'an or begging for alms, loitering, and sometimes committing petty crime, African children challenged French efforts to impose order. Using police records, child and social welfare documents, court records, and other sources, I contend that as international and domestic pressure pushed colonial governments to engage in more child "protection" during the 1920s and 1930s, officials began to redefine their enforcement activities along these lines, sometimes considering African children as victims who needed their help. But policing, surveillance, and documentation remained a priority amid the shift to child protection, partly because children continued to threaten order and stability. Indeed, discipline and protection functioned in tandem to promote order in the colony. At the same time, efforts to police the public square brought individual children to the attention of the colonial state, often for the first time, producing records about them and propelling the shift toward documented childhood.

As they lived out their daily lives and moved through spaces the French colonial state now claimed to control, Africans encountered multiple, overlapping, and likely bewildering legal and regulatory landscapes. The colonial state, of course, implemented a security and justice apparatus—police, gendarmes, prisons, courts, lawyers, and judges—to ensure order and promote their civilizing mission. This apparatus relied heavily on the *indigénat*, a system implemented in 1887 that gave French administrators the authority not only to arrest African subjects but also to fine or imprison them for up to fifteen days without trial, as punishment for a wide variety of minor offenses. More significant crimes and misdemeanors, and all civil issues, went to "Native Tribunals" where French magistrates (assisted by African assessors) or African chiefs issued decisions based on so-called customary law. Customary law, which developed out of French efforts to collect and distill rules, practices, and punishments particular to each cultural area they governed, varied by region and ethnic identity and often reflected the priorities of the older men who had worked with French officials as informants. In addition, officials modified punishments and offenses that they found distasteful or backward, replacing many of them with modern French penal practices like imprisonment or fines.[4]

The *indigénat* did not apply to the *originaires*, who fell instead under the jurisdiction of French courts and the French penal code (of 1810, with later modifications). *Originaires* could have civil matters decided in French courts according to the French civil code or they could pursue civil matters in the Muslim Tribunals, where, with French oversight, qadis could issue decisions in line with Islamic family law, inheritance practices, and so on.[5] This bifurcation in civil and legal status between colonial subjects and citizens became an enduring feature of French rule in Senegal, and as such it had significant impacts on African children's lives and on the very definition of African childhood.[6]

Like their adult counterparts, "subject" children fell under the jurisdiction of Native Tribunals when they were accused of wrongdoing, while *originaires* found themselves in French courts, answering to French penal law. But both French and Native Tribunals held minors to a different standard than adults, acknowledging that by virtue of their youth and inexperience, most children lacked criminal capacity. Relying on articles 66–69 of the French penal code in cases involving *originaires* in French courts, and on the 1903 and 1924 decrees on "Native Justice" in cases involving colonial subjects in Native Tribunals, courts decided whether to treat young African defendants as minors or adults, a process that depended significantly on a determination of whether the defendant had reached sixteen, the age of criminal responsibility.[7] The penal code and these colonial decrees also gave courts the right to decide whether to return to their families these minors acquitted because they lacked "discernment" (criminal responsibility), or whether—and for how long—to send them to a house of correction.[8] Setting aside for now the fact that there was nothing self-evident or straightforward about determining a young person's chronological age, I explore below the impact of this system on African children's daily lives.

Beyond these core bodies of colonial law, administrators implemented a tangle of additional ordinances, decisions, and decrees—some applying to the entire federation or to all of Senegal, others strictly local—that affected Africans' interactions with colonial public spaces. Officials intended many of these regulations to improve health and sanitation in the areas under their jurisdiction, usually with an eye to protecting the health of resident Europeans. In Nianing, for example, an 1889 decree on sanitation and public order required people to sweep the areas in front of their homes each day, restricted disposal of wastewater and trash to specific sites, prohibited drumming after 9:00 p.m. in areas near Europeans, limited other noisy activities, and required certain building materials in neighborhoods where Europeans lived.[9] Later ordinances, including one signed by Lieutenant Governor Camille Guy in 1903, tasked residents of towns across the colony with ensuring there were no mosquito larvae hiding in their homes or water reservoirs; prohibited laundry, bathing, and other activities in public water sources; required town residents to obtain permission to keep livestock and set rules for where and how they could be kept; and imposed other sanitation regulations.[10] Other rules targeted how people spent their time in public, limiting drumming, grain pounding, and other loud activities to daytime hours, for example, and defining begging and vagabondage as punishable crimes. The reliance on French law and the presence of a sizeable French population in the communes meant that these towns followed the metropolitan practice of arresting people who lacked jobs and places to stay, and whose idleness in public spaces threatened order and challenged French moral sensibilities. Courts might sentence adults arrested for vagabondage to several months in prison; French law prevented those under age sixteen from doing prison time, but courts could—and did—remove them from public spaces by ordering their internment in a "house of correction." In 1923, the governor general signed a decree defining and banning vagabondage across French West Africa, essentially inventing an offense where none had previously existed in a bid to establish greater control over Africans' use of public spaces.[11]

There is no doubt that, once implemented, many of these rules could make people safer, improve sanitation, protect drinking water, and encourage a certain vision of modernity and order, especially in cities and towns. At least some Africans saw opportunity in these changes, turning to the police and the courts when they were victims of crimes, for example, or using the possession of a driver's license to help them obtain employment. For its part, the colonial state used laws and regulations, police, and the courts to "improve" Africans' hygiene, morality, cultural practices, and legibility, and to turn Senegal into a modern, bureaucratic colony. These systems also served the interests of the resident French community, aiming to protect them from diseases, noise, unpleasant smells, and chaotic public spaces, and as such they not infrequently reflected French—not universal or scientifically grounded—sensibilities and preferences.[12]

Laws, ordinances, and expectations, of course, were only as good as enforcement, and we can learn a lot about the effects and limitations of these public space regulations by tracing police efforts to address violations. Regular logs of police activity in Senegal during the 1920s and 1930s, submitted daily in larger jurisdictions like Saint-Louis and Dakar and weekly in other administrative centers like Louga or Kaolack, shed light on Africans' (mis)conduct and offer brief glimpses into the demographics of crime, misdemeanor, and infraction in colonial Senegal. Dakar police reports did not usually include ages for anyone the police arrested, investigated, or ticketed, limiting our insight into the demography of crime in that city, but other jurisdictions estimated ages for minors (and, rarely, for everyone), allowing identification of a few trends. Although African men accounted for a large majority of the rule-breakers who encountered the police during the years for which I have at least some data (1924–27, 1934–38), their number included a few African women, a few French men, and many minors. Women and girls most commonly drew police attention by committing hygiene violations, such as illegal dumping of waste, failure to remove trash or sweep a courtyard, having mosquito larvae in their property, and so on, though they did not usually account for a majority of violations. The records also show that police occasionally arrested African women and older girls for alleged misdemeanors, especially fighting or assault. Arrested minors tended to be African boys whose attributed ages were between fifteen and twenty, and they were most often accused of theft or vagabondage (or both).[13]

The rest of this chapter explores how African children's lives changed due to colonial efforts to secure and maintain order in public spaces, focusing on three domains that had a particularly significant impact on minors: implementation of hygiene policy; efforts to reduce child-begging and vagabondage; and the reliance on arrests, trials, and sentencing to deal with misbehavior. It argues that French interventions did succeed in constraining African children's activities in and interactions with public spaces, especially in larger towns with sizeable European populations, changing how people thought about what childhood should be. At the same time, the police, hygiene agents, and court officials responsible for these interventions produced records of surveillance, ticketing, arrests, trials, and court decisions, contributing to the development of documentary childhood. Change was neither as complete nor as fast as French officials would have liked, however, since children and their families continued to engage in many of the practices that had not been deemed problematic prior to colonial rule. And ultimately, during the decades-long effort to force children to comply with French ideas about law and order, contests over access to and conduct in the "street" led to subtle shifts in French rhetoric, as officials and other began to think of African children not only as potential delinquents in need of discipline but also as victims who could benefit from French "protection."[14] Yet despite the softer tone, the state still emphasized order, legibility, and documentation among the children under French "protection," and relied on policing and surveillance to achieve these goals.

Hygiene, Sanitation, and Surveillance

Hygiene and sanitation regulations might have had the greatest impact on the largest number of children since they created new restrictions and required new practices in daily life. These ordinances and decrees affected chores that often fell to children, limiting where and when people could dispose of trash, dirty water, and other household wastes; requiring regular cleaning of courtyards and streets; and mandating removal of mosquito larvae. They also constrained people's ability to attend to personal needs by banning public urination and regulating the disposal of "fecal matter." Yet, as Kalala Ngalamulume has found for Saint-Louis, compliance would have been extremely difficult due to the limited or nonexistent infrastructure provided by the French, who struggled for decades in the late nineteenth century to figure out how to provide residents with clean water and who still had not installed adequate sewers by the 1910s.[15] The state never invested sufficiently in sanitation and public works even in Senegal's capital, and other parts of the colony suffered from similarly insufficient infrastructure, even if they did not have quite the same challenges that its island location posed for Saint-Louis.

Children were well represented among violators of hygiene ordinances, and the longstanding expectation among African families that girls should handle many household chores made them particularly likely to draw attention from the police, who issued fines and tickets. From late July through November 1924, for example, the Saint-Louis police ticketed at least twenty-six people for hygiene and sanitation violations in that town, and twelve of them—seven girls and five boys—were under age twenty. Their number included N'Doye Fall Diop, who lived with her mother in Saint-Louis. Noting that she was about ten years old and that her mother was "civilly responsible" for her, a hygiene agent wrote her a ticket when she dumped "fecal matter" into the river not far from her home at a time that the July 1903 Saint-Louis sanitation decree did not permit. Ousmane Kayeré, age ten and from Guet N'Dar, emptied his household's trash on the riverbank about ten meters from the water's edge, violating the same July 1903 decree and resulting in an encounter with the police. Young Ousmane admitted the violation, and the officer wrote him a ticket, noting that his father should be held civilly responsible. And finally, eighteen-year-old Aïssa N'Diaye, who lived with her mother in Sor, was ticketed because "despite a warning," she failed to "clean the courtyard of her home where there was household trash (bones, debris from fish and peanuts)" in violation of a June 1912 municipal ordinance on sanitation. Emphasizing her status as a dependent and legal minor, the police report indicated that her mother was civilly responsible for her behavior since her father was deceased.[16]

People may not have known much about the sanitation regulations, as suggested by a particularly useful set of 133 police statements regarding offenses committed in Saint-Louis from mid-July through November 1924 and June 1925. These statements suggest that each time they came upon someone engaging in prohibited behavior and stopped the person for questioning, officers not only had to get the person to admit to the behavior but also had to explain why it constituted an infraction. Even if the African residents lacked a thorough understanding of the rules—and we do not know how or whether they would have received notification of these regulations—some of those stopped and ticketed had heard about them in previous encounters with hygiene agents. Indeed, among the 133 police statements from Saint-Louis in 1924 and 1925, 16 involved violators under age twenty-six who had received prior warnings about the prohibited conduct; at least 4 of these individuals were legal minors, under age twenty. Yet these "already warned" residents, like many of their neighbors who had not yet been stopped by the hygiene police, continued to commit infractions.[17] While this behavior might have reflected a lack of understanding or a lack of resources and other options, it is certainly possible that some residents intentionally defied the rules.

Significantly, anecdotal evidence from these police statements suggests that some people, including minors, explicitly and knowingly refused to comply with French hygiene policy. Maymouna Sy, for example, a fifteen-year-old girl who lived with her parents, chose not to cooperate with the hygiene agents who questioned her about, in their words, having "neglected to clean the courtyard of her habitation." In a strikingly defiant statement, she rebuked the two agents, both African men, saying, "You are nothing but hygiene agents, I do not obey hygiene agents. You can fine me, I will pay."[18] In these short phrases, Maymouna communicated her disdain for the officers and the French notions of order and cleanliness they were paid to defend, while also asserting her intention to decide for herself when and how to clean her home. Understanding that she could not roll back French hygiene regulations, she laid out a clear refusal to follow them, a course of action made possible by her ability to pay the fine.

Fama Niang, a cloth dyer who was about twenty years old (but who was listed as a minor, with her father taking on civil responsibility), went even farther, accusing hygiene agents of orchestrating her alleged violation. Questioned about the presence of "numerous mosquito larvae in a dye pot," she responded, "It is not surprising that you found mosquito larvae in my pot of dye, it is you yourselves who brought them into my house. I will not give you my name, you can bring whomever you want and I will not give my identity to anyone." It took several hours and the involvement of the chief gendarme of the sector to establish who she was and to complete the violation paperwork. Authorities were so taken aback by her "outrageous words" that they wrote a second police statement of violation about the incident.[19] By responding like this, Fama Niang revealed that she understood the hygiene rules but rejected the corruptible system they helped create. Like Maymouna Sy and others, often girls or women, Fama Niang registered her discontent with French policies that made her daily life more difficult.[20]

Fama Niang's protest also speaks to another important aspect of French efforts to control public space through hygiene regulations and other rules and laws: the state's reliance on the idea that identity could be proven and used to hold people responsible, despite the fact that most people had no identity documents.[21] Hygiene officers noted in many of the citations issued from July to November 1924 that the person who had violated hygiene rules did not have a birth certificate or could "not present a single proof of identity." Indeed, the recipient of their reports took to underlining and otherwise emphasizing this fact in the margins of the page, as if to express astonishment that people *still* lacked these basic records of civic life.[22] Yet the hygiene violation procedure itself—like other bureaucratic, legal, and juridical processes through which the state intervened into Africans' daily lives—resulted in an increase of documented personhood and, important for our purposes, of documented childhood in Senegal. As they filled in the procès-verbal form, agents listed not only the violator's name but also their age, profession, address, and parents' names, meaning that the basic elements of an identity document were all included (though of course they could be manipulated since in the absence of an identity document, agents would have had to solicit this information from the violator in question).

It is for this reason that Fama Niang's refusal to reveal her identity was such a powerful critique of the state and that it produced such consternation among the flustered hygiene officials.

While it is clear that police continued to issue dozens of hygiene-related tickets well into the 1930s, evidence does not permit me to trace change over time in interactions between hygiene police and African minors in the colony because most police records do not include the ages of people ticketed for these sorts of violations. Even so, it is hard to imagine enforcement not having any impact on people's behavior, and especially that of children who, if they attended school even for a short time, studied hygiene as an academic subject. It is also striking that the correspondence from the 1930s in which officials worked out the details of what would become French West Africa's child-protection policies includes lengthy discussions of the region's disease burden, vaccinations, growing interest in dispensaries, and plans to improve maternal-child health but does not complain about noncompliance with sanitation and hygiene policies. Perhaps this meant that Africans had begun to alter their behavior.[23]

Religious Practice or Nuisance?
Qur'an Schools and Alms-Seeking in Urban Senegal

Even as the enforcement of French hygiene ordinances and other rules governing the use of public spaces impacted children's ability to perform ordinary chores for their families, French officials critiqued—and sometimes attempted to regulate—Qur'an schools, a cultural institution that provided socialization and religious training to Muslim children. As I have explored elsewhere, officials obsessed over the fact that Qur'an schools consistently attracted more students than their own colonial schools, and they worried that religious teachers, at best, relied on outdated (rote) pedagogy to encourage memorization of the Qur'an, and at worst, spread radical Islam. These concerns prompted the French administration to try—largely unsuccessfully—to regulate Qur'an schools on four occasions from 1857 to 1903, after which the French approach to African Islam shifted substantially toward rapprochement.[24]

Fear of radical Islam and the desire to promote French schooling only partially account for French distaste for Qur'an schools, however. Indeed, these schools seemed to many French observers to be exploitative or overly severe, running counter to a growing policy interest in child protection. Furthermore, by convening out of doors and sending students into the streets to beg for alms, Qur'an schools posed significant challenges to French efforts to maintain discipline and order in public spaces. As they worked toward child protection and aimed to clear public spaces of noise and mendicancy, officials attempted to reorder childhood for a significant proportion of Senegal's African children and eventually to recast Qur'an school students, or *talibés*, as exploited victims in need of rescuing. Their attempts to intervene and to track *talibés* of course led to increased documentation, but Qur'an schools were more difficult to penetrate than many other African institutions. Indeed, though French efforts had some effect, they neither removed Qur'an schooling as an important formative experience nor eliminated these schools and their students from public spaces, attesting to the tenacity of children, their families, and their teachers, and the centrality of Qur'an schooling to African (Muslim) childhood.[25]

Memorizing and, as historian Rudolph T. Ware III explains, ultimately embodying the Qur'an were crucial steps toward adulthood taken by Muslim boys and, to a lesser extent, girls. To gain this knowledge, children studied with marabouts, or Islamic religious teachers, who generally taught outdoors in courtyards, on verandas, or under trees, and whose teaching methods—rote memorization, writing in locally produced ink on wooden tablets, loud recitation—irked many French residents and officials. In addition to guiding students in their efforts to memorize the Qur'an, these religious schools taught humility, perseverance, and honor. Reflecting the widespread belief that true education required suffering, marabouts inculcated these values by requiring *talibés* to perform agricultural labor and domestic tasks, providing difficult living conditions, sending them out to beg for alms (food and money, known in Wolof as *yalwaan*), and punishing them harshly, often with corporal punishment, when their performance—in their studies or their chores—was insufficient. In entrusting their sons to a marabout, especially if those sons were to be live-in students (*njàngaan*), parents formally transferred rights in their sons' labor, clearing the way for marabouts to use that labor in the service of education and as remuneration for their services as teachers. As Ware points out, despite some variation in the daily schedule and amount of time devoted to each activity, alms-seeking, labor, and study were part of the practice of Qur'an schooling in the region from the earliest written references to it to the contemporary era.[26]

Yet these practices, combined with concerns about radicalization (especially before about 1910), led many French officials and observers to criticize Qur'an schools. Indeed, Qur'an schools offended French sensibilities about propriety, order, and discipline and seemed to promote child exploitation through the requirement that students work and beg. A 1911 letter from Lieutenant Governor Henri Cor, which drew on a report from médersa teachers Souleyman Seck and a Monsieur Zanettacci, for example, made this position clear. Not only did Cor complain about pedagogy, lack of infrastructure, and poor sanitation in Qur'an schools; he also accused marabouts of fraud and abuse. "Teaching" in a Qur'an school, he claimed, "is merely pretext for exploiting the religious sentiment of the masses by using the boys who are entrusted to them to go door to door begging on their behalf, and for the young girls to work as domestics in their houses." In his opinion, the administration should intervene to protect the interests of African families.[27] This letter, and the report it drew on, deployed some recognizably modern language of child rights and child protection, as Ware has found, even as it also suggested that the French were most concerned about African children when they moved through and made noise in public spaces. Despite Governor General William Ponty's rejection of much of this letter, especially its calls for more regulation, it was clear that the administration and French residents were not going to leave Qur'an schools and *talibés* alone.

A variety of other sources support the idea that Europeans' negative attitudes about Qur'an schools stemmed at least as much from their aversion to child-begging and intolerance for noise as from concerns around child welfare. In his April 1909 report, for example, the police commissioner of Saint-Louis railed against the city's Qur'an schools, which apparently had been the target of numerous complaints. He found it appalling that in neighborhoods where Europeans lived, "young natives gathered in the courtyards of houses cry out at the top of their lungs, verses from the Qur'an that the Marabout himself writes on their tablets, and all this from 7 in the morning to 5 in the evening. Sundays and holidays are not respected," he continued, "and sick people, children who are kept awake all the time by such piercing cries, suffer a lot from the current state of things." Although police had spoken to the marabouts about the problem, he noted, nothing had changed.[28] A few months later, the same official noted that the noise emanating from Qur'an schools continued to annoy many Europeans, who had sent a steady stream of complaints to the station. The schools, he grumbled, were "distributed around the European quarter" instead of being confined to African neighborhoods, allowing the "piercing cries, which the young blacks emit from morning to evening, [to] inconvenience the neighbors, principally children and the sick."[29] Even if the young *talibés* were studying in private courtyards, their loud recitations entered public spaces that the state was supposed to discipline and control, a situation that required French intervention, the police commissioner implied.

After years of criticizing Qur'an schools for noise pollution and alleged child exploitation, officials began in the 1930s to address the longstanding distaste for child-begging through the child-protection initiatives pursued in French West Africa in the years before and during the Popular Front government.[30] Having promulgated a September 1936 law aimed at protecting women and child workers, the governor general sought feedback from across the federation on its implications within each colony and how it might be expanded. Among other questions, he asked the lieutenant governors and other officials to reflect on when and in what contexts African children "found habitually in the street turning to begging" should be interned in a rehabilitation facility and how the state might prevent children from participating in the informal economy as street hawkers, sellers of prepared foods, and the like. Few if any African children worked for wages in the formal economy in the mid-1930s, so the lieutenant governor of Senegal naturally was more concerned with the implications of this law for family life and for children in the streets, and he asked local officials including cercle commandants (who were in charge of territorial districts called cercles) to conduct inquiries among the populations they administered.[31]

This request produced a series of letters and brief reports from across Senegal in late 1936 and early 1937 that offer snapshots of officials' impressions of child-begging and hawking at that time. Although the commandants of some cercles, including Thiès, Kolda, Matam, and Ziguinchor, claimed that they had no child beggars, other officials described the phenomenon in considerable detail and expressed the desire to eliminate it.[32] E. Némos, the commandant of Sine-Saloum, noted that there were two main categories of child beggars in his territory—"the blind and the pupils of certain marabouts"—and observed that the number of child beggars ballooned during the trading season and at any time the population tended to have more money on hand. Imposing penalties on parents, as called for in the new law on women and child workers, would, he believed, cut down on the number of blind beggars sent to Kaolack from far away. Turning to the second group of child beggars, Némos described their marabouts as "unscrupulous," termed this begging an "abuse," and mentioned a recent news article that had called for "serious monitoring of Qu'ran schools." Yet despite his portrayal of Qur'an students as victims and his use of rhetoric associated with children's rights advocacy, Némos urged caution. He had reservations, he explained, about imposing penalties on parents who had entrusted their children to marabouts, since this practice was associated with religious beliefs and accepted "custom."[33]

Similarly, though the commandant of Bas-Sénégal claimed that no children made their living from begging in the cercle he administered, he included a thorough description of the child-begging he had witnessed in Saint-Louis. These young beggars were students at the colonial capital's numerous Qur'an schools, and their number included children from Saint-Louis and villages some distance away. Saint-Louis residents understood that children begged to earn their keep and to pay marabouts for their teaching, and as such they supported the practice that he acknowledged was a "deeply rooted custom." As an "integral part of the religious system," the practice of Qur'an students' engaging in begging would be extraordinarily difficult for the administration to suppress. But on the other hand, the commandant worried that the custom often served as a cover for fraud and child abuse. Deploying child-rights language, he claimed that certain "so-called marabouts, of doubtful morality" hid behind their claim to teach the Qur'an to "shamelessly exploit . . . young children originally from Waalo and Cayor who are entrusted to them by naïve and oblivious parents." These fraudulent marabouts led groups of children around the colony, begging in different areas and living in "miserable" conditions. Ultimately, he claimed, the difficult circumstances would promote "bad instincts," which could over time shift from minor "pilfering" to "plunder and theft."[34] This belied his concern not only for the children themselves but also for the maintenance of order in the colony. Begging clearly did not figure into the African childhoods imagined by these officials, who feared it might threaten the future of the colony by pushing children toward criminality and seeding instability.

These sources show that over a long period of time, French officials disapproved of child mendicancy in Senegal and wanted it to stop, even if they recognized that it served a practical or religious function.[35] While they sometimes used child-protection rhetoric in their critiques, retaining control over public spaces and eliminating irritations and obstructions were at least as important to officials as providing social welfare among Africans, if not more so. Many officials claimed that child-begging did not take place in their cercles. And all of them suggested that the administration should do something about the phenomenon. Even as they used recognizably modern language of child protection and child rights, the more pressing concern was maintaining order, keeping children in their place, and ensuring there were no encumberments in public spaces, objectives that required discipline as well as protection.

This is likely because the freedom to wander, to be aimless in the city, to look for opportunity, and—as a Qur'an student—to be mobile and to seek alms were important parts of many Africans' childhoods and not something to give up lightly. Indeed, as Rudolph Ware notes, seeking food, candles, money, and other donations had been an integral part of religious training and Muslim boyhood in Senegambia for centuries prior to colonial rule, and people continued to value the practice for its ability to teach perseverance and humility and to strengthen social ties through charity.[36] Accordingly, several African students at the William Ponty School in the 1930s and 1940s touched on children's alms-seeking in their ethnographic essays, and regardless of their opinion of the practice, they nearly always connected it to the belief that suffering was essential to a good education because of its role in producing strong character.[37] Despite his negative portrayal of Qur'an schools and marabouts' treatment of their students, for example, Serigne Fall Seck noted that many people valued the perseverance that came from the labor, alms-seeking, and other aspects of Muslim religious education in Cayor. Baba Ndiaye described his own experiences in a Qur'an school and implied that difficult conditions and alms-seeking taught him about hardship, preparing him to "accept life as hard as it can be" and to "do honor to my family and to my race." And a student named Almamy, in a very appreciative essay on Qur'an schooling among Toucouleur people in Fouta, argued that alms-seeking strengthened the relationship between Qur'an students and the larger community, as mothers ran to fill their calabashes with food and other alms.[38] In their own way, each of these writers showed how begging served a crucial function in children's training and religious education and in the community itself.

Even though an (elite) African critique of Qur'an schools was beginning to emerge by the 1940s, and officials continued to worry that the practice of begging and imposing hardship would lead *talibés* to delinquency, the state did not manage to fully regulate Qur'an schools' use of public space, nor did it successfully surveil and document a significant proportion of *talibés*.[39] Officials had never fully enforced the requirement that marabouts submit lists of their students, on the books since the 1857 regulation of Qur'an schools, and the few lists they received over the years contained minimal details. The early twentieth-century shift toward rapprochement with Muslim leaders led the state to stop regulating their religious schools, and they likely ceased all efforts to collect these lists around that time.[40] Officials' hesitation to intervene in Qur'an schools and religious mendicancy, which reflected the overall policy toward Islam and the commitment to religious freedom, along with many Africans' dedication to the practice, meant that *talibés* continued to occupy public spaces as they recited the Qur'an, prayed, and begged for alms. Their largely undocumented identities stood in stark contrast to the goals of the modernizing colonial state.

"In a State of Vagabondage": Aimless Children and Colonial Spaces

French discourse about religious mendicancy sometimes bled into a larger concern about vagabondage, conduct that many feared would lead to other forms of juvenile delinquency.[41] Like child beggars, child vagabonds occupied public spaces in ways that clashed with French aesthetics and conceptions of how those spaces should be used, and their apparently idle behavior challenged French assumptions about how children (even marginalized African children) should occupy their time. As a tool authorities could use to (re)assert control over public spaces, vagabondage was a fluid concept that criminalized a variety of behaviors which had once been tolerated, if not entirely commended, like spending time in the public arena without being productive, traveling around the region without maintaining a fixed address, or sleeping out of doors (in towns and cities, where the French wanted to create modern, urban environments).[42] Although officials increasingly adopted logics of child protection during the 1930s to describe their plans to address idleness in children, these priorities of promoting order and control in public spaces remained. The pursuit of these goals, of course, required recordkeeping, creating a documentary existence for some of the children in this marginalized population, and it was limited by some children's refusal to go along with French plans.

At least since the 1848 emancipation decree, French officials and residents had expressed concerns about the potential disorder caused by aimless, unproductive children in urban public spaces. Indeed, it was this very concern that led to the creation of guardianship in 1849, which, as discussed in chapter 1, allowed the state to entrust unaccompanied and formerly enslaved minors to private individuals to keep them working and out of vagabondage. Although the state's use of guardianship declined in the early twentieth century, officials remained concerned about the presence in the streets of unoccupied and unaccompanied children, at least some of whom had fled slavery. In January 1907, the lieutenant governor made plans to send "minors found in a state of vagabondage in the city of Saint-Louis" to the orphanage created in late 1904 in nearby Sor.[43] This was a short-lived fix—the orphanage shut its doors for good in November 1907—but a revealing one, since officials envisioned sending not only child vagabonds there but also liberated minors, juveniles ordered to a "house of correction" after courts determined that they lacked criminal capacity, "morally abandoned" children, and of course African orphans.[44] As Ibrahima Thioub has argued, officials had similar fears about many types of marginalized children during the early colonial period, and the Sor orphanage, where officials planned in early 1907 to make "no distinction" between vagabonds and orphans except in their sleeping locations in the dormitory, provides compelling evidence to this effect.[45]

Arrest, trial, and—once the state opened a new juvenile reformatory in 1912—internment offered mechanisms for cracking down on child (and adult) vagabondage, illegal for all those governed by the French penal code and extended to colonial subjects in a March 1923 decree. Thus, the concept of vagabondage was a colonial import, imposed by the state on populations that had long allowed children, especially boys, a considerable amount of unsupervised time to play, work, and gather with agemates and which accepted that children might pursue Islamic education, complete an apprenticeship, or experience fosterage away from their home community. Indeed, attempting to secure approval for the March 1923 vagabondage decree, the governor general acknowledged the clash between a French worldview that held as sacrosanct orderly and unencumbered public spaces and productively occupied people, and that of their colonial subjects. While he worried about rural to urban migration in general, the governor general was particularly alarmed by the growing population of "young people" who had escaped "familial authority" by coming to the city, and he believed his decree would allow officials to more effectively address the problem. Vagabondage, he argued, was a "'new' crime" (*délit*) and thus "could not have been anticipated, and therefore punished by custom." His decree not only made vagabondage a crime under customary law but also included provisions designed to encourage recidivists to remain in their communities of origin, attempting to curb African mobility and urbanization.[46] By criminalizing vagabondage across the federation and by arresting juveniles for the offense, the state made clear that ideal childhood did not allow for *unproductive* use of public space, even as it encouraged children to perform labor in those same spaces. This suggests significant continuity between expectations for orderly work placed on liberated minors in the second half of the nineteenth century and expectations for working-class children in the 1920s.

French concerns about young vagabonds came through clearly in a 1923 incident involving Momar Seck, described variously as approximately seventeen years old and "a young Mouride of simple mind about 18 years of age," who was arrested for vagabondage twice within a year. After his release from the Thiès (adult) prison, where he had served a six-month sentence for vagabondage, he continued to "wander" around the town and rejected the administration's efforts to "get him to work" for a chief in a neighboring village as a farm laborer. Efforts to locate family members who might care for young Momar turned up nothing. The commandant was particularly bothered that Momar kept returning to the prison and loitering near the official residence, seeming not to understand that he was expected to find a job and lodging in Thiès or to go elsewhere. Arrested for vagabondage some months later and tried as a minor this time—a strategy the commandant pursued after the lieutenant governor reminded him that the colony's reformatory was only for minors ordered there by a court—Momar ultimately found himself interned in the juvenile agricultural penitentiary at Bambey until his majority.[47]

Similarly, the authorities in Dakar were troubled by Ousmane Sèye, a boy of about sixteen years who had been born in Bathurst, Gambia, and who lacked both a "fixed address" and a "regular" job in Dakar. Police arrested him in July 1936 and charged him with vagabondage, which led to a series of court hearings the following month. Although Ousmane at first vigorously denied that he was a vagabond, claiming that he was employed and giving a false address, the court went to some lengths to prove otherwise, reconvening twice to accommodate an appearance from the marabout Ousmane had identified as his landlord. When the marabout denied knowing young Ousmane, the boy admitted that he had been spending the night "in mosques or under verandas" ever since his father had gone to prison, and that he did odd jobs in the market to earn a few cents. Although this was enough for the court to determine that he was indeed in a "state of vagabondage," it acquitted him as a minor who lacked criminal understanding but ordered him interned in the juvenile reformatory in Carabane until he turned eighteen.[48]

These cases exemplify the French administration's concern with maintaining order, stability, and cleanliness in public spaces. Neither of these young people was engaging in any truly dangerous criminal behavior, but because they loitered in spaces and in ways that bothered the administration, the state used the concept of vagabondage to bring them before the court. In both cases, these young people lacked families to care for them—Momar's family could not be found and Ousmane's father was in a colonial prison—but instead of providing care in an orphanage or social welfare institution, the administration used the justice system to mandate their internment in a juvenile reformatory. This suggests that despite the proliferation of health initiatives, the expansion of colonial schooling, and the creation of orphanages in the interwar period, child "protection" in Senegal continued to prioritize order, discipline, and surveillance above everything else. Indeed, as I explore elsewhere in this book, even the institutions that seemed to provide care (schools and health clinics, for example) upheld the colonial state's linked goals of protection and discipline. Not only can we trace a throughline between surveillance of liberated minors and internment of juvenile delinquents, as Thioub has argued, but we can also extend that line to the state's efforts to control and surveil children as they moved through public spaces in the 1920s and 1930s.[49]

These examples are also compelling because they shed light on young people's efforts to make their own way in the colonial city, and show how their actions could call into question the state's power and image of itself as a protector. For his part, Momar Seck refused to accept the farm job the Thiès commandant found for him, explaining that he did not "feel at ease" there. Instead, he kept returning to Thiès, where he must have felt more at home. Ousmane Sèye, on the other hand, attempted to hide his status as an unaccompanied minor, eking out an existence carrying packages in the market and sleeping wherever he could find a place to rest. Seeming to understand the legal ramifications of being deemed a vagabond, he tried hard to shield himself from this label. It is telling that officials did not envision a scenario whereby these young people could be cared and provided for while they attended school and engaged in leisure activities, a notion of childhood that was increasingly available—even expected—for white middle- and aspiring middle-class children and even for some Black elites.[50] Instead, representatives of the colonial state found the presence in colonial urban space of unsupervised and unproductive young Africans so worrisome that they had to be removed.

The state's emphasis on child protection during the 1930s led to some reconsideration of child vagabondage, and reforms pursued in France and Madagascar seem to have at least briefly influenced authorities in French West Africa to see child vagabondage through a lens of victimization.[51] At around the same time, authorities in Senegal and their counterparts in Dakar were exploring the feasibility of a plan to create—away from the temptations of the city—a "center for the reeducation of children habitually engaging in mendicity," which would cater especially to the blind children who begged in the streets but which could also take in some *talibés*, if this could be done without offending religious sentiments. Yet after the health service submitted an exorbitant cost estimate for a facility designed for two hundred children (80% blind, 20% sighted), both administrations decided to put the plan on hold indefinitely.[52] This shows that even as officials refused to allow that child-begging and vagabondage might be valid components of childhood training, they were unwilling to spend the money that more modern approaches to child "protection" required, and instead continued turning to the police, courts, and the reformatory to force some children to change their ways.[53] Although the rhetoric of protection allowed some to see these children as victims of circumstance, poverty, misguided religious beliefs, and so on, the imperatives of order and stability, and the realities of the bottom line, remained paramount.

Petty Theft and Other Minor Crimes

Even as the colonial state concerned itself with begging, hygiene violations, vagabondage, and other behaviors that had not posed problems prior to colonial rule, officials also sought to control and punish conduct that African societies joined them in condemning (for example, theft, arson, homicide, destruction of property, assault, kidnapping, and rape).[54] But significantly, the colonial state replaced family- or community-based discipline with official, bureaucratized proceedings modeled on French juridical infrastructure. Furthermore, not only did both types of colonial courts favor the "house of correction" to try to rehabilitate wayward minors—all of whom came from places without Indigenous cultures of confinement—they also imposed lengthy periods of internment, separating children from their families and communities for years.[55] As in all other contacts with the police, justice, and penal systems, those minors engaging in petty and more serious crimes would have seen their identities recorded and documented, their personhood and misdeeds written into existence. Yet even in moments when they were most susceptible to intervention and reshaping from the colonial state, at least some minors tried to tell their own stories.

The state invested most heavily in policing in the larger towns, where French residents worried about security, crime, and juvenile delinquency as African urban populations grew. In 1913, the justice service annual report commented proudly on the increasing numbers of cases tried (overall) in Saint-Louis, due largely to better enforcement of laws already on the books. And at the same time, officials boasted of declining crime—and especially juvenile crime—in the second arrondissement. Minors had accounted for only 12 of the 269 successful prosecutions of crimes, or *délits*, in Dakar, Rufisque, and Thiès over the year, and the report noted that this was a "very low percentage if one takes into account the level of corruption among the general population, which is higher in the towns."[56] Data compiled for the Native Tribunals in 1936 suggest even lower incidence of juvenile crimes and noncriminal violations, indicating that only 1 boy and 1 girl under age sixteen were accused of crimes in that year, while 3 boys and 2 girls under sixteen allegedly committed noncriminal violations of one kind or another. The fact that 77 men and 1 woman were accused of crimes, while 4,643 men and 2,285 women were cited for noncriminal violations, suggests that the low juvenile statistics did not stem from a lack of police involvement.[57]

Yet even if certain official statistics revealed occasional downward trends in juvenile crime, officials remained concerned about it, police kept arresting young people, and courts continued to hear cases involving juveniles. These arrests at least sometimes stemmed from a disconnect between local ideas about children and misconduct and the French penal code or customary law. Local practice had long treated some misconduct as childish mistakes that required parental discipline and necessitated social repair or restitution, and simply did not see other behaviors, like vagabondage, as problematic at all. Children and their families thus must have found it strange that the French approach to justice led to the arrest and trial of minors for petty theft or loitering. Yet these types of offenses were most common. Indeed, of the fifty-three arrests of minors that I have identified across four administrative cercles in the mid-1930s, thirty-six involved allegations of theft and twelve involved allegations of vagabondage. Six more minors were arrested for alleged fraud, embezzlement, or falsification. This group of records included seven minors arrested for various types of assault but none arrested for other violent crimes.[58] These statistics suggest that colonial rule subjected minors to increased policing and surveillance and sought to constrain and control them in new ways.

It is difficult to discern how African children experienced and reacted to these shifts in the legal landscape, since extant sources do not include their testimony on these issues, and indeed include very little testimony from children on any topic. But in a couple of court transcripts, the African minors on trial crafted narratives of their (mis)behavior in ways that might indicate an ongoing process of learning about and understanding the implications of colonial law. In a July 1923 trial in the Native Tribunal in Tivaouane, where an approximately ten-year old orphan named Ismaël Sy stood accused of stealing "five packs of cigarettes and two flasks of cologne" from a boutique in Pire, for example, he did not seek to excuse or apologize for his actions. Rather, perhaps put at ease by the fact that the presiding officer, both assessors, and the court secretary were African, he admitted to stealing the items from Amadou Diop's shop and then answered questions forthrightly and concisely, as in the following exchange:

> Q: What did you want to do with the cigarettes you stole?
> R: Smoke.
> Q: At your age, my child, one mustn't smoke.
> R: I will not smoke any more.
> Q: And the cologne?
> R: So I could perfume myself.
> Q: Where is your father?
> R: Deceased.
> Q: And your mother?
> R: Also deceased, from the plague.
> Q: With whom do you live?
> R: I was with my uncle in Tivaouane, but he left me and I no longer know where he is.
> Q: What were you doing in Pire?
> R: I had gone there on a walk (*J'y étais allé en promenade*).[59]

Although the lack of information about body language and tone of voice, and the mediated nature of colonial court testimonies prevent me from drawing conclusions about frame of mind, it is worth noting that Ismaël's words do not imply he was terribly worried about the trial or remorseful for his pilfering. And if he was not concerned, perhaps it was because, as the tribunal acknowledged, local custom held that "a theft committed by a child the age of Ismaël Sy (10 years) is not reprehensible." Yet as it turns out, the circumstances *were* dire, and despite acquitting him of any criminal responsibility, the tribunal ordered Ismaël's internment in the juvenile "penitentiary at Bambey until his majority," that is, for eight to ten years, because he had stolen the items and lacked family to care for him.[60] This case encapsulates the state's tendency to simultaneously pursue control and protection as it worked to reform childhood and maintain order in the colony.

On trial in Kébémer in August 1927 on charges of pickpocketing, fourteen-year-old Maïssa Diop showed more awareness of the legal process and perhaps what was at stake. In his first court appearance, he told the French police commissioner, presiding in lieu of a judge, and the two Wolof assessors that he had been born in Saint-Louis, which would give him certain citizenship rights as an *originaire* and require trial under French law instead of local custom. This claim delayed the proceedings for five days, while Maïssa tried—unsuccessfully—to procure a copy of a birth certificate to substantiate his citizenship status. After the delay, the trial began with testimony from the alleged victim (twelve-year-old Mamadou Sylla), from the African police officer who had investigated the theft, and from the woman young Maïssa allegedly tapped to safeguard the stolen money (Hama Fall). Together, these witness testimonies suggested that Maïssa pickpocketed Mamadou Sylla, stealing forty francs, while the younger boy was standing in line to buy a ticket at the train station. Alerted by Mamadou, the police officer took Maïssa to the police station and put him in prison, where he eventually admitted to the theft and told the officer where to recover the stolen forty francs. The officer, Abdoulaye Touré, made sure to describe Maïssa as a boy of "poor character" who "spends all his time committing thefts."[61]

Events unfolded differently in Maïssa's account, however, which portrayed him as an innocent who had simply gathered money that had fallen to the floor. After picking up the money, Maïssa claimed, he left the train station, asked Hama Fall to hold onto it for him, and returned to the station where the police officer searched him as fear prevented him from telling the officer what had happened. When asked why he had not returned the money to Mamadou Sylla right away, young Maïssa explained, "I was afraid to do it because there were a lot of people at the train station." This story did not convince the court, which believed he had indeed stolen from Mamadou. Although Maïssa's age (fourteen years) led the court to acquit him because he lacked criminal "discernment," it also prompted his internment in a penitentiary until the age of majority (twenty years). In issuing this decision, the tribunal noted that this was at least the fourth petty theft he had committed in only eight months, and that his parents could not prevent his bad behavior.[62] His effort to excuse his conduct suggests that he was at least somewhat aware of French law, court proceedings, and their potential ramifications, and that he perhaps wanted to avoid being sent to a juvenile institution. He thus strategically crafted a narrative of himself as an opportunistic collector rather than a thief. Yet regardless of their efforts to justify or make light of their conduct, courts determined that Ismaël Sy and Maïssa Diop, along with dozens of other minors who had committed petty theft or vagabondage, were in fact juvenile delinquents who required long periods of internment to prevent new offenses and to encourage their rehabilitation.

In doing so, the courts sent a clear message that the French police and justice systems aimed to eliminate such behavior from colonial public spaces, imposing discipline and protection on young people who did not comply.

This commitment to controlling and cleaning up public spaces guided policy, policing, and surveillance throughout the period, even amid concerns about the "severity" of juvenile punishments that emerged during the late 1920s and 1930s. Indeed, in a 1929 report on the juvenile reformatory in Carabane, the local French administrator argued that interning minors for so many years for relatively unimportant offenses constituted a "serious psychological error." Yet instead of criticizing policing or ill-fitting colonial regulations, he advocated changing the approach to rehabilitation.[63] In 1938, a different administrator expressed similar concerns about long internments for insignificant offenses like larceny or vagabondage and called for a mandate that courts consider returning minors to their families for rehabilitation as the law allowed. But like his predecessor, he did not question policing of minors or the regulation of public spaces themselves.[64] These critiques reflected larger shifts in French rhetoric about and policy toward African children that, by the 1930s, positioned efforts to address juvenile delinquency as an important component of "child protection." In this context, officials began in 1937 to discuss and then draft several reforms to juvenile justice, which would have created separate juvenile courts, deemphasized the use of reformatories for some older children, and kept children under thirteen out of reformatories altogether.[65] Yet neither the drafting process of the late 1930s nor the delayed implementation of the resulting reforms in 1952 changed the approach to policing. Instead, emblematic of the state's efforts to maintain order and control, policing and surveillance of public spaces continued to shape children's daily lives.

Conclusion

As it sought to establish and maintain order in public spaces, the colonial state did not spare children from its efforts to enforce regulations pertaining to sanitation and hygiene, mobility, the appropriateness (or lack) of productive activity, begging and charity, sounds and smells, and so on. Rather, African children, like adults, drew the attention of the police when they performed activities that might once have been ordinary and unproblematic, and when they engaged in conduct—like theft—that their societies and families did not condone. Colonial rule not only placed significant new restrictions on how public space could be used but also imposed a different approach to dealing with challenges to the state's vision of order and to handling crime and punishment. Under the French system, minors could be ticketed, and their parent or guardian required to pay a fine to the state on their behalf; they could be arrested and tried in a French court or a Native Tribunal for a huge range of offenses; and they could be interned for long periods in a juvenile reformatory run by and for the colonial state. Although direct evidence is lacking, it seems likely that those who encountered the colonial penal and justice systems in this way would have been profoundly affected. Furthermore, representatives of the disciplinary state documented African minors, often for the first time, since many African families did not record births with the French civil state. It is quite significant, then, that the tickets, arrest records, trial transcripts, and internment orders produced through police and judicial processes included all the individual identifying information the state had begun to expect from its subjects.

These changes also likely impacted many African children who did not experience the state's legal and repressive power directly, especially in cities and towns that had a more significant police presence. By witnessing or hearing about other children's encounters with colonial police and courts, they would have learned about French expectations for colonial African childhood, which required children to have a home and parents or guardians, attend school or hold a job or apprenticeship, follow a rash of hygiene restrictions and safety rules imposed by local governing bodies, and never amble about in public spaces. They of course could not engage in conduct that would have gone against their community norms, in addition to violating French law, such as theft or assault. Although French rhetoric shifted in the late 1920s and 1930s away from viewing African children mainly as potential threats to colonial order and stability and toward treating them as unfortunate victims of their circumstances who would best be saved through French intervention, the state's need to discipline and surveil remained. Despite a softer tone and a new emphasis on social welfare, children continued to experience discipline, surveillance, and policing, and they continued in various ways to push back against it, shaping the documented and disciplined colonial African childhood that emerged.

CHAPTER 5

The Body

HYGIENE, MEDICINE, AND CHILDREN'S HEALTH

In an early draft of his 1934 report on child protection, Governor General Jules Brévié was especially keen to tout recent expansion in biomedical care targeted at children. The Dakar School of Medicine had opened in 1918 to train African medical assistants, and the colony had created new dispensaries. Furthermore, medical officials "began visiting schools, vaccinating, establishing individual [medical] records," he explained, noting that "at the slightest ailment little schoolchildren were brought to the dispensary where they received care, advice, remedies."[1] Yet even as he stressed the humanitarian nature of these French initiatives, Brévié hinted at other motivations when he wrote that dispensaries allowed the French "to watch over children" (*veiller sur l'enfant*), revealing that, like many other French policies targeting African children, medical interventions incorporated both protection and discipline.[2] This report, ultimately intended for the Colonial Ministry in Paris, prompts us to ask what it meant for colonial doctors, teachers, and officials to "watch over" African children's health, and it points us toward three fruitful areas of inquiry: vaccinations, school medical visits, and medical records. Each of these initiatives has a much longer history than Brévié's report allows, and they were linked in important ways.

This chapter explores how hygiene and health animated French efforts to reform African childhood from the 1870s to the 1930s, focusing on smallpox vaccinations, the increasingly important connection between biomedical practice and colonial schools, and the production of documentation related to children's medical encounters. Setting aside the issue of whether French hygiene interventions improved African children's health outcomes, this chapter explores their impact on ideas about and experiences of childhood in colonial Senegal and asks how they affected colonial power. Smallpox, long present in both Western Europe and West Africa, garnered considerable French attention and resources and defined most African children's earliest encounters with colonial biomedicine, largely because, even if it was not the deadliest to Europeans, it was the one infectious disease the French could reliably control with a vaccine. In both France and Senegal, smallpox disproportionately impacted young children, so children naturally became targets of French vaccination campaigns. Beginning in 1904, all children were supposed to receive smallpox vaccines, and colonial schools became a key locus of enforcement in ways I explore below. The emphasis on vaccination against smallpox, I suggest, paved the way for other, more intensive health interventions in colonial schools, which functioned as a space where the state could explore methods to medicalize African childhood and make it more hygienic. Together, vaccinations and school-based medical interventions generated significant quantities of data about African children's health, and in recording this data colonial officials involved with hygiene initiatives contributed to the development of documentary childhood in Senegal.

Biomedical interventions focused on children reflected the larger health priorities of the colonial state, which, as Kalala Ngalamulume argues, can be divided into three eras. In the nineteenth century, French concerns about African health were wholly and unapologetically self-serving. Europeans worried about what they saw as the filth and potential for contagion of African homes and bodies; the French used health concerns as justification for racial segregation, and they sought to control disease among Africans as a way of protecting themselves. Health interventions reflected a more limited understanding of disease transmissions, especially before the acceptance of germ theory in the late nineteenth century. Although the protection of European life always remained top of mind, priorities shifted in the early twentieth century as economic development imperatives demanded a growing and healthy workforce. Accordingly, Governor General Ernest Roume's public health decree of 14 April 1904 expanded the health infrastructure in French West Africa, created sanitary police and hygiene committees for the federation, and claimed new powers for the government during epidemics, among other reforms. Additional decrees issued not long afterward added to or modified the 1904 reform. Particularly significant was the February 1905 decree creating the Native Medical Assistance (Assistance

Médicale Indigène, or AMI) program, which provided free biomedical care to Africans across the colony. By the 1920s and 1930s, amid the effort to justify French colonialism by portraying it as humanitarian and reflecting the French state's emphasis on social welfare policies at home, and amid growing concerns about extremely high infant and child mortality rates, the colonial administration made a much more sustained and serious effort to provide medical care to Africans. These programs targeted mothers, babies, and young children but also provided new avenues for children ages five and over to receive medical care in clinics and, crucially, through their schools.[3]

As this brief historical overview suggests, colonial health policy in Senegal became increasingly focused on surveilling and intervening with African bodies, shifting over time from a primary focus on the quarantine and mobility restrictions (along with some vaccinations) believed to best protect Europeans to promoting biomedical health encounters and vaccinations on a much larger scale. African children were always key to French biomedical interventions, and their importance seemed to grow as medical policy developed. Not only were they crucial for the future economic success of the colony and more susceptible to smallpox but they became sympathetic figures at the center of French efforts to refashion the public image of colonial rule. And furthermore, the very dependence and vulnerability of African children could allow them to be surveilled, vaccinated, treated, and documented when they entered colonial spaces such as schools, reformatories, and urban streets. French medical practices, discourses, and habits of documentation produced knowledge about African children for the benefit of the colonial state but also aimed to reshape African childhood by normalizing biomedical care. Yet, because these initiatives required children to participate, show up, and comport themselves in particular ways, children's actions or inaction ultimately limited the state's ability to fully refashion and record childhood.

Smallpox and African Childhood

Producing high fevers and skin lesions, or pox, smallpox caused death in some 30 percent of cases, and it resulted in significant scarring and sometimes blindness among those who recovered. Endemic in Senegal in the late nineteenth century, smallpox turned epidemic in parts of the colony every few years, and French colonial authorities struggled to stem these outbreaks. Recovery from the disease conferred some immunity, leaving children—anyone born since the last epidemic—at the greatest risk of infection.[4] This association with childhood, found in Senegal and France alike (along with many other places), is one reason the disease and French attempts to surveil and control it affected so many African children. Indeed, children underwent vaccination, and many entered the colonial record as their results were recorded and tracked, or as they were reported as smallpox victims by the sanitary police. Smallpox, French interventions into epidemics and transmission, and African reactions thus had a significant impact on childhood itself.

Familiar with smallpox for centuries prior to European colonization of the region, West Africans had developed a constellation of tools for responding to the disease, protecting people from it, and addressing its impacts on the community. In Senegal, early French observers noted that people simply accepted it as a fact of life, a challenge that many children had to pass through on their way to adulthood. Yet significant evidence also shows not only that Africans in Senegal and elsewhere in the region knew the symptoms of smallpox and tried to stay away from sick people but also that some, especially in Muslim communities, used a process called variolation, or inoculation, to protect themselves. Variolation entailed removing matter from the pustules of an infected person and inserting it into a small incision on the body of a healthy person to produce a mild case of smallpox. Although the person was contagious while infected and a small percentage of variolated people died of smallpox, the procedure ultimately conferred protection against future infection. Significantly, Africans often underwent variolation during childhood, though the timing depended on the prevalence of smallpox since the procedure could only be used during an outbreak.[5] While African communities did not keep written records of variolation, it is perhaps significant that the procedure resulted in scarring, a kind of inscription on the body that would indicate a certain immunity.

French (and European/American) understandings of many infectious diseases changed radically in the later nineteenth century, as scientists worked out germ theory and investigated methods of disease transmission, and as tropical medicine became a respected subfield. Smallpox was something of an exception, since European doctors had used a cowpox-derived vaccine, developed by Edward Jenner in 1796, to significantly reduce transmission rates of smallpox in some European countries. French doctors and colonial administrators hoped to repeat these successes in Senegal, and by the 1880s, they began launching large-scale vaccination campaigns in colonial towns, outposts, and villages. Even though French people had used variolation before the development of the vaccine, French medical personnel and officials condemned the practice in Senegal, since it could lead to severe illness and disease transmission, and since they rightly thought its use undermined attempts to convince Africans to accept the vaccine. Noting that Muslims seemed most likely to stand by variolation, they frequently blamed marabouts for its prevalence.[6] This represented a significant clash over understandings of health and healing, and it often depended on the bodies of African children, who were prime targets for both variolation *and* vaccination.

For the information needed to enforce quarantines, respond to outbreaks with vaccines, maintain an understanding of the disease landscape, and ultimately gear up for mass vaccination campaigns, officials relied on police commissioners and the sanitary police, who were responsible for tracking the spread of disease. Police reports indicated the number of children and adults in each neighborhood or village who were suffering from smallpox, along with an accounting of those who were recovering or who had died from the illness. Occasionally, reports included names, ages, and other identifying information. In January 1889, for example, the police commissioner in Saint-Louis sent the names, ages (seven to fifteen), and addresses of six children who had contracted smallpox and of two more whose health was improving. To collect this information, the police commissioner likely had to rely on the power of his office to intervene into family and children's affairs at a moment of vulnerability. Indeed, less than two months later, a doctor for the colony observed that because "during an epidemic, the large majority of the native population carefully hides the sick from doctors," the police commissioner was best positioned to provide data on the occurrence of smallpox in Saint-Louis.[7] The reliance on police to enforce health policy is suggestive of the power imbalances that animated biomedical planning in Senegal and informed children's early encounters with representatives of the colonial state.

Sanitary police also relied on neighborhood chiefs and community members for information about smallpox cases, and they sometimes worried that these individuals were not being forthcoming. This fear seemed to be justified when, in March 1888, the police commissioner, asked by the colony's head doctor to follow up on a lead, verified the existence of multiple cases in Sor that the neighborhood chief had not reported. He also found that the cadi (Muslim judicial official) of Saint-Louis had not reported the smallpox death of his own young son. Acting on suspicion of additional smallpox cases the next month, a hospital official discovered and reported on "2 children of 7 to 8 years with developing pustules in the courtyard of the Lezongar home. 3 others recovering at M. Pécarrère's house." Railing against the "deceptions" that were obscuring the full extent of the outbreak, the head doctor criticized the police for failing to collect sufficient information, essentially making a case for even more involvement of the police in the implementation of public health policy.[8] Despite French complaints that chiefs failed to report cases in their jurisdictions and that residents hid sick family members—especially children—from medical personnel, Africans sometimes cooperated with requests for case counts and other information. In January 1895, for example, the chief of Guet Ndar reported that "two children of this village were stricken with smallpox." The interior director who received his report then communicated with the chief doctor and the mayor of Saint-Louis about the cases so that they could determine whether to order an investigation.[9]

Keeping up with the spread of disease in the more remote French outposts and in rural areas presented bigger challenges. Some of these areas had sanitary police, doctors, or hygiene agents who could assist in keeping the administration informed. Administrators also found out about epidemics from chiefs, from public rumor, and by conducting their own investigations while touring the areas under their charge. Thus, in January 1898, the administrator of the Cayor cercle wired the governor general about the nine smallpox cases (seven of them in children) that he had discovered in Pire-Goureye and the isolation and disinfection measures he had ordered in response. The region needed a visit from a vaccinating doctor, he intimated. And in February 1903, the resident in Yang Yang also requested a vaccinating doctor since he had recently received reports of ten smallpox cases in different parts of the province, as well as a notice of additional cases in Jolof Oriental from the chief of that canton.[10]

Indeed, the initial recording of information about smallpox cases, significant whether it consisted only of case counts or also included personal information, could trigger additional interventions from representatives of the colonial state. Often, a report of a smallpox case—especially one in an urban area—prompted a visit from a colonial doctor. This was the case in June 1888, when an official (probably the chief doctor) checked in on a young smallpox patient, Benita Soumaré, a day or two after the police commissioner reported that the girl, "age 8 to 10 years," exhibited a mild case.[11] Reports of smallpox could offer justification for the administration to take extreme measures to try to contain the disease, isolating sick people (including children) a distance away from the village, burning homes, and burying personal property thought to be contaminated. These approaches, better known to historians for their use to address plague in Dakar and the surrounding areas during the 1914 epidemic, allowed the state to assume considerable power in the lives and material circumstances of children and their families.[12]

Even when officials did not pursue such drastic measures, the process of surveillance and documentation had a real impact on African childhood, bringing many children to the attention of the colonial state, producing direct encounters between children and the colonial doctors, and generating records of these encounters and the children who experienced them. Sanitary police and doctors tracked and counted smallpox patients—including children—at all stages of the disease, perhaps not realizing or not caring that people in many of these communities feared that counting children would invite envy and bad luck.[13] This insensitivity to cultural norms, along with the repressive responses that medical intervention could involve, may explain why many African families hid smallpox victims from the state. Yet regardless of taboos, numerous children were documented, tracked, and made legible to the colonial state vis-à-vis this illness.

Vaccination initiatives, including weekly or daily sessions at established locations in the colonial towns and mobile vaccination campaigns in the countryside, also shaped children's experiences and produced a new sort of documentation. Kalala Ngalamulume has suggested that the French administration began regularly providing smallpox vaccines in 1852 with the goal of reaching all unvaccinated children but that interest among Africans was limited at this early date. In an effort to overcome what the interior director called "lack of concern and negligence, if not marked opposition" to the vaccine among "native populations," the administration began in the 1860s to require a certificate attesting to a child's successful smallpox vaccination or recovery from the disease to enroll in school. In March 1870, officials launched a drive to vaccinate all nonimmune children who attended French schools and—significantly—the Qur'an schools of the colonial capital, and they envisaged doctors working in the other French posts following suit. This position was reiterated by an 1889 sanitary commission policy that called on "soldiers and pupils at schools [to] have themselves vaccinated, to reduce the grip of the disease."[14] Such policies likely resulted in some increased compliance with vaccination policies—in May 1870, for example, one official made the somewhat ludicrous claim that all schoolchildren and most other children in Saint-Louis had been vaccinated only two months into a campaign—but the fact that officials continued to discuss the issue and propose new requirements, and the continued incidence of smallpox in the colony, suggests that many chose not to comply.[15]

To address the spread of smallpox in rural areas, the French administration relied on information supplied by the commandants, doctors, and African chiefs working in these regions, and frequently found themselves scrambling to respond to outbreaks with limited vaccine doses and human resources.[16] The appointment of temporary "vaccinating doctors," which dated to the 1890s if not before, was an early strategy to move toward population-level disease control. The doctors given these assignments traveled to affected areas with a quantity of vaccine, administering it to as many people as possible, though prior to the reforms of the early twentieth century, shortages in medical personnel and vaccine doses constrained these efforts. People sometimes responded positively to vaccination campaigns, lining up to receive their doses, but many rejected the idea. Doctors sometimes treated other health issues while on tour, and the head of the health service referred to this as the best possible "means of propaganda for the vaccine," a comment that belies the challenge of getting Africans to accept this intervention. The same concern came through in the 1897 decision to focus vaccination efforts on territories under chiefs known to be receptive to the French, having attended the colonial School for Sons of Chiefs and Interpreters.[17]

As they had done with smallpox cases, French officials and medical personnel documented vaccinations—a much bigger and more comprehensive undertaking—to provide data on the successes and limitations of the program, to begin to create medical histories for individual people, and, most immediately, to facilitate follow-up. If a week after receiving the cowpox-derived vaccine a pustule had appeared on the patient's body, doctors considered the vaccination to have taken effect, and the patient to be protected from smallpox. As they commonly did in Europe during the nineteenth century, doctors in Senegal hoped to source vaccine matter from successfully vaccinated children, a process that required some children to remain—and even travel—with vaccinating doctors to facilitate arm-to-arm vaccination. If French thinking on this practice reflected British ideas, then children were particularly valued due to their association with innocence and the presumed greater benefit of lymph from their bodies.[18] Whatever the logic, it is clear these initiatives were important to colonial medical strategies in Senegal in the later nineteenth century, since in February 1871 the chief doctor instructed the police to be sure to record "the children presented [each Monday], so that we can, by bringing them back to the hospital the following Monday, take note of the results of the operation and use the vaccine that they will be able to provide." And several months earlier, the police commissioner had offered to supply the Interior Department with the names of all schoolchildren and others who had recently been vaccinated.[19]

Although some Africans accepted—even readily—French vaccination initiatives, many did not, especially in the early years. Even in Saint-Louis, where Africans had much longer exposure to French medical practices and institutions, it could be difficult to achieve compliance, explaining why some doctors advocated for mandatory smallpox vaccination for all, and why the administration implemented vaccine requirements within institutions they controlled like colonial schools. The colony's chief doctor expressed some frustration with this state of affairs in an 1888 letter, observing that while the most recent vaccination drive had reached over six hundred people, including the students attending the girls' and boys' schools, in general the "natives of St Louis, of Guet N'Dar, of N'Dar Toute, of Sor did not present themselves."[20] Africans were suspicious of this foreign intervention, accepted smallpox as a normal childhood rite of passage, preferred to undergo the more familiar variolation procedure in their own communities, or had enough experience with past epidemics to realize the next one was years away; they likely had other reasons for rejecting the smallpox vaccine as well.[21] Children themselves regularly removed the vaccine matter that had just been placed into the wound on their arm, either intentionally or because they did not understand that they needed to let the wound heal. Indeed, one vaccinating doctor noted that mothers needed to be repeatedly reminded to "let their child's arm dry [i.e., produce a scab] before covering it. It is necessary to watch the children," he continued, "who, out of fear or anger, hasten to scratch (*gratter*) the sore spot."[22]

And furthermore, even if they allowed their children to receive the French vaccine, many African parents rigorously challenged the notion that their children should be used to incubate vaccine for others. Indeed, a Dr. Rigollet, who worked as a vaccinator in Senegal in the early 1890s, listed numerous drawbacks to using human vaccine sources, not the least of which was "the natives' repugnance, impossible to overcome except by force, toward letting their children do this, and that would have the effect of keeping a number of parents from having their children vaccinated out of the fear that they would later be taken as vaccine producers." Other doctors noted similar reactions. Furthermore, a Dr. Girard noted in an 1888 report that French people did not want to receive a vaccine containing lymph from a Black patient, showing that at least in French West Africa, people did not accept the idea of a universally innocent childhood. Instead, as we might expect, race shaped not only the experiences of childhood but also the very idea of what made a child a child.[23]

In the discourse and practice around smallpox transmission, surveillance, and vaccination in late nineteenth-century Senegal, then, we can discern contestation over whether colonial medical practitioners or marabouts should treat children's bodies—through vaccination or variolation—to protect them from smallpox, whether the disease should be left to run its course, and whether children's bodies should be used in service of state interests to produce more vaccine matter. This power struggle over access to and control of African children within colonial medicine and in other arenas would continue far into the twentieth century, as explored elsewhere in this book. French resistance to receiving vaccine matter from Black children, while unsurprising, suggests that the French not only saw African children as culturally "backward," uncivilized, and morally suspect but feared African children's bodies themselves as possible sources of contamination. There were no universal ideas about children in this way of thinking. Tensions related to the use of vaccine from human sources likely declined in the early twentieth century, when the government general instructed officials in each of the federation's colonies to create a vaccine-production center that would use lymph from livestock. Senegal had already been producing some vaccines in the hospital laboratory, but in 1906 a separate laboratory in Sor began to turn out vaccine matter for use in vaccination campaigns, medical clinics, and other efforts.[24]

Vaccination and Health Intervention after the 1904 Public Health Reform

Local production of vaccine was crucial to solving longstanding challenges of supply, reducing logistical challenges that might have hindered the mass vaccination effort Governor General Roume called for in his April 1904 health and hygiene decree. Articles 4 and 5 of the decree required parents or guardians to ensure that all babies received the vaccine prior to their first birthday and that children be revaccinated by ages eleven and twenty-one, supporting these mandates through free vaccination and follow-up clinics. The decree also outlined a specific approach to recordkeeping that would have important impacts for the development of documentary childhood in the colony. Administrators were to provide lists of children who had not yet been (successfully) vaccinated and lists of those who were eleven or twenty-one. The vaccinating doctor had to record each vaccination on those lists, noting the total number administered in each village and, when possible, the names of those who were vaccinated. Once the doctor verified that the vaccine had produced an immune response, the patient or parents received a vaccination certificate. The procedure was to unfold similarly in the protectorate, though with the involvement of focused vaccination missions or agents of AMI.[25] Since civil registration remained extremely limited at this time, especially outside the communes, this decree was aspirational, but it also conveyed a hope that administrators, with the help of local chiefs, would be able to compile relevant lists of names. Despite these limitations, the 1904 decree established the expectation that all people would receive two doses of smallpox vaccine as children and a third shortly after reaching legal majority, and that they would receive a document recording these prophylactic efforts.

The number of people who underwent smallpox vaccination each year was not insignificant, and although the statistics I have been able to locate only rarely include information about age, it is clear that vaccination campaigns continued to focus on children. In 1913, against a backdrop of localized epidemics in parts of Senegal and shortages in personnel, the hygiene service managed to administer 180,242 vaccinations, even as the supervising official complained that many African families continued to avoid vaccinations and hid family members who had fallen ill with smallpox. Then, as they worked to regain ground against epidemic disease following World War I, administration officials tracked cases and deaths and targeted areas with outbreaks for vaccination campaigns. They also continued administering vaccines in the cities, where they wanted to ensure that the disease would remain under control. In 1921, officials reported 4,456 vaccinations in Saint-Louis and 648 in the surrounding areas, 4,225 in Dakar, and 4,761 in Rufisque. In 1926, officials reported giving 2,886 vaccine doses in Dakar and 149,181 doses in Senegal (the two areas were governed separately at the time), noting that 23,682 of these went to babies under age one and 71,828 went to first-time recipients older than one. And in 1936, although there had been no cases in Dakar since 1929, officials vaccinated 12,111 of the city's 92,634 inhabitants, noting that while a handful had been given in the native hospital, 11,826 people received vaccines from "the Hygiene Service on its premises and in the schools" or from "the Mobile Team doctor in the outlying areas." In the rest of Senegal, where the total population was reported as 1,697,677, and where 241 people had contracted smallpox (and 15 of them died), vaccinators gave "92,452 first-time vaccinations and 41,964 revaccinations."[26]

From about 1920, then, colonial smallpox vaccination campaigns were extensive, reaching significant percentages of the population—8–10 percent of Senegal's population might undergo vaccination in any given year, and in some years the rate was closer to 14 percent.[27] At least sometimes, officials relied on intrusive and even coercive methods to track smallpox cases and recruit vaccine recipients. As the 1913 annual report put it, officials "search[ed] methodically in each hut to discover and isolate smallpox patients hidden within."[28] Eventually, however, vaccination attracted so much interest from a subset of the population that officials wanted to weed out overly enthusiastic patients who sought revaccination before they were due, a problem the French could address by focusing on young children and documenting vaccinations at an individual level. Given the concern with children, it is likely that most of the 71,828 people over age one who were vaccinated for the first time in 1926 were in fact children, perhaps those who needed this documentation to attend school.

Yet even as these annual, and later biannual, vaccination drives produced significant successes, French officials continued to impose what we might call sanitary discipline in colonial spaces—spaces over which they had some control—to prevent the spread of smallpox and other diseases. In one undated report (but likely written in the mid-1930s), the Dakar administrator worried about the increase in begging in the streets, "especially by very young children for the benefit of the marabouts," and negative implications for the health of the city. One February day, workers for Dakar's hygiene service "apprehended 62 beggars ages 6 to 8" and took them to a clinic to vaccinate them. Most of the children had come from Fouta Toro, the official continued, where their parents had "entrusted" them to marabouts as live-in Qur'an students. During the dry season, marabouts brought these children to Dakar, where they lived in poverty and begged for alms. In addition to the fact that passersby saw such begging as a nuisance, the Dakar administrator claimed, the "migration of these individuals to Dakar offers numerous drawbacks from a public health perspective." The decision to vaccinate the young children without a thought to seeking consent from their parents or even consulting their marabout was an attempt to mitigate these risks.[29] Such sanitary discipline could affect children in private spaces too. In 1935, for example, the government general reported that the dozens of orphans and abandoned children who stayed in the workhouses of the Sisters of Saint-Joseph of Cluny and the Sisters of the Immaculate Conception were "submitted to medical control by a doctor connected to each establishment, and treated when there is a need."[30] This was so even though the Catholic orders were private organizations. And as noted above, hygiene police and other health officials sometimes brought enforcement of sanitary laws inside people's homes.

As many scholars have observed, colonial medical policy and practice was closely linked to the exercise of colonial power.[31] This was clearly the case in Senegal and French West Africa more generally, since authorities there developed a hygiene service that was informed in its early days by military medicine, and that always relied on the work of police officers and commissioners, who filled out the ranks of the hygiene police, as discussed in chapter 4.[32] This hygiene policing, and the efforts to surveil disease incidence and promote vaccination that it supported, had a particularly significant impact on African children. This was especially true of smallpox vaccination, which, thanks to regular and extensive campaigns, reached more children than many other colonial interventions intended for them, such as schooling, scouting, or sports. Vaccination involved a bodily experience—a new, colonial ritual that consisted of inserting matter into the skin which left a scar. Vaccination also represented a form of sanitary discipline that originated outside the family and community. It produced new kinds of data and knowledge about African children (and populations more broadly) that the state could use in support of planning for the future and laying claim to humanitarian initiatives, and, through its association with vaccination certificates and individual medical records, it promoted documentary childhood.

Vaccinations, Medical Visits, and Documentation in the Colonial School

Yet although mass vaccination campaigns had the potential to affect large sections of the population, institutions like colonial schools, over which the French exerted greater control, presented the opportunity to intervene much more intensively in children's lives. These interventions involved vaccinating but expanded outward to also include checkups, growth tracking, and treatment for disease. Hygiene and sanitation were of paramount importance to French education personnel, whose sense of racial superiority often led them to describe their African students as dirty and who embraced cleanliness not only for its ability to reduce disease transmission but also as a marker of morality and civilization. Colonial education policies frequently incorporated rules related to health and hygiene, boys and girls studied hygiene as a core academic subject, teacher evaluations often included sections on students' "sanitary status" (incentivizing the enforcement of hygiene-related rules), and—eventually—doctors or other health workers regularly visited many of the colony's schools to provide routine care and address illnesses and injuries. Schools, therefore, provided spaces in which the state could attempt to much more thoroughly medicalize and track

African children, producing and collecting knowledge about them and using it to inform state policy. Further, administrators and social welfare planners hoped that hygiene education and access to doctors, nurses, and medicines via the French school would lead students to encourage others to seek treatment in clinics.[33] It is no accident that by the early 1930s, schooling and health clinics had become cornerstones of colonial child "protection" plans. As such, this partnership between schools and biomedical practice increased the state's influence over the physical bodies and embodied experiences of Senegal's children, and officials' efforts to create medical records helped produce documentary childhood in colonial Senegal. Yet at the same time, African children's and parents' responses rendered these changes incomplete.

The link between medicine and schooling did not, of course, begin in the 1920s and 1930s. Indeed, from the 1870s if not earlier, French officials, teachers, and doctors envisioned medical intervention and colonial schooling working in tandem to reshape African childhood. In the late nineteenth century, scholarship applicants and applicants for admission to certain colonial schools had to see a doctor to obtain medical paperwork—a health certificate or proof of vaccination—and for a few months at least, boarders at the School for Sons of Chiefs and Interpreters received treatment from a colonial doctor during his regular visits to their school.[34] This vision was enshrined in a section of Governor General Roume's 1904 public health decree, which not only required smallpox vaccination as a condition of enrollment in all schools but also tasked teachers with enforcement and medical surveillance. Teachers' obligations now included making sure that all students were vaccinated, sending new students who could not prove their status "to the doctor to be vaccinated," and notifying the administrator about any "children of about eleven years who must be revaccinated." Furthermore, they had to report any incidence of infectious disease in their schools so that appropriate measures could be taken to minimize its spread. A report of a smallpox case resulted not only in the sick person staying away from school for forty days but also in the "revaccination of all the teachers and pupils" who were not sick.[35] By promoting the examination and medicalization of African children's bodies in the colonial school, this decree aimed to significantly impact childhood experiences in Senegal and improve the state's knowledge of African children's health.

The government moved to further build out the health infrastructure with a series of decrees in the early twentieth century, including one in January 1905 that established municipal hygiene services in the communes, a February 1905 decree forming the AMI program to provide biomedical care in more remote areas, and a January 1906 decree creating native medical assistants to support the AMI program. In this context, and to assist in implementation of the 1904 public health reform, hygiene and education administrators began to develop medical infrastructure within schools themselves, creating dispensaries, providing medicines and first-aid supplies to teachers, and/or dispatching doctors to the schools on so-called medical visits. In 1907, the Saint-Louis hygiene service began sending a municipal doctor to the schools to conduct medical examinations, recording the details of each student's medical and treatment history on a newly created form. While at the schools, the doctor probably also administered smallpox vaccinations. Dakar, Rufisque, and the rest of the second arrondissement adopted similar procedures, and the 1907 annual report specified that "educational medical records were kept. Filters were installed, and the rules of school hygiene were observed." In addition, students with malaria received quinine to treat the disease, allowing them to attend school much more regularly.[36] At around the same time, an official doctor began conducting medical examinations of all candidates for admission into French West Africa's specialized training schools to ensure that candidates were physically equipped for their program of study and, simultaneously, to create the medical documentation required for admission.[37] Thus, by the first decade of the twentieth century, the state had linked schooling to a more intensive medicalization of childhood in a bid to reform African hygiene practices and had begun to normalize the collection of information about schoolchildren's bodies and health.

Yet Africans often challenged the new expectations, especially in the early years, and at least some colonial officials understood the political—and potentially unpalatable—nature of any decision to send a biomedical doctor into a colonial school to attend to African children. Thus, when the director of the girls' school in Dakar requested a house call in November 1904 to address what she called the "poor sanitary state of our native pupils," the head of the education service and other officials concluded that it was premature to arrange such an intervention. Worried that this visit might alienate Muslim parents, whom the French already struggled to convince of the utility of schooling for girls, officials declined to fulfill the director's request. Instead, they suggested she use "persuasion" to convince her students to accept French ideas about cleanliness and appeared to consider requiring medical certificates when students returned to school from the Easter break, which was months away.[38] Significantly, they did not give up on the idea of hygiene reform but merely postponed the more intensive interventions that would become commonplace within a decade or two.

Although the 1904 reform seemed poised to require some engagement with biomedicine prior to school attendance, it did not prompt an abrupt and wholesale change in behavior among African children and their families, not even those who were drawn to French schooling. Indeed, each time a teacher or official extolled the importance of hygiene education in schools, they implicitly acknowledged students' continued avoidance of biomedicine. A teacher's reflections on hygiene education at the Dakar boys' school in the early twentieth century are a case in point. In his annual report for 1906–7, the instructor of the first-year class, a Monsieur Niénat, commented on his students' growth in French and other subjects, including hygiene. Hygiene instruction, he thought, had brought about improvements in student cleanliness and in the appropriateness of their attire, and thanks to his teaching, "the sight of the medical doctor causes them less fright." Having learned some "scientific vocabulary," he continued, students accepted the idea that French doctors knew more than "their marabout doctors."[39] Similarly, in his treatise on France's "moral conquest" of West Africa, published a decade later, school inspector Georges Hardy touted schools' utility in leading Africans to accept biomedicine. Schools could support rapid progress in public health, Hardy claimed, by encouraging students to question marabouts, showing them "the way of the dispensary, having students vaccinated, dispelling the prejudices that make people fear the doctor," and emphasizing "habits of cleanliness and hygiene," among other things.[40] Yet in suggesting that hygiene instruction had made or would make a difference in student attitudes toward colonial doctors, both Niénat and Hardy admitted that African children had not necessarily embraced these biopower "benefits" with open arms.

Discourses around medical documentation—namely proof of vaccination, certificates of health, and later individual medical records—also shed light on Africans' efforts to shape the processes of medicalization. Although people *could* obtain vaccination certificates and other documents, they did not necessarily do so, even after the 1904 decree made childhood vaccinations obligatory and more closely linked vaccination, biomedicine, and schools.[41] It is often impossible to judge whether missing medical certificates and vaccination records reflected what we might call resistance—unwillingness to vaccinate or to provide documents to the colonial state, for example, or another considered objection—or whether they resulted from gaps in the archival record. Yet the colonial archives contain some glimpses of the back and forth that the state's requests for children's medical records sometimes produced.

In 1904, for example, Suzanne Loppy of Rufisque requested a scholarship for her son, Fara Diaw, which would allow him to attend a primary school in Senegal. Loppy, who was unable to sign her own name (and thus likely illiterate), sent a variety of other papers—a certificate from the school director attesting to her son's behavior and aptitude, proof that she did not owe taxes, a list of her children and dependents, and an attestation of Fara's age in lieu of a birth certificate. But she did not send the vaccination paperwork, a fact to which officials called attention when they were reviewing scholarship requests for 1905 and 1906. Diaw's family, like the families of three other candidates, had not submitted all required documents or had missed the application deadline.[42] This episode raises unanswerable but compelling questions about African families' acceptance or avoidance of smallpox vaccination: Did Loppy simply forget to include a vaccine certificate? Or was she unable to acquire one, either because she did not have immediate access to a recognized medical professional or because her son had not been vaccinated?

In other cases, it appears that an interlocutor helped families compile complete application packages, including vaccination certificates. In 1905, for example, the families of three boys who had completed primary school at the boys' school in Dakar applied for scholarships to allow their sons to attend the Lycée Faidherbe in Saint-Louis as boarders. Not only were all three request letters and all three school certificates written on the same date (11 July 1905), but the wording, syntax, and handwriting are very similar, suggesting that the same person, perhaps a teacher or school director, had helped the families. The medical certificates submitted indicated that seventeen-year-old Ibrahima Niang's recent smallpox vaccination had been successful, Amadou Guèye (age eighteen) had once suffered from the disease though his recent smallpox vaccination had not taken, and Jean Diop had received the vaccine numerous times—once recently—but it had never produced a response.[43]

In addition to suggesting that these families had help in navigating French administrative and education bureaucracies, the three application packages offer evidence of the ways school and medical infrastructures could operate in tandem to produce legible child subjects. In all three cases, the requirement for a medical certificate to apply for a scholarship triggered the families to request this documentation from the doctor on 8, 11, and 16 July 1905. It is also possible, though the available documents are inconclusive, that the requirement for a medical certificate prompted the families of Amadou Guèye and Ibrahima Niang to allow their children to be vaccinated; Jean Diop's medical certificate suggests that his experiences with vaccination extended farther back in time. Such a chain of events—the need for a vaccination certificate leading parents to have children vaccinated—seems even more likely in the case of Madjighen N'Daw, the child of a French trader, Louis Vallier, and his African wife, Maty Niang, who lived near Louga. In July 1911, Vallier wrote to request a scholarship to allow five-year-old Madjighen to attend primary school in Saint-Louis, and her file includes a vaccination certificate signed by a doctor in Louga just one week after her father wrote the letter. This suggests that even a child whose father was French (and presumably more accustomed to recording things like births, deaths, and medical encounters) obtained a medical record only when the school required it. Furthermore, her scholarship application, like those of many other children, provided the state with information about her family, her previous contact with schools, and her body/bodily health.[44]

By the 1920s and 1930s, the school-based medical infrastructure developed for the communes had spread to villages and towns across the colony, especially those with at least some administrative presence. By design, schools became centers of biomedical care, with doctors or other health agents making rounds regularly, dispensaries caring for sick students and—sometimes—community members, and teachers maintaining "little pharmacies" that could treat students' minor ailments.[45] By promoting preventative care, vaccinations, and curative care *at school*, the colonial state centered children in its efforts to improve African health and hygiene. This partnering of schools and biomedical care also ensured that African children encountered both colonial teachers at school who taught hygiene and monitored them for cleanliness and disease and colonial doctors and nurses, whose health interventions subjected children's bodies to surveillance, measurement, and evaluation. Thus, schools became spaces in which children's health was tracked by teachers, school directors, hygiene agents, and doctors, generating knowledge and records and contributing to the documentation of childhood. Yet conversely, the fact that these interventions *had* to happen at school—because families were not taking up French "hygiene" fast enough at home—underscores the fact that remaking childhood was a negotiated and faltering process.

Some medical interventions and records focused on aggregates—the populations of specific classes and even entire schools in various places across the colony. Teachers and school directors were key here, since they had long been expected to promote scientific understandings of health and disease by teaching several hours of "hygiene" per week, encouraging students to wash their bodies and clothes regularly, and serving as models for good hygiene through their own personal conduct. And of course, as noted above, teachers had disease-reporting obligations under the 1904 public health reform. To these ends, during a 1906 conference for teachers at the Normal School, the education inspector for French West Africa listed "hygiene" as one of the four most crucial school subjects in which African teacher candidates should receive training (the other subjects were French, agriculture, and manual labor instruction). Hygiene training would prepare future teachers to eliminate "certain illnesses particular to their race [and] to remove a deplorable influence from their 'sorcerers,'" he continued, noting that Normal School "students will learn to vaccinate, and to use standard remedies in a rational manner."[46] This vision for how to train African primary school teachers not only emphasized the importance of "hygiene" instruction in schools but also positioned future teachers as proponents of biomedicine and technicians who could administer vaccines and first aid, thereby intervening in African children's understandings and experiences of illness and injury.

The colonial state tracked these classroom interventions through the school inspection process, which involved regular evaluations by a school inspector of entire schools and of individual teachers. By the 1930s, teachers' performance evaluations often commented on the "sanitary status" of each class, incentivizing teachers to intervene in disease, hygiene, and "sanitary" issues. Indeed, of the eighty-eight school inspection reports from the 1930s that I was able to consult, at least fifty commented directly on "sanitary status" with an evaluative word or phrase: the situation "seems good" or was "satisfactory." Many also provided details about student illnesses, cleanliness, the availability of a dispensary and medications, and other issues, making them an important source for data on a subset of African children and their (non)compliance with French expectations. A 1935 report on the Diakhao Preparatory School is a case in point. Although he gave the school's sanitary status a "satisfactory" rating, the inspector complained that students were not especially clean and instructed the teacher to "use the 2 hygiene lessons planned for each week to oblige the students to bathe and to wash their clothes."[47] A few years later, similar preoccupations animated the inspection report for the N'Dioum Rural School, which rated hygiene as "lousy" in the introductory class but "better" in the elementary grade, since "the students are better dressed and cleaner." The report also mentioned a doctor's visit to the school and commented that students had received smallpox vaccines a few months before.⁴⁸ These reports and numerous others like them reveal that the colonial state's decades-old effort to medicalize and sanitize African childhood was—at best—incomplete. With child-protection programs and French hopes for a more hygienic colonial future riding on the cooperation of African schoolchildren, it is telling that many of those enrolled in the 1930s had to be vaccinated at school because their families chose not to—or were unable to—comply with a vaccine mandate dating to 1904. And the fact that many schools incorporated bathing and laundry time into the school day because children did not meet French standards of cleanliness at home offers evidence of the faltering and contested nature of efforts to remake (and clean up) African childhood.⁴⁹

Other school-based medical interventions had significant impacts at an individual level (though of course also implications for population-level public health), especially insofar as they led to more encounters between specific children and representatives of the state, and to the creation of knowledge about and records connected to individuals. Indeed, by the mid-1930s, schools across French West Africa offered colonial doctors access to African children, who were examined, vaccinated (as needed), and given a health record at school. In a 1934 letter to the colonial minister, Governor General Brévié emphasized the surveillance and documentary outcomes of these practices. Every pupil, he wrote, receives "an individual health record, stored and kept current by the school director, following the doctor's instructions. These records constitute complete health files, allowing [us] to follow and to usefully treat pupils in the middle of their studies."⁵⁰ In a separate report produced that same year, the governor general again highlighted the importance of student health records to the goal of child protection, proclaiming that in schools in Dakar and across French West Africa, "schoolchildren are the object of all of our care. They have an individual health record (*une fiche sanitaire individuelle*), and their health status is verified by a doctor-inspector."⁵¹

In contrast to the governor general's categorical assertions, school inspection reports offer more nuance, showing that even as the process of creating student medical records at school generated detailed knowledge about individual children, education and medical personnel were still working out the deployment and format of these records through the 1930s. Indeed, while some schools maintained medical records by the mid-1930s, others failed to keep these records up to date, and still more were just starting to create them. Attempting perhaps to underscore the importance of collecting this information and to ensure some uniformity, the state distributed preprinted health forms that doctors and teachers had to complete for each student beginning around 1935–36.⁵² Although

I have not been able to find any of these records in the archives, a February 1933 inspection report for the Podor Regional School offers a detailed description of the kind of information they contained. "For each pupil," the doctor collected "information on hereditary and personal medical history, visual and auditory acuity, splenic index, illnesses contracted during the time at school. The children are measured and weighed at regular intervals and those with deficiencies are cared for preemptively." Students' physical growth became part of their school medical record too. A Doctor Besnes(?), the colonial doctor who evidently launched the medical records program in this school, had also established medical records for students in the administrative circle's other schools, stating that "sanitary surveillance of the schools accounts for an important part of his task."[53] The inspector praised this work, putting it forward as a model that should be expanded to all the colony's schools. It thus seems likely that medical encounters at schools across the colony resulted in the collection of similar information as individual medical records were created.

By the 1930s, then, colonial schooling and biomedical intervention had become closely linked: students (and others in the community) accessed biomedical care through the local school, especially if they lived outside the communes, and each school-based medical encounter produced data for a young student's individual school medical record. Crucially, in colonial Senegal schools *and* dispensaries, teachers *and* doctors were part of the state apparatus, and as representatives of the colonial state, they attempted to impose French hygiene standards while also producing and collecting knowledge. At the same time, medical records could serve a crucial function for individual students in this era when few people possessed identity documents like birth certificates. While school medical records could not establish birth, citizenship, or nationality, they could support other kinds of claims, and they were often used as part of requests to travel or to gain admission to spaces controlled by the colonial state. The medicalization of childhood under colonial rule thus not only changed many children's experiences by introducing new ideas about health and hygiene and increased the state's involvement in children's lives but also represented a significant step toward the documentation of childhood in Senegal.

Conclusion

The history of French efforts to contain and control smallpox and to vaccinate people—especially children—against it offers insights into some of the ways that colonial health policy functioned on a mass scale and raises questions about how ultimately quite large numbers of children encountered the medical apparatus of the colonial state. It also offers hints into how this sort of mass health campaign produced paperwork and documentation that not only made children more legible to the colonial state but could also be used by vaccine recipients, as children or adults, for their own ends (as identity documents or in applications). Yet even as some children and their families responded positively to state efforts to promote and document vaccination, others avoided the initiatives. The trends that I have discussed in this chapter—increases in the state's interest in and interventions into children's health, mitigated by children's and their families' (in)action—continued into the postwar period, as evidenced by a renewed focus on maternal and child health, part of France's efforts to reform and reassert control. While significant numbers of mothers took advantage of the opportunity for free prenatal consultations and health checks for their young children, the response fell short of French targets, suggesting that colonial health policies had some impact on African children but that the hoped-for transformations remained incomplete.[54]

Schools provide a window into how French officials worked to implement their ideals of hygiene intervention to a greater extent among a population they much more fully controlled. And they were central to the state's child-protection initiatives by the 1930s and into the postwar period, as suggested by the governor general's 1940 report, which noted that schools were important, among other things, because they offered hygiene instruction, shaped children's health via "periodical school medical controls," provided financial support to allow needy children to attend school, and offered a reliable source of food for children whose families did not have enough.[55] These sorts of interactions and the records they produced contributed significantly to a reimagining of childhood experience—one that was monitored and evaluated by colonial doctors, and where children's health statistics were recorded and conserved by the colonial state. This process helped to write and surveil a new sort of documented childhood into being. Indeed, most or all African children would ultimately have to participate in this documented childhood in order to be recognized by the state, to receive benefits, to access rights, and to establish legal personhood.

CHAPTER 6

The Document

CHRONOLOGICAL AGE AND AFRICAN CHILDHOOD IN COLONIAL SENEGAL

During the General Council session of 1911, Galandou Diouf, who represented Rufisque, complained that the colony's schools were consistently turning away African students "who reach the age of 16 years or who have exceeded that age." In unenrolling these students, school directors were trying to comply with a 1907 education reform limiting primary school access to children under age sixteen. Diouf took issue with this measure, which disproportionately affected African students since they often enrolled in French schools only after completing years of Qur'an schooling or needed extra time to learn French, and he called on his colleagues to support his resolution demanding that it be "abandoned" and that affected students be allowed to return to school. Others voiced their support, with J.-J. Crespin criticizing the administration for withholding schooling from "gifted and willing young people," and Louis Guillabert pointing out the illogic of such a restriction in a place like Senegal, which had struggled with low school enrollments. Diouf's resolution received unanimous approval.[1] But the issue did not go away, and in response to councilors' questioning during the 1912 session, the government's representative maintained that the policy was necessary to ensure "separation" at school between adults and "children under sixteen." Unpersuaded, the angry councilors voted unanimously in favor of another resolution calling on the administration to allow students over age sixteen to continue their studies.[2]

This incident highlights the increasing salience of chronological age, in this case—age sixteen—in defining childhood and, crucially, in determining access to certain rights, statuses, or opportunities in colonial Senegal. Indeed, the French reliance on chronological age to mark off the status of "child" or "minor" in this and a wide variety of other policies and procedures sent the message not only that chronological age mediated people's encounters with the state but also that the state could impose its own chronological endpoint on African childhood. And the debates in the General Council in 1911 and 1912 over access to schools suggest that this message had begun to shape people's personal experiences and perhaps to shift how they thought about colonial childhood. Councilors often raised issues in session that their constituents had brought to their attention, and Galandou Diouf, a Black man and *originaire*, was particularly well connected to African residents, voters and nonvoters alike. Diouf's objections to the age restrictions in schools likely reflected complaints he had heard from Africans, suggesting that as they worried about the negative effects of the policy on their children, Africans were beginning to think of childhood as something that could be defined—at least by the French colonizers—with reference to chronological age.

This chapter explores how the French dependence on chronological age in its various efforts to discipline, "protect," and document African children imposed new ideas about how to measure and define childhood on Senegal's population but also created spaces in which Africans could challenge these ideas. These efforts were consistent with the emergence of what Corinne Field and Nicholas Syrett call "bureaucratic age" in many modern states, that is, the processes by which states moved to render their populations more legible by standardizing collection of vital records and documenting ages.[3] In colonial Senegal, the state's emphasis on chronological age, part of a larger shift toward documentation of individual identities that scholars have examined in different parts of the world, faced difficulties not only in the lack of birth registration and other documentation but also in the very different imaginary of age—and childhood—at work in African worldviews. Yet even though they recognized that Africans defined childhood differently and that most did not register births with the state, officials do not seem to have questioned the idea that African childhood should, like French childhood, be marked off based on chronological age.[4]

This reliance on chronological age went far beyond fulfillment of the state's basic bureaucratic functions, like collecting individual taxes and managing military enlistment or conscription, to encompass officials' efforts to portray French colonial rule as an endeavor that would both improve African well-being and ensure France's future in the region by focusing on African children. Since chronological age could determine whether a person should be subject to state surveillance, tried in court as a child or an adult, or allowed to access certain benefits and programs, this mechanism for rendering identity and measuring capacity or dependence structured Africans' encounters with the state. And given the state's emphasis on programs construed as protecting *children*, its use of chronological age required African children and their families to familiarize themselves with a new way of defining childhood, an approach that, over the long term, would come to be widely accepted in Senegal. Yet on the other hand, I argue, French reliance on chronological age in a place where most people did not yet keep track of it created spaces in which Africans could maneuver by presenting themselves as one age or another in pursuit of a specific goal.[5]

The Age(s) of Children in Rules, Regulations, and Codes

As officials in Senegal worked to promote the ideals of child protection, order, and the rule of law, they relied on the construct of chronological age to make numerous decisions about people's status before the state and the privileges or restrictions that status afforded. Indeed, assessments of chronological age shaped decisions about when to end guardianship over a liberated minor, whether a young person—or their guardian—had to pay the fine incurred by a hygiene violation, whether courts should treat a defendant as an adult or a child who lacked "discernment," when to release a detainee from a reformatory, and whether a person was too old to enroll in primary school. Although different numbers marked the divide between child and adult across the various sites and institutions discussed in this book, and though these ages occasionally changed, the consistency with which the state referenced and tracked chronological age sent the message that it was natural, evident, and central to the very idea of "the child." This ultimately had material effects on children's lives. Indeed, in structuring how young people interacted with guardianship, police, the courts, schools, and more, the French reliance on chronological age fundamentally challenged how Africans understood and experienced childhood in Senegal.

As officials went about the work of running a colonial administration and recording details of this work, they generated numerous lists of various subsets of the population, including children, who had had an encounter with the state for one reason or another. These lists often included names and basic demographic information—current address, birthplace, parents' names, and (approximate) age or birthdate—information the state needed to make people more legible and, when it came to young people, to determine whether they should be categorized as a "child" ("minor") or an adult. This of course gave the state insight into the population and gave officials points of reference for future administrative decisions. In addition, whether or not this was the state's intent, listing names in inventories, registers, and record-books began to construct documented histories and identities that could have significant impacts on children's lives at the moment they were created and going forward.

As envisioned by Governor Auguste Baudin in 1849, the guardianship system oversaw recently liberated *minors*, entrusting them with individuals who pledged to "raise them well and care for them until their *majority*."[6] This took place only after judicial authorities, using procedures that remain obscure, determined an estimated age or birth year for those liberated from slavery, adding it to the liberation register and the liberty certificate that served as proof of freedom. Those determined to be eighteen or older ("major"), on the other hand, were released on their own recognizance. In theory, age should also have determined the end point of guardianship for those incorporated into the system, since the state's tutelage was supposed to end at the age of legal majority. In practice, many remained under guardianship well into legal adulthood, due to the state's insufficient oversight and guardians' interest in maintaining access to their wards' labor for as long as possible.[7] After the reforms to guardianship of 1903 and 1904, more frequent surveillance allowed the state to track and emancipate from guardianship at least some of those who had reached majority, but even under the improved system, notifications sometimes came late or not at all.[8] Yet although attaining majority often did not result in changes in status for liberated minors (especially since slavery was associated with perpetual junior status), and despite the problems in applying the state's own rules, guardianship emphasized the centrality of chronological age to French ideas about childhood, since the beginning and end of this status turned on an assessment of whether a person was under or over age eighteen.

Similarly, when children encountered the colonial legal apparatus, chronological age had an outsized impact on their status before the police and courts. Hygiene agents or police held a parent or guardian "civilly responsible" for hygiene violations of legal minors (by the 1920s, "minors" were those under age twenty-one), for example, and it was this responsible person who had to pay the fine.[9] Judges also relied on age rendered in years—whether derived precisely from a birth certificate or estimated during an arrest or court proceeding—to determine whether a defendant should be tried as an adult or considered a minor. Here, sixteen was one key age, since the French penal code of 1810, which applied to *originaires* and shaped official thinking in responding to all juvenile crime, indicated that when minors under age sixteen violated the law "without discernment" (or lacking legal understanding), courts should acquit them but should also require a period of rehabilitation. In Senegal, given officials' mistrust of African parents, courts usually ordered internment in a reformatory. Since the 1810 penal code required that detainees be released from internment upon reaching legal majority, this age (twenty under the 1810 code, but eighteen or twenty under other rules) also took on critical importance.[10]

In the areas were customary law applied, age sixteen also stood as the divide between minority and majority, according to the governor general's 1924 reorganization of the "native" justice system in French West Africa. Although the decree called on "native" courts to determine the age of criminal responsibility according to the "most widely followed custom" in areas under their jurisdiction, it also indicated courts should treat those "who are or who appear to be under sixteen" as minors whenever custom would hold younger children criminally responsible.[11] Only seven years later, another decree established additional guidelines, indicating that sixteen was the minimum age of "penal majority" in the Native Tribunal, allowing consequences after trial to include the "return of the delinquent to his parents, or to a notable native, or his removal to a house of correction," and confirming the court's role in establishing duration of internment while cautioning that a minor could not be interned "beyond his eighteenth year."[12] Thus, although both the French penal code and local customary law set *penal* majority at sixteen, their pronouncements about internment implied different ages of *legal/civil* majority in the two systems: twenty for the *originaires* for whom French law applied, and eighteen for "native minors" governed by customary law as laid out in 1931. Complicating this even further, a reform proposed in 1937 but set aside until the 1950s would have extended the age of majority to twenty-one for those justiciable under French law, allowing the state to intervene even later and longer in the lives of *originaires*.[13]

A report on the Special Professional School in Carabane, the only juvenile reformatory in French West Africa at the time, brought this discrepancy to light in 1938. E. Némos, the report's author and the superior administrator of Casamance, pointed out that since both customary and French courts often ordered internment until a minor reached the age of majority, *originaires* and subjects faced different sentence lengths based on nothing more than their status before the court. At the time of his most recent inspection of the reformatory, he wrote, eleven of the detainees had been tried in French courts and thirteen had appeared before Native Tribunals, meaning that this inequity affected real people, and he argued that all African minors should be judged and sentenced under the same rules. Although a reader of Némos's report, likely the governor of Senegal (its intended recipient), noted in its margins that officials could not apply the same legal regime to *originaires* and subjects, he was more receptive to Némos's suggestion that courts could simply agree that no one of any status should be interned in a juvenile reformatory past age eighteen.[14] This suggestion became policy across French West Africa a few months later, when the head of the judicial service instructed all magistrates and court officials to use internment sparingly and to ensure that, whether ordered there by a French or a native court, no minor would remain in a reformatory past his eighteenth birthday. Crucially, courts now had to ensure that each minor's file included a birth certificate or other court-produced document to attest to their age.[15] This new requirement emphasized the importance not only of chronological age but of *documented* age, centering these ideas in the construction of African childhood.

If chronological age was baked into legal procedure and court practices in Senegal—in no small part because it was a feature of both metropolitan and colonial law—it mediated access to children's institutions like schools in a somewhat more fluid way as interested parties debated student age and the appropriateness of upper age limits for school enrollment. These debates reflected the central tension between the goal of attracting African students to colonial schools and the perceived need to avoid wide age ranges within the same classrooms. This could be hard to achieve given that Africans often started at a French school after attending a Qur'an school for years and were therefore significantly older than their French or *métis* classmates. Even those Africans who enrolled at a younger age were at a disadvantage, since most African families did not speak French at home and the need to learn the language sometimes required students to repeat grades. Thus, student ages could vary significantly, as in a Dakar primary school that in 1905 had seventeen students over the age of sixteen (two of them were about twenty-five years old) out of a total student population of 271.[16] The problem was widespread and persistent, with many schools enrolling twice as many students age thirteen and older as they did students under thirteen, according to the 1917 annual report.[17] At least some teachers, officials, and French parents expressed real concern about such mixing, routinely drawing on racist assumptions as they did so. Frequent references to unspecified "moral" hazards glossed the widespread idea that Black children were more sexually precocious, a belief that was made explicit in a 1906 incident in which a Black girl, age eleven or twelve, lifted the skirt of her six-year-old French classmate and said something obscene. A furious letter from the younger girl's father prompted an investigation, which led to the older girl's suspension for this "immoral" act.[18] Questions about whether schools could successfully teach older students stemmed from the widespread belief that the intellectual capacity of Black children declined as they grew up—dulled, some believed, by Qur'an schooling—and from assumptions that they would create discipline problems.[19]

These concerns prompted several efforts over the years to impose an upper limit, usually age sixteen, on eligibility for primary school enrollment. In 1893, for example, the Ploërmel school limited its four regular primary grades to students aged six through sixteen, and created an "annex" with two levels, one for beginning students from ages ten to fifteen and the other for students aged sixteen or older. Over the next couple of years, the administration expanded and modified this approach, moving classes for older students to the evening, and later—amid complaints that older children showed up tired after a full day at Qur'an school—limiting these evening classes to adults.[20] Enforcement seems to have posed problems, and the administration issued additional decrees in 1907 and 1911 that limited primary school enrollment to students aged sixteen and under.[21] Although some evidence suggests that schools began to enforce these age restrictions, the issue of age limits remained unsettled. Accordingly, in April 1913, the still new *Bulletin de l'enseignement de l'Afrique Occidentale Française* published a selection of essays by teachers, all of them French, who expressed a range of opinions about the issue, and in July 1913 the *Bulletin* revealed that, amid findings that strict age limits had inhibited educational progress in Senegal, the Superior Council of Primary Instruction was now advocating a more flexible approach.[22] New rules in place by 1935, however, veered back toward rigid age restrictions, requiring that children enter preparatory school by age eleven, elementary school by age thirteen, regional school by fifteen, and superior primary school by seventeen.[23] And in early 1940, when the governor of Senegal described schooling, along with sanitary and hygiene policies, as the most important child-protection initiative, he noted that schools were designed for children from ages seven to sixteen.[24]

These discussions about age in schools and the administration's various decrees aimed at imposing age limits demonstrated the increasing importance of measuring age and contributed to its significance in defining colonial African childhood. As in court, sixteen seems to have marked the dividing line between those young enough to spend time in a primary school, envisioned as a space for children, and those who were too old. But regardless of the number selected, the association between school and chronological age was important in and of itself. Indeed, as more African children and their families engaged with French schools—this population was increasing, with over 60,000 students enrolled across French West Africa by the mid-1930s—children not only would have realized that chronological age helped identify them in school enrollment registers and to teachers but also that chronological age could afford—or limit—opportunities. Like guardianship, policing, and courtroom procedures, schooling not only elicited chronological age to make people legible to the state but encouraged those made legible to incorporate age into their own understandings of colonial institutions and policies and—perhaps—into their strategies to navigate colonial rule.

Inventing Chronological Age

While the rules, regulations, and procedures of the colonial state treated it as if it were a neutral and natural measure of who was and was not a child (and in which context), chronological age of course was neither self-evident nor objective. As I explore in the book's introduction, Senegal's African societies rendered age with reference to capacity, social status, and progress through rituals marking transitions between life stages. With the exception of those involved in the Catholic Church, who would have recorded baptisms in church registers, and some who lived in French towns or who had close ties to colonial institutions, most Africans did not typically track specific birthdates or document births prior to colonial rule.[25] Even in the communes, officials had only limited success in promoting birth registration among residents, a surprising fact since *originaires* could have used this bureaucratic function of the state to protect their children's voting rights, and since the 1916 law recognizing *originaires*' citizenship seemed to require compliance. Outside the communes, the state lacked capacity to register all births and deaths, and such registration was not even called for by law for a limited subset of African subjects until 1933.[26] As a result, even if they claimed to know their ages, most Africans would not have been able to provide a court, school, or other official with a birth certificate to prove it. And it is likely that many children, if asked their age, would not have been able to give a numerical answer that officials found satisfactory.

And yet, ages appear everywhere in colonial records—officials needed to know age so they could apply the law and institutional rules—raising questions about the production of this information. Indeed, the archives largely obscure the procedures officials used to ascertain or impose chronological ages, except when established in a *justification supplétif*, an official court document that relied on witness testimony, or where births had been declared before the state, though the records offer glimpses into the estimation, guesswork, and adjustments involved. Officials often recorded imprecise chronological ages or birthdates, indicating that a birth year or age was approximate or giving a range of ages. The machine-printed liberty certificates that officials issued formerly enslaved people before 1903 featured spaces for the individual's name, parents' names, birthplace, and approximate age, along with details about their liberation.[27] Guardianship registers, school enrollment records, juvenile penitentiary registers, and even court documents likewise reveal that officials had to estimate chronological ages, recording the number along with the word *environ*, or "about/around," as the Kaolack Tribunal did in 1928 when ordering three years' internment for "young Matar Dramé, around 14 years old" (*le jeune Matar Dramé agé de 14 ans environ*).[28] French officials or African colonial employees likely generated these estimates based on visual inspection of or interviews with the children in question, and like any record, these were subject to mistakes and subsequent alterations, done with intent or through an error in transcription.[29] Documented age, therefore, involved knowledge production, and while colonial officials had more power in these processes, Africans could engage or negotiate in various ways.

The state turned on the fiction that its data—including the ages of individual colonial subjects—was precise, accurate, and impartial, and officials sometimes had to adjust birthdates or ages to meet this expectation, especially when the state's ability to enforce French principles required it or when officials recognized a glaring error. This was perhaps most significant in court documents. Since the law—and the desire to rule as a "humane" empire—required prompt release of detainees, and courts tended to order minors interned "until majority," it was imperative for officials to have the most precise information possible about each detainee's age. Thus, when the French administration in Senegal agreed in 1926 to detain young Dramané Bakayoro, a boy from neighboring French Soudan, in the Bambey reformatory until his majority, it encountered a records problem. Because the documents sent from Soudan gave an inexact age for Bakayoro, referring to him as "13 or 14 years old," Senegal's secretary general wrote, the lieutenant governor of Soudan would need to indicate the exact release date.[30] The tension between the invented nature of documented age and the state's demand for precision also seems to have encouraged drift in certain records, whereby ages became more concretely defined as they were repeated. Although court records from October 1925 gave young Fara Diallo's age as "around 16" and said he should be interned until "the age of twenty-one," for example, the governor's internment order described him more confidently as "age 16 years."[31] Even more strikingly, when Gorgui Basse went on trial for theft in 1923, the Ziguinchor correctional court estimated that he was between thirteen and fourteen years old. A few weeks later, in his order to intern Basse at Bambey until his majority, the interim lieutenant governor rendered the boy's age—in much more settled terms—as "thirteen and a half."[32]

Fixing detainees' chronological age, however, did not solve the problem of determining the precise release dates for detainees ordered interned "until majority," whose internments were supposed to end on the relevant birthday, so officials developed workarounds. Occasionally, internment ended on the anniversary of the court's decision during the year in which the detainee would reach majority (assuming that the estimated chronological age was correct). Thus, an internment order indicated that Abdoulaye Lome, who was "born in 1916" and whose court decision was handed down on 18 May 1927, would be "interned in the Bambey penitentiary until 18 May 1936, the date on which, lacking any other specifications about the exact date of his birth, he will be presumed to have attained the age of 20 years."[33] Much more frequently, the administration ordered the release of detainees just before or on New Year's Day of the year in which they would reach majority, to ensure that the state could not be accused of knowingly detaining anyone for too long.[34] The inconsistencies in the approach to determining the endpoint of a young person's internment reflects the fluidity and lack of fixity and knowledge of chronological age, even as it also shows that officials wrestled with how to codify it (or work around its fluidity).

Officials and others involved with guardianship also glossed over uncertainties about children's ages, and they sometimes had to update records deemed incorrect during subsequent encounters with the minors in question. Guardianship commission members most often upheld existing records, sometimes explicitly confirming them, at other times not mentioning age at all. It was not terribly uncommon, however, for the commission to adjust children's ages, sometimes rather significantly, as when Vacla Arba, determined to be seven years old at her liberation in August 1903, was aged up to "around 13 to 14 years" when she appeared before the commission in January 1906 and to "around 15 years" at her next appearance in November of the same year.[35] At least in theory, these shifts in recorded chronological age could have important consequences, since they lengthened or shortened the time it would take to reach the age of majority, the age at which liberated minor status was supposed to end. Tienouma Diara, for example, who was liberated from slavery in 1896 at age ten, was on track to age out of guardianship in 1906 or 1907, since at this time guardianship was supposed to end at age twenty. But in September 1906, members of the guardianship commission estimated her age at only seventeen, effectively prolonging her time under guardianship by several years. She apparently took matters into her own hands after that, failing to show up for her next summons around a year later, since she had recently run away.[36]

Likewise, documents related to schooling offer occasional glimpses of the ways in which teachers and officials assigned ages when they could not be documented with birth certificates, and sometimes made adjustments or new estimates, even though the lower stakes produced a smaller document trail. One particularly revealing early twentieth-century document from Gorée sheds light on the procedures teachers might have used to establish ages when students lacked birth certificates and knowledge of how old they were in years. Participation in the young children's class at the Gorée girls' school had increased to twenty-seven, wrote the director, and at least ten young girls were under age five. These very young girls did not know their ages, they lacked birth certificates, and their mothers were unknown to the school, making it difficult for teachers to properly document the girls' enrollment and attendance. To address this issue, the school turned to the police commissioner, who helped determine a place and date of birth for these students.[37] This example not only shows the value teachers placed on knowing their students' ages but also emphasizes the ongoing connection between documentation and the disciplinary power of the state.

By determining chronological age, recording it, referring back to it, and updating it as needed, French officials emphasized the primacy of chronological age over most other markers of life stage and status. Although we could read this as an extraordinary bid for power and knowledge—the state's representatives could create records out of thin air and then rely on these records as evidence—we would miss something essential in doing so. Indeed, the state *depended* on chronological age, especially with regard to children, since trials and sentences, guardianship proceedings, creation of health records, school registration, and other "protection" initiatives could not proceed without it.

Yet chronological age was not a neutral and provable "fact" in this era before widespread birth registration but rather the result of something between a story told by the person whose age was being recorded and an invention based only on the recorder's assessment of reality. This very *createdness* of chronological age, and the accompanying idea that it could be—and often was—recorded incorrectly, opened up space for Africans to maneuver, to strategize around the malleability and unknowability of this supposedly neutral measurement.[38] Although the evidence is fragmentary, it suggests that at least some Africans sought to adjust their recorded chronological ages when they needed those ages to be something different, ultimately shaping not only individual Africans' access to specific types of benefits that corresponded to age but also what the French state knew or thought it knew about African children.

Claims-Making and Chronological Age

Even if chronological age was not something they had previously been inclined to track, at least some Africans quickly accepted the idea that it was important to the French, who included age requirements in public notices about scholarship competitions and admissions tests, documented ages as they registered children for school, attempted to collect the names and ages of children attending Qur'an schools, and pointed to age as a reason for refusing requests for school admission or scholarship. Africans might have encountered this reality as they sought an opportunity, or they might have heard about it from others. In April 1919, for example, Abdoulaye Seck, who worked as a civil servant in the colonial postal and telegraph office in Saint-Louis, received word that his nephew Babakar Diop was too old to apply for a scholarship for a superior primary school in France (fifteen was the age limit). At seventeen, young Babakar was only eligible for a scholarship to do classical studies in a French secondary school, which would require him to pass exams in Latin and Greek, among other subjects.[39] From these letters, and others like them, recipients (and anyone else who read them or heard about them) would have learned not only that the French administration valued numerical age as a measurement but also that the association of specific ages with specific individuals could provide or foreclose on opportunities in the French system. Given that age was, as French officials put it, "poorly defined" in many African communities, Africans could respond creatively and strategically to French reliance on it.

Some students accepted the importance of chronological age to the French administration and used age-based claims—many of which lacked documentation—in requests for exceptions, special favors, or alternative pathways to obtain their goals, especially as officials implemented more age limits in the early twentieth century. This is what Ibra Abdoul (Aziz), son of the deceased Almamy of Lao, seems to have been up to as he sought readmission to the Sons of Chiefs Section of the Normal School. Born apparently in 1886, Ibra learned in October 1904 that he had exceeded the age limit of fifteen, beyond which students were not supposed to be admitted as boarders to the Normal School.[40] Discouraged, he wrote repeatedly to the governor general and other officials over several weeks, arguing variously that he had previously attended the School for Sons of Chiefs for three years but had "not yet finished my instruction," that he deserved an exception since his father had been a "faithful servant" who had been killed a few years prior, and that he should be admitted as a day student if he was too old to board at school. He accepted the association of eligibility with chronological age, describing himself in nearly every letter as eighteen years old and noting that he exceeded the age limit—fifteen years—for enrollment as a boarder. Yet at the same time, in at least one letter, he made the case that he was "still young," as he pleaded with the governor general to admit him despite his age.[41] In his letters, Ibra acknowledged that French officials required information about chronological age and accordingly included his age each time he wrote about himself. Strikingly, he also pushed back against the idea that the state could choose a specific chronological age as the endpoint of African childhood by contending that he should still be accepted as a schoolboy even though he was eighteen.

Other young people or their parents took a somewhat different approach, trying to finesse chronological ages to fit within French requirements and sometimes even producing documents to support their claims. In a report made after a 1913 visit to the École Rurale de l'Avenue Faidherbe in Dakar, for example, the school inspector revealed his suspicion that several students were attending this primary school despite exceeding the upper age limit of sixteen. Although Biram Niang had presented a birth certificate at the time of enrollment showing 1899 as his birth year, the inspector thought the date was incorrect and insinuated that the entire birth certificate was a fake. Abdoulaye Diop, on the other hand, had somehow been allowed to enroll in school without a birth certificate. Neither student was under age sixteen, the inspector contended, and thus neither belonged in the primary school's daytime classes, though they could attend evening adult classes instead. Rather than recognizing the resourcefulness of these students, who may have gone to some lengths to get around French efforts to exclude them from school, the inspector reprimanded the (African) teacher, who was also the school director, for the shortcomings of his recordkeeping.[42] Yet I think we should reflect for a moment on these incidents, which likely were *not* isolated (they were simply the few detected). If the inspector was correct that these students had passed their sixteenth birthdays (the records contain no insight into how the inspector came to his conclusions about their age), it is worth noting that the students had enough motivation and knowledge of the importance of chronological age to, in Niang's case obtain a false document, and in Diop's case convince school personnel that he was the appropriate age. These cases hint at some of the ways Africans could work within or around the construct of chronological age to pursue their goals.

Another case involving education and age limits confirms that Africans not only tried to maneuver around French age requirements but also had sophisticated understandings of certain bureaucratic procedures. When Alpha Diol, canton chief of Dakar, requested a scholarship to allow his son Matar Diol to attend the Lycée Faidherbe Saint-Louis, he described Matar as "about twenty years old" and noted that he had earned his primary school certificate in 1905, the year before. Regarding Diol's request, the lieutenant governor informed the Dakar delegate that because a 1904 decree had set nineteen as the maximum age for scholarship availability, Matar was now too old to qualify.[43] When the delegate in turn notified Alpha Diol that his son was too old, the chief responded by challenging the legitimacy of his son's birth record, which indicated 1885 as the birth year, and by presenting an alternative certificate from the Muslim Tribunal that showed the boy's age as seventeen and a birth year of 1889. Although the delegate discounted the document from the Muslim Tribunal, he asked whether they should reexamine the whole issue of Matar's eligibility. The head of the education service declined, maintaining that despite the discrepancy in the birth documents, Matar was too old to receive a scholarship.[44]

This striking example suggests that this chiefly family—well positioned to have some insight into French bureaucratic demands and expectations—had come to appreciate the administration's dependence on chronological age as a measure of a person and as a means of accessing opportunity, and that they sought to use gaps and tensions in the knowledge of age to Matar's advantage. Furthermore, recognizing the importance not only of chronological age but also of documentation, they turned to the Muslim Tribunal, a parallel court that was staffed by African colonial employees and approved by the colonial state, to generate a documented competing claim. After hearing from four African witnesses, the cadi of Dakar came through, issuing a decision that the state's birth registry had erred, and that according to "public" knowledge, Matar Diol had been born on 17 April 1889. This new birthdate, documented by the Muslim Tribunal on 5 October 1906, several days *after* Matar's family learned that he was too old to qualify for a scholarship for the Lycée Faidherbe, reworked his age so that it fell well below the scholarship cutoff of age nineteen.[45] While I have not found evidence that anyone officially discredited the Muslim Tribunal's decision, it is clear that the administration did not accept it, and by May 1907 Matar had been admitted to the Sons of Chiefs Section of the Normal School, where his age was recorded as twenty-one.[46] If this incident foregrounded the importance and potential flexibility of chronological age, it also shows how Africans sometimes sought to challenge or subvert French ideas about when African childhood should end, and when young Africans should be able to access spaces meant for children.

While desire to access the benefits of schooling for a longer period of time could lead students to claim younger chronological ages, both the guardianship and court systems could have the opposite effect, since young people could be removed from guardianship or released from juvenile detention when they reached the age of the majority. In a striking departure from trends in British colonial Africa, where young defendants positioned themselves as minors to receive a lighter punishment, the extreme differences in sentence length between adults and minors in early twentieth-century Senegal incentivized young people to make sure that the court treated them as adults.[47] This goal might have motivated Samba Tène as he encountered the colonial legal apparatus in 1926 following an arrest on theft charges in April of that year. Tried and convicted by the lower-level court in Podor shortly after his arrest, Samba escaped only a few days into his three-month prison term, managing to evade the authorities until 10 October 1926. His recapture raised new questions for the local administration about how to proceed, bringing Samba's story—and possibly also his strategy—to light in the archival record.[48]

Significantly, the April court judgment and an October entry in the Podor prison register indicated that Samba was "about 18," which meant that the trial court had treated him as an adult. But a few days after Samba's rearrest in October, the French administrator in Podor rejected the earlier estimate, claiming instead that Samba was "at most, 14 years old." This claim recast Samba as a minor who required rehabilitation at a juvenile facility under article 54 of the 22 March 1924 judicial decree and called into question the three-month prison sentence he had received when the court believed he was an adult. Precisely because he recognized the potential impact of this reassessment of Samba's age, the Podor administrator sought the lieutenant governor's guidance on how to proceed. Should *he* send Samba Tène to the Bambey penitentiary, he asked (since, the letter implied, he could not return this child to prison), or would *the court* need to issue a new judgment in the case, "ordering Samba Tène's internment at Bambey, either for the duration of his sentence, or until his majority?"[49]

The Political Bureau's response underscored the thorny problems posed by chronological age in regimes where documentation of births remained minimal, and it also privileged the existing—if manufactured—record. Any change to Samba's situation would have to come from the judiciary, the official cautioned, and a decision to intern him at Bambey would first require a "judgment certifying that his real age is in fact that which you attribute to him." Likely wanting to spare the court the annoyance of a new court proceeding involving witness testimony to establish Samba's age, and recognizing that the appeal deadline had already passed, the official instructed the Podor administrator to retain the original sentence, of which only about two months remained. He advised modifying conditions in consideration of the lingering questions about Samba's age, however, suggesting that they "isolate young Samba Tène," presumably to protect him from the negative influence of other prisoners, and shield him from prison labor beyond his strength.[50]

This case is tantalizing precisely because we do not know who determined Samba's age. The fact that he escaped from the adult prison only a few days into his sentence suggests that he was not resigned to his fate. Perhaps he knew that adults received short prison sentences compared to minors sent for rehabilitation and used the uncertainties around chronological age to his advantage. Conversely, perhaps the Podor administrator wanted to reclassify Samba as a minor to allow the state to intervene in his life for a longer period, or because the official did not like the idea that a young thief could be returned to the region in which he had to maintain order after a few short months. Extant evidence does not provide an answer to these questions, but I think that the questions themselves are instructive. They suggest that the creation of a person's chronological age could provide an opening, a possibility, even a strategy.[51]

An attempt to contest the state's determination of age was also at the heart of Amadou Sall's efforts to secure the release of his stepdaughter Léonie Guèye in 1925. Léonie had been imprisoned with other women in the adult facility in Saint-Louis after her third arrest for theft in July 1922. As I discuss in chapter 2, her detention raised significant moral concerns among officials, who struggled to determine whether the adult facility or the all-boy juvenile reformatory posed a greater moral hazard. Officials had decided to keep her among the women in the adult prison, but the change in location had not altered the plan to detain her until she reached majority at age twenty (or eighteen). Following an unsuccessful attempt to get her out of prison in 1924, Amadou Sall tried again in February 1925, asking the lieutenant governor for "mercy in freeing my daughter, Léonie Guèye." Léonie was "of age" (*majeure*), he claimed, and he would see to it that she stopped stealing. He had contacted the attorney general first, he added, and that official had recommended he notify the lieutenant governor that Léonie was "now of age."[52] Yet, although he expressed interest in ending her "irregular situation," the lieutenant governor rejected the idea that he could release her on the grounds that she had reached legal majority. This was mathematically impossible, since the courts had recorded her age as thirteen when she was sentenced less than three years earlier, and he did not entertain the idea of revising that record. Instead, he sought information about Léonie's conduct in prison and her parents' moral and financial situation to help him decide whether to release her to her stepfather's supervision. The prison warden's positive assessment came quickly, but the inquiry into her parents' situation took more time.[53] As he waited for a decision, Sall sent another letter, reiterating his desire to be reunited with his daughter and noting that he was "old" and had "only the mother of the girl in question" to be with him. Ultimately, the lieutenant governor ordered Léonie's "provisional release and return to her family."[54]

Although he did not deploy numbers as evidence, Sall made two age-related arguments in his 1925 requests for clemency. In his first (February) letter, he claimed that Léonie was "of age" twice in just a few lines. Significantly, this term could express both social-relational and chronological conceptions of age, and we do not know Sall's intent. Did he mean to claim that Léonie had reached adulthood according to the standards and assumptions of their society (she likely had gone through puberty, and she could have been married in absentia)? Did he intend, as the lieutenant governor believed, to cast doubt on the administration's initial calculation of her chronological age? Was he trying to be ambiguous in order to hedge his bets? The reference to his own old age in his second (April) letter was a moral claim, based on social constructions of elderhood (as requiring support and care of younger family members). Perhaps it reveals a desire to use terms and concepts the French would find compelling.[55]

Whatever his precise motivation, it is significant that Sall based his argument for Léonie's release on claims about her age, and especially that he deployed the concept of the age of majority. Even though he did not connect majority to a specific number, to a measurement of time lived, it seems likely that the French emphasis on chronological age had shaped his thinking and his strategy for securing her release. Similarly, Samba Tène might have influenced the court's determination that he should be tried as an adult rather than a minor, a determination that had significant impact since adult sentences were typically much shorter than the length of time courts ordered minors interned. These stories, along with those of Alpha and Matar Diol, Biram Niang, Abdoulaye Diop, and Ibra Abdoul (Aziz) offer insights into how some Africans sought to maneuver within and around the concept of chronological age to access benefits, change their circumstances, or otherwise make claims on the state. These individuals left traces, often fragmentary, in the archives, and as such their stories likely reflect much larger shifts in how Africans engaged with the idea of chronological age.

Conclusion

This chapter shows that colonial officials in Senegal depended on knowledge and documentation of Africans' chronological age to run the colonial bureaucracy and to ensure that they followed procedures and the rule of law. This knowledge was particularly important in structuring the state's interactions with children, since the various laws, policies, and procedures aimed at children applied to populations (liberated minors, penal minors, legal or civil minors, schoolchildren, and so on) defined by a chronological age or age range. Yet early on, most Africans did not register births with the civil state—indeed, the state did not have the capacity to handle widespread birth registration—and most did not know their birthdates or ages rendered in years. Furthermore, most of Senegal's societies considered age as a reflection of a person's capabilities, social standing, and progress through community rituals, and not as a measure of a precise quantity of time elapsed since birth.[56] For French bureaucracy to function properly and for the state to increase the legibility of the people it governed, then, officials had to determine (or impose) chronological ages, documenting them each time they created a record of an individual person. As Africans became more familiar with how the state functioned and its reliance on age in numerous policies and procedures, they began to use age as a tool themselves.

It also seems likely that Africans expanded their understanding of age in order to productively engage with French institutions, and some began to refer to chronological age as they described themselves in correspondence, court testimony, and elsewhere, much like Ibra Abdoul (Aziz) did in the letters I discuss above or like prominent politician Lamine Gueye did in his 1966 memoir. Noting that he had been born in 1891, Gueye wrote that his parents sent him to Qur'an school "at the age of six," that he started at the Ploërmel primary school at age twelve, and that before age eighteen he received funding for attendance at the médersa.[57] This phrasing suggests that Gueye not only structured his memory of childhood according to chronological age but that he accepted this as normal and natural. Ultimately, even as some people challenged the state's power to impose its version of legibility on them, the idea of measuring childhood at least in part by chronological age increasingly shaped Senegalese thinking and was taken up, after 1960, by the independent state of Senegal. Over the course of the twentieth century, chronological age not only mediated people's relationships with the state; it also came to shape understandings of childhood and children's identity. Tracked and recorded on certificates, court documents, attendance lists, registers, and more, chronological age was central to the idea of the documented child in Senegal.

Conclusion

In May 1992, Senegal signed on to the African Charter of the Rights and Welfare of the Child, an agreement developed by the member states of what was then called the Organization of African Unity (now the African Union) that went into effect in November 1999. Underscoring the "special safeguards and care" children required, the charter called on its parties to protect and improve children's lives and welfare, laying out a variety of specific rights, freedoms, and goals to guide state actions in doing so. In pledging to abide by this agreement, Senegal, along with all other parties to it, implicitly accepted its definition of "child," stated clearly in article 2: "For the purpose of this Charter, a child means every human being below the age of 18 years." And strikingly, among the many rights and protections included in the charter was the right to "name and nationality" (art. 6), which indicated that "every child should be registered immediately after birth."[1] This language was consistent with the United Nations Convention on the Rights of the Child of 1989, signed and ratified by Senegal in 1990, which defined a child as a person under eighteen, unless "under the law applicable to the child, majority is attained earlier" (art. 1); called for prompt birth registration; and advanced the idea that each child has a right to have and to "preserve" a name and nationality (arts. 7 and 8).[2] These concepts were enshrined in Senegal's domestic law well before the country signed these international agreements, with the Family Code of 1972 defining a "minor" as a person who "has not yet reached eighteen years" (art. 276) and requiring—as had the 1961 law creating a single civil registration process in Senegal—all "births, marriages and deaths" to be added to the vital records registers, or the État-Civil (art. 30).[3]

These documents suggest that Senegal—its government, if not the general population—had come by the 1970s and 1980s to embrace age-based definitions of childhood and to expect birth registration as a universal norm, greatly advancing the trends I describe in this book. This makes sense, given that independent

Senegal operated in an international system of states in which certain norms, such as identity registration, were expected and widespread. Indeed, scholars have frequently shown that identity registration of citizens, resident foreign nationals, and others was crucially important to modernizing states, and Senegal was no exception. Documented identity has become essential in the modern world, allowing states to track their populations, levy taxes, attempt to secure their borders, protect residents' rights, provide social welfare, and complete many other bureaucratic functions. As proof of nationality and citizenship, identity documents also provide certain protections to the individuals who carry them, allowing people to make various kinds of claims on the state. Conversely, those who lack identity documents are at an immense disadvantage, potentially unable to access the rights and benefits to which they are entitled, vulnerable to exploitation, and more easily rendered stateless.[4] As such, it is logical that the Senegalese state has been working to expand birth registration and identity documentation more broadly, and that many Senegalese citizens now register births and deaths with the state and carry a national ID card.

With financial support from a variety of sources including foreign-aid and international nongovernmental organizations, the Senegalese state has made important strides in civil registration and identity documentation, especially in the last few decades. Indeed, while in 2005, only 55 percent of births were declared with the state, some 77.4 percent were declared in 2017 as the state worked to expand access by adding new physical locations where people could register births and by offering mobile phone–based platforms to do so.[5] Yet despite what many would see as progress, numerous problems, challenges, and debates remain. As Senegal, like many other countries in the Global South, began to implement biometric identification systems, for example, it received support from international partners for various pilot projects and rollouts, resulting in a patchwork of systems that do not necessarily integrate with each other and potentially imperiling the goal of a comprehensive, technology-driven vital registry and identification system. The involvement of multiple international partners—consultants, technology advisors, donors, and so on—also raises questions about sovereignty. And conversely, these systems lead to ethical concerns about the uses to which states will put the additional information they learn about their citizens in their implementation. At the same time, biometric systems do not guarantee the elimination of confusion, manipulation, or fraud, as scholars Séverine Awenengo Dalberto, Richard Banégas, and Armando Cutolo contend. Indeed, these systems rely on other identity records, which are often established through oral testimony and witness accounts and can be entirely fraudulent.[6] It would seem that some of the themes I discuss in this book, such as the importance of records to state surveillance and discipline, or people's efforts to challenge and maneuver within state systems, continue to play out in contemporary Senegal, albeit in very different ways.

The technical, even scientific, appearance of contemporary civil registration and personal identification systems, combined with their reliance on precise measurements of identity and age—identities connected to precise birthdates, minor status corresponding to those under the chronological age of eighteen—sends the message that such concepts are neutral and universally applicable. And the adoption of eighteen as the "magic age" at which a child transforms into an adult, not only in international conventions and charters like those I discuss above but in the domestic laws and procedures of Senegal and many other countries around the world, likewise suggests that the category of "child" is natural, self-evident, and consistent across cultures.[7] Indeed, amid contemporary debates about how to ensure that children can access the rights and protections of various international agreements, including the right to civil registration and identity documentation, we sometimes lose sight of the variations in the definition of childhood across cultures, and we often obscure the historically contingent nature of childhood and of children's experiences. I have tried to complicate these assumptions in this book, which not only explores the history of the documentary *colonial* state as it collected and recorded information about Africans, including children, at both the population and individual levels, but also shows how various child-focused initiatives of the colonial state, and—crucially—children's responses to them, shaped individual children's lives and the very understanding of childhood itself.

This book, then, offers in part a study of a historical precursor to late colonial efforts to create a French West Africa identity card, which, as Dalberto shows, Africans eagerly sought as a means to access rights and benefits, and of a precursor to postcolonial Senegal's emphasis on identity documentation, vital statistics registration, and, more recently, biometrics.[8] Although I am not proposing a throughline between these histories, I do think there are certain important connections. As I show, the French colonial state created and maintained numerous records of children's names, ages, and various interactions with state institutions and their representatives. Tracking children's experiences under guardianship, school enrollment and grades, violations of law or sanitation regulations, vaccinations and medical encounters, and more began to normalize the documentation of children's lives and the idea that the state had a right to, and perhaps *should*, maintain these sorts of records. Documentation—of chronological age, vaccination status, school attendance, and the like—in turn became increasingly useful to children and their families as they attempted to make certain kinds of claims on the state. Although the dynamics of vital registration and biometric identification in contemporary Senegal differ in important ways, I do think that the historical account offered here sheds light on the processes by which Africans began to accept the idea of documentation, to acquiesce to it, and, in some cases, to find it potentially beneficial.

This book also explores the historical contingencies within the colonial state and among African children and their families that produced shifts in how Africans experienced childhood and how childhood came to be defined. On one hand, it traces how the French colonial state sought to discipline, surveil, and ultimately "protect" African children through specific institutions and practices—guardianship, schools, juvenile reformatories, policing and hygiene enforcement, vaccination, and medical interventions. The rules that governed these children's institutions or that structured African children's encounters with representatives of the state communicated specific expectations for colonial African childhood, ultimately forming an image of a "protected" child who was obedient and loyal, attended school, received biomedical care, prepared for a future in agriculture or a manual trade, understood hygiene, and did not encumber public spaces by loitering or being loud in them. Officials could present this prototype to the Colonial Ministry and to the international community as evidence of French compassion and care for colonized children. Yet the book also highlights how African children acted in their own interests, sometimes going along with the state and sometimes challenging its initiatives. Over time, however, certain programs, such as schooling or childhood vaccination, came to be accepted as typical childhood experiences, likely incorporating ways they had been shaped by children's reactions to earlier initiatives. As children encountered the state's disciplinary apparatus in its various guises—in schools, public streets, courtrooms, reformatories, and medical clinics—they faced efforts to categorize them based on chronological age and to impose new expectations for children's behavior and activities. By navigating and responding to these encounters, children contributed to shifts in the definition of African childhood under colonial rule and made clear that the state could not redefine childhood on its own. My book thus reminds us that "child" is a historically contingent and constructed category, and that it will continue to be so in the future.

Select Bibliography of Archival Sources and Serial Publications

Archives

Les Archives Générales de la Congrégation du Saint-Esprit, Chevilly-Larue, France (AGCSE)
    3i2.17: Journaux de communauté et divers, 1887–1973
    3i1.22a3: Mission de Thiès

Archives Nationales de la République du Sénégal, Dakar, Senegal (ANS)
    Fonds Sénégal Colonial
        Sous-Série 1G: Enseignement
        Série F: Sécurité publique au Sénégal: Police, gendarmerie, prisons (1840–1956)
        Sous-Série 10D: Administration centrale de la colonie du Sénégal (1785–1964)
        Série H: Santé et assistance publique, fonds Sénégal colonial, 1817–1960
        Sous-Série 2M: Justice pénal
        Série R: Agriculture, élevage, eaux et forêts, pêche dans la colonie du Sénégal, 1864–1959

    Fonds Afrique Occidentale Française (AOF)
        Série J: Enseignement jusqu'en 1920
        Série K: Travail et main d'œuvre-esclavage
        Sous-Série 1G: Études générales, monographies, thèses
        Sous-Série 2G: Rapports périodiques des gouverneurs, administrateurs, et chefs de services depuis 1895
        Sous-Série 13G: Sénégal: Affaires politiques, administratives et musulmanes (1782–1959)
        Sous-Série 21G: Police et sûreté
        Sous-Série 22G: Statistiques générales et démographiques
        Sous-Série 1H: Santé
        Sous-Série 2H: Assistance

Série H: Santé, AOF, archives anciennes
Série M: Justice, AOF, archives anciennes
Sous-Série 6M: Justice, Sénégal
Série O: Enseignement de l'AOF, 1895–1958
Série R: Agriculture, élevage, eaux et forêts, pêche en AOF, 1820–1959

Archives Nationales d'Outre-Mer, Aix-en-Provence, France (ANOM)
    Fonds Ministériels
        SEN/X: Sénégal et dépendances—Culte, instruction publique, beaux-arts
        SEN/XI: Police, hygiène, et assistance, 1816–1895
        SEN/XIV: Esclavage et traite, travail et main d'oeuvre

Institut Fondamental de l'Afrique Noire, Dakar, Senegal (IFAN)
    Cahiers William Ponty / William Ponty Notebooks (CP)

Serial Publications

L'Afrique Occidentale Française en [year]: Rapport d'ensemble annuel
Budget de la Colonie du Sénégal, exercise [year]
Budget des pays de protectorat: Exercise [year]
Bulletin de l'enseignement de l'Afrique Occidentale Française
Bulletin d'Information et de Renseignements
Conseil Général, session extraordinaire de [year]
Conseil Général, session ordinaire de [year]
Journal Officiel de l'Afrique Occidentale Française
Journal Officiel de la République Française, Lois et Décrets
Journal Officiel de la République Française
Moniteur du Sénégal et Dépendances (became *Journal Officiel du Sénégal et Dépendances,* then *Journal Officiel du Sénégal*)
Rapport Général présenté à M. le Ministre de l'intérieur par l'Académie de Médecine sur les vaccinations et revaccinations pratiquées en France et dans les colonies françaises pendant l'année [year]; became L. Camus, *Rapport Général présenté à M. le Ministre du Travail, de l'Hygiène, de l'Assistance, et de la Prévoyance Sociale par l'Académie de Médecine sur les Vaccinations et Revaccinations pratiquées en France, et aux colonies pendant les années [years]*
Recueil de législation, de doctrine et de jurisprudence coloniales
Recueil Jurisprudence AOF

Databases

Liberated Minors Database
  Contains data compiled from the following ANS files: H173, H174, H175, H176, H177, H178, H206, 1F1, and K23
Minor Detainees Database
  Contains data compiled from the following sources: ANS files: 3F25, 3F26, 3F27, 3F28, 1F150, H284, 1R118, 2G32/84, 6M273, 6M364; AGCSE file: 312.17; *Journal Officiel du Sénégal*; *Conseil Général, session ordinaire de [year]*

Notes

Introduction

1 Alioune Diop, "Histoire d'un écolier noir (par lui-même)," *Bulletin de l'enseignement de l'Afrique Occidentale Française* 20, no. 76 (1931): 25–29. Diop would go on to cofound the pan-African literary and political journal *Présence africaine*, in 1947.
2 He may have written this narrative in response to a call for essays on "School Life in AOF: Inquiry into the Black Child of AOF," which had gone out in 1929 and again in 1930. See *Bulletin de l'enseignement de l'Afrique Occidentale Française* 18, no. 70 (July–December 1929): 15–16.
3 Celebrated Nigerian writer Chinua Achebe referred to himself as a "British-Protected Child" to gesture toward the in-betweenness he felt during and after his time in British colonial schools. See Achebe, "The Education of a British-Protected Child," in Achebe, *The Education of a British-Protected Child: Essays* (New York: Knopf, 2009), 3–24.
4 See, for example, Gouverneur Général, p.i., to Gouverneurs des Colonies du Group and M. le Gouverneur Administrateur de Circonscription de Dakar et Dépendances, 26 October 1938, 2H13, Archives Nationales du Sénégal, Dakar (hereafter ANS); Secrétaire Général for Gouverneur, Sénégal, to Gouverneur Général, AOF, 1 January 1940, 2H13, ANS.
5 Sous-Directeur for Ministre des Colonies to Messieurs les Gouverneurs Généraux, Gouverneurs des Colonies, Commissaires de la République au Togo et au Cameroun et l'Administrateur des îles Saint-Pierre et Miquelon, 24 August 1933, 2H13, ANS; Gouverneur Général AOF to Ministre des Colonies, 30 March 1934, 2H13, ANS; Comité National de l'Enfance, *Congrès International pour la Protection de l'Enfance, Paris, 4–9 Juillet 1933, IX Section: Section Coloniale*, vol. 4, *La protection de l'enfance indigène dans les colonies françaises* (Paris: Imprimerie Beurq, 1935). On child welfare and global movements to address it, see Emily Baughan, *Saving the Children: Humanitarianism, Internationalism, and Empire* (Oakland: University of California Press, 2022).
6 Barbara Cooper, *Countless Blessings: A History of Childbirth and Reproduction in the Sahel* (Bloomington: Indiana University Press, 2019), chaps. 5–6.
7 "La Protection de l'Enfance en AOF," n.d. [March 1934], 2H13, ANS; Gouverneur Général AOF to Ministre des Colonies, 30 March 1934, 2H13, ANS.
8 Gouverneur Général AOF to Ministre des Colonies, Dakar, 30 March 1934, 2H13, ANS.

9 For a similar discussion of chronological age in the very different context of British East Africa, see Corrie Decker, *The Age of Sex: Custom, Law, and Ritual in Twentieth-Century East Africa* (Madison: University of Wisconsin Press, forthcoming), chaps. 5–6.

10 Philippe Ariès, *Centuries of Childhood: A Social History of Family Life*, trans. Robert Baldick (New York: Knopf, 1962); Joseph M. Hawes and N. Ray Hiner, eds., *Children in Historical and Comparative Perspective: An International Handbook and Research Guide* (Westport, CT: Greenwood Press, 1991); Heidi Morrison, "What Is the Global History of Childhood?" in *The Global History of Childhood Reader*, ed. Heidi Morrison (New York: Routledge, 2008), 1–8; Paula S. Fass, ed., *The Routledge History of Childhood in the Western World* (London: Routledge, 2013).

11 Abosede A. George, *Making Modern Girls: A History of Girlhood, Labor, and Social Development in Colonial Lagos* (Athens: Ohio University Press, 2014); Temilola Alanamu, Benedict Carton, and Benjamin N. Lawrance, "Colonialism and African Childhood," in *The Palgrave Handbook of African Colonial and Postcolonial History*, vol. 1, ed. Martin S. Shanguhyia and Toyin Falola (New York: Palgrave Macmillan, 2018), 389–412; S. E. Duff, "Childhood and Youth in African History," *Oxford Research Encyclopedia of African History*, 25 March 2021, https://doi.org/10.1093/acrefore/9780190277734.013.230; S. E. Duff, *Children and Youth in African History* (Cham, Switzerland: Palgrave Macmillan, 2022); Robin Phylisia Chapdelaine, *The Persistence of Slavery: An Economic History of Child Trafficking in Nigeria* (Amherst: University of Massachusetts Press, 2021); Decker, *The Age of Sex*. For a very brief overview of French discourses and policies related to children in French West Africa, see Lisa McNee, "The Languages of Childhood: The Discursive Construction of Childhood and Colonial Policy in French West Africa," *African Studies Quarterly* 7, no. 4 (2004): 20–32.

12 Kelly M. Duke Bryant, *Education as Politics: Colonial Schooling and Political Debate in Senegal, 1850s–1914* (Madison: University of Wisconsin Press, 2015), 14–19. Although the scholarship on childhood in French colonial Africa is minimal, several excellent studies have appeared recently. See, for example, Rachel Jean-Baptiste, *Multiracial Identities in Colonial French Africa: Race, Childhood, and Citizenship* (Cambridge: Cambridge University Press, 2023), and Jessica Catherine Reuther, *The Bonds of Kinship in Dahomey: Portraits of West African Girlhood, 1720–1940* (Bloomington: Indiana University Press, 2025).

13 Corinne T. Field and Nicholas L. Syrett, "Introduction: Chronological Age: A Useful Category of Historical Analysis," AHR Roundtable, *American Historical Review* 125, no. 2 (2020): 370–84, 374 (quotation). See also Duff, *Children and Youth in African History*, 4–7, and Corrie Decker, "A Feminist Methodology of Age-Grading and History in Africa," *American Historical Review* 125, no. 2 (2020): 418–26.

14 Defining childhood is made even more challenging by the fact that colonial administrations, missionaries, and reformers often referred to adult Africans using terminology of childhood (calling them "childlike," for example), as a way of reinforcing their belief that African societies were at an early stage of development, that they required European tutelage and guidance, and that they were not ready for self-government. On these points, see Duff, "Childhood and Youth in African History," and William B. Cohen, "The Colonized as Child: British and French Colonial Rule," *African Historical Studies* 3, no. 2 (1970): 427–31.

15 "Young" or "youth" can also be glossed as *ndaw* (which likewise means "small"). The Guy-Grand dictionary from 1923 includes the word *dara* to describe girls who had reached the age of reason, but I have not found a comparable term in other dictionaries. This dictionary also added a note that *gune* could be used for a child up to around age twelve, in this way translating a Wolof category into terms that made sense to French readers. Missionnaires de la Congrégation du S. Esprit et du S. Coeur de Marie, *Dictionnaire Français-Wolof et Wolof Français, nouvelle édition, contenant tous les mots du Dictionnaire de Dard, du Vocabulaire du baron Roger, du Dictionnaire manuscrit de l'abbé Lambert, revue, corrigée, considérablement augmentée et précédée des principes de la langue Wolofe* (Dakar: Imprimerie de la Mission, 1855), 91, 138; V.-J. Guy-Grand, *Dictionnaire Français-Volof, précédé d'un abrégé de la grammaire Volofe*, 2nd ed. (Dakar: Mission Catholique, 1923), 214, 346; A. Kobès and O. Abiven, *Dictionnaire Volof-Français* (Dakar: Mission Catholique, 1923), 104; Abdoulaye Sadji, *Education africaine et civilisation* (Dakar: SAFEP, Imprimerie A. Diop, 1964), 39–51; Jean-Léopold Diouf, *Dictionnaire wolof-français et français-wolof* (Paris: Éditions Karthala, 2003). For a linguistic analysis of these and other terms relating to childhood, see Jacqueline Rabain-Jamin, "Enfance, âge et développement chez les Wolof du Sénégal," *L'Homme* 167–68 (2003): 49–65.

16 Almamy, Mémoire de fin d'études normales: Système d'éducation traditionnelle des Torobés, 1948, XV-Se-558, Cahiers Ponty, Institut Fondamental d'Afrique Noire, Dakar (hereafter CP, IFAN). For an analysis that uses many of the same William Ponty notebooks to explore childbirth and values of childhood in the Sahel, see Cooper, *Countless Blessings*, 100–105.

17 Ibrahima Ben Mady Cissé, Mémoire de fin d'études normales, 1949, XV-Se-562, CP, IFAN. See also Almamy, Mémoire; Seydou Diallo, Mémoire de fin d'études normales: L'enfant dans le milieu familial, 1949, XV-Se-564, CP, IFAN; Malick S. Fall, Mémoire de vacances: L'enfant dans le milieu familial, 1949, XV-Se-24, CP, IFAN; Fodé Fanné, Mémoire de fin d'études normales: L'enfant dans le milieu familial, 1949, XV-Se-26, CP, IFAN; and Amadou Sylla, Mémoire de fin d'études normales: La formation morale de l'enfant dans un milieu indigène, 1949, XV-Se-15, CP, IFAN.

18 L. J. B. Bérenger-Féraud, *Les peuplades de la Sénégambie* (1879; repr., Nendeln, Lichtenstein: Kraus, 1973), 8, 13; Alexandre Bernard Etienne Antoine Lasnet et al., *Une Mission au Sénégal: Ethnographie, botanique, zoologie, géologie* (Paris: Augustin Challamel, 1900), 46–47, 116–19. Despite the profound racism and essentialism of these texts, they do provide some useful observations about late nineteenth-century cultural practices.

19 Coutumes du Sénégal, Thiès, 1907, 1G330, ANS; Report on Customs, Bakel, 15 May 1907, 1G330, ANS. See also Cercle de la Haute Gambie, 1907, 1G330, ANS; Report on Sarakholé Customs, 1907, 1G330, ANS; and Abdou Salam Kane, "Coutume civile et pénale Toucouleur (Cercle de Matam)," in *Coutumiers juridiques de l'Afrique Occidentale Française*, vol. 1, *Sénégal*, comp. Comité d'études historiques et scientifiques de l'Afrique Occidentale Française (Paris: Librairie Larose, 1939), 66, 68.

20 Coutume des Sérères N'Doute (Cercle de Thiès), d'après M. J. C. Fayet, Administrateur-adjoint des Colonies, 1937, in *Coutumiers juridiques*, 202; Coutume Sérère de la Petite-Côte (Cercle de Thies), d'après M. Dulphy, Administrateur des Colonies, 1936, in *Coutumiers juridiques*, 244, 302. It is perhaps also significant that the maternal uncle, in consultation with the father, decided when a boy was ready for circumcision

21 In her 2022 dissertation, Na'ama Morag-Zamonski portrays labor—for the family, community, and marabout (Islamic teacher)—as a normal part of African children's lives in the 1930s and 1940s. Despite some concerns about such work, especially when performed for a marabout, French officials and entrepreneurs sometimes forced children to work in factories or mines or included them in adult corvée labor. See Morag-Zamonski, "Being a Child in French West Africa: 1930–1950" (PhD diss., Ben Gurion University of the Negev, 2022).

22 On *métis* children and communities in French West Africa, see Owen White, *Children of the French Empire: Miscegenation and Colonial Society in French West Africa, 1895–1960* (Oxford: Oxford University Press, 1999); Emmanuelle Saada, *Empire's Children: Race, Filiation, and Citizenship in the French Colonies*, trans. Arthur Goldhammer (Chicago: University of Chicago Press, 2012); Hilary Jones, *The Métis of Senegal: Urban Life and Politics in French West Africa* (Bloomington: Indiana University Press, 2013); Kelly Duke Bryant, "French Fathers and Their 'Indigenous Children': Interracial Families in Colonial Senegal, 1900–1915," *Journal of Family History* 42, no. 3 (2017): 308–25; and Jean-Baptiste, *Multiracial Identities in Colonial French Africa*.

23 George, *Making Modern Girls*, 6. Audra A. Diptee, in contrast to George, emphasizes the particularity of African childhood as envisioned by colonizers in the nineteenth and twentieth centuries, and as articulated in international human rights activism and agreements from the mid-twentieth century through the contemporary period. And Dónal Hassett demonstrates that by construing African and French children very differently, French administrators effectively limited African war orphans' access to financial support from the French state following World War I. See Audra A. Diptee, "Notions of African Childhood in Abolitionist Discourses: Colonial and Postcolonial Humanitarianism in the Fight against Child Slavery," in *Child Slavery Before and After Emancipation: An Argument for Child-Centered Slavery Studies*, ed. Anna Mae Duane (New York: Cambridge University Press, 2017), 208–30, and Dónal Hassett, "*Pupilles de l'Empire*: Debating the Provision for Child Victims of the Great War in the French Empire," *French Historical Studies* 39, no. 2 (2016): 315–45.

24 On gender differences as they related to Africans' maneuvering around chronological age in colonial Kenya, see Decker, "A Feminist Methodology of Age-Grading."

25 Mary Jo Maynes, "Age as a Category of Historical Analysis: History, Agency, and Narratives of Childhood," *Journal of the History of Childhood and Youth* 1, no. 1 (2008): 114–24; Mona Gleason, "Avoiding the Agency Trap: Caveats for Historians of Children, Youth, and Education," *History of Education* 45, no. 4 (2016): 446–59; Lynn M. Thomas, "Historicising Agency," *Gender and History* 28, no. 2 (2016): 324–39; Stephanie Olsen et al., "A Critical Conversation on Agency," *Journal of the History of Childhood and Youth* 17, no. 2 (2024): 169–87.

26 Sarah Maza, "The Kids Aren't All Right: Historians and the Problem of Childhood," *American Historical Review* 125, no. 4 (2020): 1266.

27 Peter N. Stearns, "Challenges in the History of Childhood," *Journal of the History of Childhood and Youth* 1, no. 1 (2008): 35–42; Christopher J. Lee, "Children in the Archives: Epistolary Evidence, Youth Agency, and the Social Meanings of 'Coming of Age' in Interwar Nyasaland," *Journal of Family History* 35, no. 1 (2010): 25–47; Gleason, "Avoiding the Agency Trap," 452, 458; Nell Musgrove, Carla Pascoe Leahy, and Kristine Moruzi, "Hearing Children's Voices: Conceptual and Methodological

Challenges," in *Children's Voices from the Past: New Historical and Interdisciplinary Perspectives*, ed. Kristine Moruzi, Nell Musgrove, and Carla Pascoe Leahy (Cham, Switzerland: Palgrave Macmillan, 2019), 9–19; Jennifer Beinart, "Darkly through a Lens: Changing Perceptions of the African Child in Sickness and Health, 1900–1945," in *In the Name of the Child: Health and Welfare, 1880–1940*, ed. Roger Cooter (London: Routledge, 1992), 220–43. In her wonderful book on girlhood in Dahomey, Jessica Reuther adopts an innovative approach, combining scattered fragments of written evidence about multiple children to create "collective biographies" that she supplements with visual evidence. Reuther, *The Bonds of Kinship in Dahomey*, 14–18.

28 Musgrove, Leahy, and Moruzi, "Hearing Children's Voices," 18–20; Marie Rodet and Elodie Razy, "Introduction: Child Migration in Africa: Key Issues and New Perspectives," in *Children on the Move in Africa: Past and Present Experiences of Migration*, ed. Elodie Razy and Marie Rodet (Suffolk, UK: James Currey, 2016), 6–8.

29 For analysis of a different sort of student writing, see Kelly Duke Bryant, "'Dear Monsieur Administrator': Student Writing and the Question of 'Voice' in Early Colonial Senegal," in Moruzi, Musgrove, and Leahy, eds., *Children's Voices from the Past*, 85–105.

30 This excludes students attending night classes meant for adults.

31 For useful surveys of the literature on African youth and the major themes it has explored, see Richard Waller, "Rebellious Youth in Colonial Africa," *Journal of African History* 47 (2006): 77–92; Nicolas Argenti and Deborah Durham, "Youth," in *The Oxford Handbook of Modern African History*, ed. John Parker and Richard Reid (New York: Oxford University Press, 2013), 396–413; and Jamaine M. Abidogun, "Youth and Popular Culture in Colonial Africa," in Shanguhyia and Falola, eds., *The Palgrave Handbook of African Colonial and Postcolonial History*, 1:479–506. And for one considering children and youth together, see Duff, "Childhood and Youth in African History."

32 James C. Scott, *Seeing Like a State: How Certain Schemes to Improve the Human Condition Have Failed* (New Haven, CT: Yale University Press, 1998), 2–6.

33 Michel Foucault, *Discipline and Punish: The Birth of the Prison*, trans. Alan Sheridan (New York: Vintage, 1995), 189–90.

34 For example, Megan Vaughan, *Curing Their Ills: Colonial Power and African Illness* (Stanford, CA: Stanford University Press, 1991), 8–11.

35 Frederick Cooper makes a similar point for a later time period, focusing on adult issues (like family allowances and voting rights). See Cooper, "Voting, Welfare and Registration: The Strange Fate of the État-Civil in French Africa, 1945–1960," in *Registration and Recognition: Documenting the Person in World History*, ed. Keith Breckenridge and Simon Szreter (London: Oxford University Press, 2012), 400–407. Ishita Pande explores similar themes regarding colonial India. See Pande, "Power, Knowledge, and the Epistemic Contract on Age: The Case of Colonial India," AHR Roundtable, *American Historical Review* 125, no. 2 (2020): 407–17. Susan J. Pearson's study of birth registration in the United States shaped my thinking on the subject, though she focuses much more than I do on the people recording births and advocating for better data, mandatory reporting, and so on. See Pearson, *The Birth Certificate: An American History* (Chapel Hill: University of North Carolina Press, 2021).

36 Veena Das, "The Signature of the State: The Paradox of Illegibility," in *Anthropology in the Margins of the State*, ed. Veena Das and Deborah Poole (Santa Fe, NM: School of American Research Press, 2004), 227; Jane Caplan and John Torpey, "Introduction," in *Documenting Individual Identity: The Development of State Practices in the Modern World*, ed. Jane Caplan and John Torpey (Princeton, NJ: Princeton University Press, 2001), 1–7; Bianca Premo, "Meticulous Imprecision: Calculating Age in Colonial Spanish American Law," AHR Roundtable, *American Historical Review* 125, no. 2 (2020): 396–406. For an essay exploring similar issues related to documentation and African children in East Africa, see Sarah Walters, "'Child! Now You Are': Identity Registration, Labor, and the Definition of Childhood in Colonial Tanganyika, 1910–1950," *Journal of the History of Childhood and Youth* 9, no. 1 (2016): 66–86. And on the shortcomings and opportunities of French efforts to make marriages more legible in colonial Soudan, see Emily S. Burrill, *States of Marriage: Gender, Justice, and Rights in Colonial Mali* (Athens: Ohio University Press, 2015), chap. 6.

37 Séverine Awenengo Dalberto and Richard Banégas, eds., *Identification and Citizenship in Africa: Biometrics, the Documentary State and Bureaucratic Writings on the Self* (London: Routledge, 2021), especially the essay by Dalberto, "The French West African Identity Card in Senegal: The Challenges and Meanings of Legal Identification in the Era of Imperial Citizenship," trans. Rachel Robertson, 129–36; Kévin Fouquet, "L'état civil sénégalais aujourd'hui, de l'enregistrement à l'archivage: Les difficultés d'un outil de bonne gouvernance et de respect des droits humains," *La Gazette des archives* 259, no. 3 (2020): 115–28; Eva Magdalena Stambøl and Leonie Jegen, "Colonial Continuities and the Commodification of Mobility Policing: French Civipol in West Africa," in *Postcoloniality and Forced Migration: Mobility, Control, Agency*, ed. Martin Lemberg-Pedersen et al. (Bristol, UK: Bristol University Press, 2022), 76–92.

38 On terminology related to slavery, see P. Gabrielle Foreman et al., "Writing about Slavery/Teaching about Slavery: This Might Help," 26 March 2025, https://www.pgabrielleforeman.com.

39 Bernard Moitt, *Child Slavery and Guardianship in Colonial Senegal* (Cambridge: Cambridge University Press, 2024), 58–66; Bernard Moitt, "Slavery and Guardianship in Postemancipation Senegal: Colonial Legislation and Minors in *Tutelle*, 1848–1905," in *Child Slaves in the Modern World*, ed. Gwyn Campbell, Suzanne Miers, and Joseph C. Miller (Athens: Ohio University Press, 2011), 144; Trevor R. Getz, *Slavery and Reform in West Africa: Toward Emancipation in Nineteenth-Century Senegal and the Gold Coast* (Athens: Ohio University Press, 2004), 83.

40 Sarah Fishman, *The Battle for Children: World War II, Youth Crime, and Juvenile Justice in Twentieth-Century France* (Cambridge, MA: Harvard University Press, 2002), 15–17; Miranda Sachs, "'A Sad and . . . Odious Industry': The Problem of Child Begging in Late Nineteenth-Century Paris," *Journal of the History of Childhood and Youth* 10, no. 2 (2017): 188–205.

41 Duke Bryant, *Education as Politics*, 12–19; Yves Hazemann, "Un Outil de la conquête coloniale: L'école des Otages de Saint-Louis (1855–1871; 1892–1903)," *Cahiers du Centre de Recherches Africaines* 5 (1987): 135–37.

42 For example, Commandant de cercle de Saldé to Gouverneur, 31 October 1886, J5, ANS.

43 Moitt, *Child Slavery and Guardianship*, 89–91; Martin Klein, *Slavery and Colonial Rule in French West Africa* (Cambridge, UK: Cambridge University Press, 1998), 28–29,

71–74; Mbaye Guèye, "La fin de l'esclavage à Saint-Louis et à Gorée en 1848," *Bulletin de l'Institut Fondamental de l'Afrique Noire* 28 (1966): 651.

44 This was true to a point. The Frères de l'Instruction Chrétienne (Ploërmel Brothers) left the colony, turning over their boys' schools to secular teachers. The Sisters of Saint-Joseph de Cluny stopped providing public schooling for girls, though they continued to run a workshop and private orphanage, to offer religious education for girls outside of regular school hours, and to work in hospitals. The Fathers of the Séminaire du Saint-Esprit had just closed the government-funded penitentiary-school but continued to operate their own orphanage, mission schools, and seminary. See Abigail R. Warchol, "Care-Taking as Civilizing: Catholic Orphanages and the *Mission Civilisatrice* in Saint-Louis, Senegal, 1936–1949" (MA thesis, University of North Carolina at Chapel Hill, 2019), and Elizabeth A. Foster, *Faith in Empire: Religion, Politics and Colonial Rule in French Senegal, 1880–1940* (Stanford, CA: Stanford University Press, 2013), 69–84.

45 Alice L. Conklin, *A Mission to Civilize: The Republican Idea of Empire in France and West Africa, 1895–1930* (Stanford, CA: Stanford University Press, 1997), 38–106.

46 Sylvia Schafer, *Children in Moral Danger and the Problem of Government in Third Republic France* (Princeton, NJ: Princeton University Press, 1997).

47 Conklin, *A Mission to Civilize*, 212–23; Alexander Keese, "Colonialism and Decolonization in French Sub-Saharan Africa," in *The Routledge Handbook of Francophone Africa*, ed. Tony Chafer and Margaret A. Majumdar (London: Routledge, 2024), 23–42.

48 Tony Chafer, "Conflicting Modernities: Battles over France's Policy of Adapted Education in French West Africa," in *France's Modernising Mission: Citizenship, Welfare and the Ends of Empire*, ed. Ed Naylor (London: Palgrave Macmillan, 2018), 5–13; Harry Gamble, *Contesting French West Africa: Battles over Schools and the Colonial Order, 1900–1950* (Lincoln: University of Nebraska Press, 2017), chap. 3; Ghislaine Lydon, "The Unraveling of a Neglected Source: A Report on Women in Francophone West Africa in the 1930s," *Cahiers d'études africaines* 37, no. 147 (1997): 555–84; Baughan, *Saving the Children*, 78–104.

49 Whereas French pronatalism motivated the state to try to ensure that all French children could become productive citizens, child protection in the colonies was aimed at ensuring a healthy, compliant, subject workforce and promoting the idea of France as a humanitarian empire. On developments in France, see Fishman, *The Battle for Children*, 31–43, and Timothy B. Smith, "Assistance and Repression: Rural Exodus, Vagabondage and Social Crisis in France, 1880–1914," *Journal of Social History* 32, no. 4 (1999): 821–46. On related developments across the French Empire, see Martin Thomas, *The French Empire between the Wars: Imperialism, Politics and Society* (Manchester, UK: Manchester University Press, 2005), chap. 5.

Chapter 1

1 Régistre destiné à Inscrire les délibérations, les procès-verbaux des Séances et les transactions du Conseil de Tutelle des Enfants mâles, mineurs et sans Parens à St Louis (hereafter Régistre-Tutelle), 22 June 1849 entry, M3, ANS.

2 Arrêté qui institue des conseils de tutelle à St Louis et à Gorée pour les affranchis mineurs orphelins, 13 April 1849, M3, ANS; Klein, *Slavery and Colonial Rule*, 25; Moitt,

"Slavery and Guardianship in Postemancipation Senegal," 143–45; Kelly M. Duke Bryant, "Changing Childhood: 'Liberated Minors,' Guardianship, and the Colonial State in Senegal, 1895–1911," *Journal of African History* 60, no. 2 (2019): 209–28; Moitt, *Child Slavery and Guardianship*, 58–62. At least until the 1860s, guardianship also structured the state's efforts to provide for orphans.

3 Régistre-Tutelle, 1849–57, M3, ANS; Enregistrement tutelle, 1858–74, M3, ANS; Richard Roberts and Martin A. Klein, "The Banamba Slave Exodus of 1905 and the Decline of Slavery in the Western Sudan," *Journal of African History* 21, no. 3 (1980): 375–94; Klein, *Slavery and Colonial Rule*, 132–37, 159–77; Kelly M. Duke Bryant, "A 'Sentiment of Humanity'? Child Protection, Surveillance, and State Guardianship in Senegal, 1895–1910," in *Diverse Unfreedoms: The Afterlives and Transformations of Post-Transatlantic Bondages*, ed. Sarada Balagopalan, Cati Coe, and Keith Green (New York: Routledge, 2020), 38–39; Liberated Minors Database.

4 Lieutenant Gouverneur to Gouverneur Général, 4 May 1904, K23, ANS.

5 Thanks to Corrie Decker for helping clarify this point.

6 Guèye, "La fin de l'esclavage à Saint-Louis et à Gorée," 637–67; Joshua Goodwin et al., "The Registers of Slave Liberation in Colonial Senegal: Preliminary Analysis of the Evidence from 1894 to 1903," *Esclavages et Post-esclavages* 5 (2021), https://journals.openedition.org/slaveries/5495; Marion Pluskota, "Freedom of Movement, Access to Urban Centres, and Abolition of Slavery in the French Caribbean," *International Review of Social History* 65 (2020): 106–8.

7 Moitt, *Child Slavery and Guardianship*; Moitt, "Slavery and Guardianship in Postemancipation Senegal." See also Ousseynou Faye, "Un aspect négligé de l'histoire sociale de la colonisation: Les domestiques dans la vie de relations à Dakar de 1885 à 1940: Etude d'un salariat urbain à la périphérie du monde du travail," *Annales de la Faculté des Lettres et Sciences Humaines, Université Cheikh Anta Diop de Dakar* 23 (1993): 79–95; Klein, *Slavery and Colonial Rule*, 29, 71–75; Getz, *Slavery and Reform in West Africa*, 82–84; and Cati Coe, "Domestic Violence and Child Circulation in the Southeastern Gold Coast, 1905–28," in *Domestic Violence and the Law in Colonial and Postcolonial Africa*, ed. Emily S. Burrill, Richard L. Roberts, and Elizabeth Thornberry (Athens: Ohio University Press, 2010), 54–73.

8 Faye, "Un aspect négligé"; Ibrahima Thioub, "La gestion de la marginalité juvénile dans la colonie du Sénégal: De l'abolition de l'esclavage aux écoles pénitentiaires, 1848–1906," *Cahiers Histoire et Civilisations* 1 (2003): 117–30; Ibrahima Thioub, "Juvenile Marginality and Incarceration during the Colonial Period: The First Penitentiary Schools in Senegal, 1888–1927," in *A History of Prison and Confinement in Africa*, ed. Florence Bernault, trans. Janet Roitman (Portsmouth, NH: Heinemann, 2003), 79–95.

9 Gleason, "Avoiding the Agency Trap," 452, 458; Mona Gleason, "The Archived Child: Strategies for Amplifying Children's Contributions to History," *Qualitative Inquiry* 30, no. 10 (2024): 764–73.

10 Initially, Governor Baudin created a separate committee of women, charging it with guardianship of girls, but he eliminated this committee after only a couple of weeks, giving the guardianship councils responsibility for all unaccompanied children. He also staffed the council with a few additional members. Arrêtés on Guardianship, 13 April 1849, M3, ANS; Arrêté Overturning 13 April 1849, 1 May 1849, M3, ANS;

Arrêté on Guardianship Councils, 25 May 1849, M3, ANS; Moitt, *Child Slavery and Guardianship*, 68–74. The records do not reveal how council members determined whether a child was an "ex-captive" or an "orphan." Although some entries are clear, describing children of free status with recently deceased parents, for example, or including the name of the former enslaver of an "ex-captive" child, many are not, the likely result of slippage in the usage of these terms. Moitt suggests that council members or officials may have categorized as orphans any child whose parents could not be found.

11 Régistre-Tutelle, 8 June 1849 entry, M3, ANS.
12 Régistre-Tutelle, n.d. [July 1849] entry, M3, ANS; Moitt, *Child Slavery and Guardianship*, 74–75.
13 Moitt, "Slavery and Guardianship in Postemancipation Senegal," 145–47; Moitt, *Child Slavery and Guardianship*, 93–98.
14 Arrêté on Guardianship, 13 April 1849, M3, ANS; Speech by the President of the Guardianship Council, May 1849, M3, ANS.
15 État alphabétique des individus dont la Tutelle Officielle s'est occupée, depuis 1849 jusqu'au 1er janvier 1864, M3, ANS; Enregistrement tutelle, 1858–74, M3, ANS.
16 In addition, on the request of their parents, guardianship councils also arranged apprenticeships for many boys who were not liberated minors. The terminology used in the records is inconsistent, however, and it is therefore nearly impossible to determine with certainty whether an apprenticed boy (or any child who appeared in guardianship records) was also a liberated minor (or "ex-captive," to use the term that often appears in these early records). Régistre-Tutelle, 1849–57 (especially 31 December 1849 entry), M3, ANS; Enregistrement tutelle, 1858–74, M3, ANS.
17 Régistre-Tutelle, 9 March 1850 entry, M3, ANS.
18 Enregistrement tutelle, 1858–74, entries for no. 10—Yoro and no. 90—Abile, M3, ANS. First entrusted, in May 1863, to a Madame Lejuge, who found her to be a "*mauvais sujet*," Abile was then placed with Kati-Demba, followed by Mme. Vve Taillarder.
19 Régistre-Tutelle, 5, 22 June, 25 July 1849 entries, M3, ANS.
20 Laïta Fall's Certificat de liberté, 18 November 1901, 1F1, ANS; Procureur Général to Gouverneur Général, 26 December 1901, M13, ANS; Yandé Sène to Gouverneur Général, n.d. [1901], 13G76, ANS; Sénégal et Dépendances, *Conseil Général, session ordinaire de 1901* (Saint-Louis, Senegal: Imprimerie du Gouvernement, 1901), 345–54; Procès-verbal, Commissariat de Police, 13 May 1904, K23, ANS; Georges Deherme, "L'Esclavage en Afrique Occidental Française: Étude Historique, Critique et Positive," in *Slavery and Its Abolition in French West Africa: The Official Reports of G. Poulet, E. Roume, and G. Deherme*, ed. Paul E. Lovejoy and A. S. Kanya-Forstner (Madison: University of Wisconsin Press, 1994), 145; Martin Klein and Richard Roberts, "Gender and Emancipation in French West Africa," in *Gender and Slave Emancipation in the Atlantic World*, ed. Pamela Scully and Diana Paton (Durham, NC: Duke University Press, 2005), 167. Jessica Reuther explores the blurred lines between child enslavement and other forms of child dependency in Dahomey at around the same time. See Reuther, *The Bonds of Kinship in Dahomey*, chap. 5.
21 Ministre des Colonies to Gouverneur Général AOF, 31 October 1903, SEN/XIV/28bis, Archives Nationales Outre-Mer, Aix-en-Provence, France (hereafter

ANOM); Lieutenant Gouverneur du Sénégal to Gouverneur Général AOF, 22 November 1903, SEN/XIV/28bis, ANOM; Gouverneur Général AOF to Ministre des Colonies, 24 November 1903, SEN/XIV/28bis, ANOM; Arrêté, 24 November 1903, SEN/XIV/28bis, ANOM; Émile Roux, *Manuel à l'usage des administrateurs et du personnel des Affaires Indigènes de la colonie du Sénégal et des colonies relevant du Gouvernement Général de l'Afrique Occidentale Française* (Paris: Augustin Challamel, 1911), 234–35; Klein, *Slavery and Colonial Rule*, 131–33; Moitt, "Slavery and Guardianship in Postemancipation Senegal," 147–50; Moitt, *Child Slavery and Guardianship*, 139–46. The public orphanage, which opened in Sor (outside Saint-Louis) in December 1903, had been discussed for years as colonial and elected officials searched for a way to address "morally abandoned," orphaned, and unruly children. Although short-lived—it closed after less than three years—the timing of its opening reflected the state's increasing interest, in the context of secularization in France, in challenging the Catholic mission's efforts to reach the colony's children through orphanages, schools, and the recently closed penitentiary-school. See Arrêté, 22 November 1907, H177, ANS; Thioub, "La gestion de la marginalité juvénile," 125–28; and Foster, *Faith in Empire*, 54–56, 69–84.

22 Lieutenant Gouverneur du Sénégal to Gouverneur Général AOF, 4 May 1904, K23, ANS; Gouverneur Général AOF to Lieutenant Gouverneur du Sénégal, 8 June 1904, K23, ANS; Arrêté, 1 October 1904, K23, ANS; Thioub, "La gestion de la marginalité juvénile," 123–24; Moitt, "Slavery and Guardianship in Postemancipation Senegal," 150–52.

23 État des mineurs libérés confiés à des personnes de Saint-Louis, October 1904, H173, ANS; Président de la commission des mineurs affranchis to Secrétaire Général, 5 January 1907, H177, ANS; Administrateur Dolisie, commandant le cercle de Thiès, to Gouverneur, 12 February 1909, H178, ANS; Président du Tribunal to Lieutenant Gouverneur, 19 June 1909, H178, ANS; Président du Tribunal to Lieutenant Gouverneur, 18 September 1909, H178, ANS; Roux, *Manuel à l'usage*, 234.

24 Conklin, *A Mission to Civilize*, 73–106.

25 Dénombrement de la population européenne et indigène des Colonies de l'Afrique Occidentale Française, 1 September 1904, 22G20, ANS; Klein, *Slavery and Colonial Rule*, 23–29, 37–58, 79–83, 110, 119, 132; Klein and Roberts, "Gender and Emancipation in French West Africa," 165–66; Liberated Minors Database.

26 Arrêté creating conseils de tutelle, 13 April 1849, M3, ANS; Conseil de tutelle, president's speech, n.d. [May 1849], M3, ANS; Arrêté, 24 November 1903, SEN/XIV/28bis, ANOM; Gouverneur Général AOF to Procureur Général, 8 June 1904, K23, ANS; Liberated Minors Database. Officials continued to send most newly liberated minors to private individuals even after the 1903 reform, due to the insufficiency or lack of availability of institutional settings.

27 Liste des mineurs affranchis placés en apprentissage chez divers entrepreneurs et ouvriers de Saint-Louis, n.d. [1904], K23, ANS; Liste des enfants mineurs destinés à l'École Pinet-Laprade, n.d. [1904], K23, ANS; Lieutenant Gouverneur du Sénégal to Gouverneur Général AOF, 2 May 1904, K23, ANS; Président du Tribunal to Maire, Dakar, 16 October 1904, 1F1, ANS.

28 This was likely true in earlier periods too, but evidence is lacking.

29 Liberated Minors Database. The guardian's profession was not indicated for 510 liberated minors.

30 Liberated Minors Database. On liberated minors as domestics, see Faye, "Un aspect négligé," 80–85.
31 F. Bonnard to Secrétaire Général, 18 April 1905, 1F1, ANS; C. Gaure to Secrétaire Général, 31 January 1906, 1F1, ANS; Coumba Siguita to Secrétaire Général, Saint-Louis, 3 November 1909, H206, ANS.
32 Alexis Béziat to Secrétaire Général, Saint-Louis, 5 February 1906, 1F1, ANS; V. Peignet to Secrétaire Général, Dakar, 5 December 1907, H177, ANS.
33 Administrateur en chef P. Godel to Lieutenant Gouverneur, 6 July 1909, H206, ANS. Aïssatou was also called Aïda.
34 Tableau de recensement des mineurs de la commune de Rufisque, 15 March 1906, 1F1, ANS.
35 This fits into a larger pattern, widespread in colonial Africa, of European officials, entrepreneurs, and colonists employing African boys and men as domestic servants. Reflecting the racist notion that Africans were perpetual children, these employers tended to refer to all male servants as "boys," regardless of their actual age or social stage. See, for example, Marco Gardini, "Working as a 'Boy': Labour, Age, and Masculinities in Togo, *c.* 1975–2005," in Razy and Rodet, eds., *Children on the Move in Africa*, 104–22, and Karen Tranberg Hansen, *Distant Companions: Servants and Employers in Zambia, 1900–1985* (Ithaca, NY: Cornell University Press, 1989), 65–70.
36 Note from Chef du 1er Bureau to Secrétaire Général, 5 May 1905, 1F1, ANS; Veuve H. Bancal to Secrétaire Général, 20 March 1908, H174, ANS.
37 Pécarrère to Président du Tribunal de Saint-Louis, Dakar, 20 January 1906, H175, ANS.
38 On French concerns that formerly enslaved people would simply stop working, precipitating a collapse of the colonial economy, see Klein, *Slavery and Colonial Rule*, especially 178–85. On metropolitan policy, see Schafer, *Children in Moral Danger*.
39 Roux, *Manuel à l'usage*, 234. Rhetoric about the importance of mass schooling notwithstanding, the colonial administration never devoted sufficient funding or staffing to colonial schools in Senegal and would not have been able to make schooling available to all. On colonial education, see Duke Bryant, *Education as Politics*.
40 Commissaire de police to Secrétaire Général, 14 December 1905, H175, ANS. Physical and sexual abuse were not uncommon, and several others ran away from guardians following this sort of mistreatment. See, for example, Secrétaire Général to Commissaire de police, 5 September 1906, 1F1, ANS, and Commissaire de police to Secrétaire Général, 5 September 1906, 1F1, ANS.
41 Président de la commission des mineurs affranchis to Secrétaire Général, 23 October 1906, H175, ANS.
42 Liberated Minors Database. Since the circumstances leading to flight are normally impossible to discern from the inventories, analysis of context and possible motivation is based on qualitative evidence regarding a smaller number of cases. Furthermore, given that commissioners could not find over 450 children who entered guardianship in Saint-Louis, it is likely that many episodes of flight went unreported.
43 Summons for J.-J. Crespin/Balla Fall, 20 November 1906, H173, ANS; Illegible [Service des contributions directes] to Président, 21 November 1906, H173, ANS; Note from Chef du 1er Bureau to Secrétaire Général, 5 May 1905, 1F1, ANS. Returned to J.-J. Crespin by the secretary general, Balla Fall ran away again, ending up in a town along the rail line where he worked for a Monsieur Morilhon as a cook. See Illegible [Service des contributions directes] to Président, 21 November 1906, H173, ANS.

44 Certificate de Liberté for Niélé Diara, 2 August 1898, H175, ANS; Commissaire de police to Secrétaire Général, 25 October 1906, H175, ANS; Secrétaire Général to Commissaire de police, 27 October 1906, 1F1, ANS. This child's name was spelled Niélé Diaro in other documents.

45 Secrétaire Général to Commissaire de police, 5 September 1906, 1F1, ANS; Commissaire de police to Secrétaire Général, 4 February 1911, H178, ANS; Baca Sar to Secrétaire Général, 27 April 1906, 1F1, ANS; Commissaire de police to Secrétaire Général, 30 April 1906, 1F1, ANS; État de mineurs, Saint-Louis, 24 July 1907, H177, ANS. The guardian's name appears variously as Baca Sar, Baka Sar, Bakar Sar N'Diaye, and Baka Sar N'Diaye.

46 Kelly M. Duke Bryant, "Runaways, Dutiful Daughters, and Brides: Family Strategies of Formerly Enslaved Girls in Senegal, 1895–1911," *Women, Gender, and Families of Color* 7 (2019): 37–55. Jessica Reuther makes a similar point about girls in Dahomey. See Reuther, *The Bonds of Kinship in Dahomey*, chap. 4.

47 Secrétaire Général to Commissaire de police, 27 October 1906, H175, ANS; Commissaire de police to Secrétaire Général, 31 October 1906, H175, ANS; Président de la commission des mineurs to Chef de Bureau, 30 October 1907, H177, ANS.

48 See, for example, État de mineurs affranchis confiés à Saint-Louis, November 1905, H173, ANS; État de mineurs affranchis confiés à Saint-Louis, August 1906, H173, ANS.

49 État de mineurs affranchis confiés à Saint-Louis, April 1905, H173, ANS; Duke Bryant, "Runaways, Dutiful Daughters, and Brides," 41–44.

50 Cercle de Thiès, Mineurs affranchis, 15 March 1906, 1F1, ANS. For another example from outside the main towns, see Administrateur Saldé to Secrétaire Général, telegram, 1 April 1909, H178, ANS, and Klein, *Slavery and Colonial Rule*, 205–15. On labor as an economic strategy for children and families in a different African context, see Jack Lord, "Child Labor in the Gold Coast: The Economics of Work, Education, and the Family in Late-Colonial African childhoods, c. 1940–57," *Journal of the History of Childhood and Youth* 4, no. 1 (2011): 86–115.

51 Président de la commission to Secrétaire Général, 26 November 1906, H173, ANS; Secrétaire Général to Président du Tribunal chargé de la Commission, 17 December 1906, H173, ANS.

52 Edouard Duprat to Secrétaire Général, 12 November 1904, 1F1, ANS; Edouard d'Erneville to Président de la Commission chargée des mineurs affranchis, 24 January 1908, H174, ANS; Vve Paul Deproge to Secrétaire Général, 14 September 1909, H206, ANS.

53 James C. Scott, *Weapons of the Weak: Everyday Forms of Peasant Resistance* (New Haven, CT: Yale University Press, 1985).

54 Madame Le Franc to Secrétaire Général, 20 August 1906, 1F1, ANS; Henri Roumégaux to Secrétaire Général, 27 August 1906, 1F1, ANS; Commissaire de police to Secrétaire Général, 1 September 1906, 1F1, ANS; Secrétaire Général (by order of Chef du 1er Bureau) to Commissaire de police, 11 September 1906, and replies, 12 September 1906, 1F1, ANS; Secrétaire Général to Madame Directrice de l'ouvroir, September 1906, 1F1, ANS. Bernard Moitt interprets Cécilé's experiences a bit differently; see Moitt, *Child Slavery and Guardianship*, 117–18.

55 Procès-Verbal, Commission des mineurs affranchis, Tivaouane, 10 October 1908, H178, ANS; Administrateur J. Godel to Lieutenant Gouverneur, 22 July 1909, H206, ANS; Administrateur en chef Godel to Lieutenant Gouverneur, 21 October 1909, H206, ANS; Secrétaire Général to Administrateur Tivaouane, November 1909, H206, ANS.

56 They shared this preoccupation with employers of female domestics elsewhere in colonial and postcolonial Africa. See Hansen, *Distant Companions*, 84–139; Sacha Hepburn, "'Bringing a Girl from the Village': Gender, Child Migration, and Domestic Service in Post-Colonial Zambia," in Razy and Rodet, eds., *Children on the Move in Africa*, 69–84; and Waller, "Rebellious Youth in Colonial Africa," 83. For a study of colonial authorities' efforts to surveil white women who worked in commercial sex, see Caroline Séquin, *Desiring Whiteness: A Racial History of Prostitution in France and Colonial Senegal, 1848–1950* (Ithaca, NY: Cornell University Press, 2024).

57 Monsieur Fréau to Secrétaire Général, 27 September 1906, H175, ANS; Commissaire de police to Secrétaire Général, 25 October 1906, H175, ANS; Charles Pellegrin to Secrétaire Général, 3 January 1907, H175, ANS. Previous guardians had already returned both girls to the administration. I have found only one example of a guardian complaining about a male ward who did not sleep at home, but in contrast to complaints about girls, it contains no references to moral failings or inappropriate sex. See Note for Secrétaire Général, 22 July 1905, 1F1, ANS.

58 On enslaved women and girls and sexuality, see Klein and Roberts, "Gender and Emancipation in French West Africa," 165.

59 Lieutenant Gouverneur Sénégal to Gouverneur Général AOF, 4 May 1904, K23, ANS. I have not found evidence that African guardians complained about the sexual conduct of their wards.

60 Klein, *Slavery and Colonial Rule*, 246–48.

61 Secrétaire Général to Commissaire de Police and response, 5 September 1906, 1F1, ANS.

62 Liberated Minors Database. In addition, one guardian complained about a liberated minor boy spending nights outside the home, one male ward was reported as being a father, and three male wards married, suggesting a significant gender difference in the experiences of male and female liberated minors. All these statistics are likely well below actual numbers.

63 Liberated Minors Database; État de mineurs, 28 April 1905, H173, ANS; État de mineurs, 29 May 1905, H173, ANS. The same 1905 reports also indicated that three boys were either "happy" or "content," and a report from Dakar in November 1908 stated that two boys said they were "enchanted" with their circumstances. See Juge-Président, p.i., du Tribunal de Dakar to Secrétaire Général, 24 November 1908, H178, ANS.

Chapter 2

1 Commissaire de Police [Thiès], inquiry report, 15 February 1892, 3F26, ANS; Directeur de l'Intérieur to Commissaire Principal de Police, 28 February 1892, and Commissaire

Principal de Police to Directeur de l'Intérieur, 29 February 1892, 3F26, ANS; Directeur de l'Intérieur to M. Hovelt, 29 February 1892, and Inspecteur Hovelt to [Directeur de l'Intérieur], 1 March 1892, 3F26, ANS; Directeur du Pénitentiaire to Secrétaire Général, 13 January 1900, 3F26, ANS. Moussa also went by the names of Mamady and Pierre.

2 Secrétariat Général to Procureur Général, 13 February 1892, 3F26, ANS; Directeur de l'Intérieur to Procureur Général [demand]/Procureur Général to Directeur de l'Intérieur [response]/Directeur de l'Intérieur to Directeur de l'établissement pénitentiaire de Thiès [second response], 5 March 1892, 3F26, ANS; Directeur de l'École-Pénitentiaire de Thiès to Directeur de l'Intérieur, 8 March 1892, 3F26, ANS.

3 Prior to 1903, the head prosecutor ordered such transfers. In 1903, the governor general reassigned the guardianship program to the secretary general, who became responsible for transfers. Directeur de l'Intérieur to Procureur Général, 5 March 1892, 3F26, ANS; Procureur Général, Decision: Bakary, 1 March 1893, 3F26, ANS.

4 Directeur de l'Intérieur to Commissaire Principal de Police, 28 February 1892, 3F26, ANS.

5 Andrew Burton, "Urchins, Loafers and the Cult of the Cowboy: Urbanization and Delinquency in Dar Es Salaam, 1919–61," *Journal of African History* 42 (2001): 199–216; Waller, "Rebellious Youth in Colonial Africa," 83–88; Laurent Fourchard, "Lagos and the Invention of Juvenile Delinquency in Nigeria, 1920–1960," *Journal of African History* 47 (2006): 115–37; Simon Heap, "Processing Juvenile Delinquents at the Salvation Army's Boys' Industrial Home in Lagos, 1925–1944," in *Children and Childhood in Colonial Nigerian Histories*, ed. Saheed Aderinto (New York: Palgrave Macmillan, 2015), 49–76; George, *Making Modern Girls*.

6 Foster, *Faith in Empire*, 55–65; Thioub, "La gestion de la marginalité juvénile"; Thioub, "Juvenile Marginality"; Ousseynou Faye, "Assister ou punir l'enfant: Quelle expérience pour l'état colonial au Sénégal?" *Cahiers Histoire et Civilisations* 1 (2003): 17–29; Dior Konaté, *Prison Architecture and Punishment in Colonial Senegal* (Lanham, MD: Lexington, 2018), 204–10.

7 Procureur de la République to Chef du Service de l'Intérieur, 11 February 1877, 3F25, ANS; Thioub, "Juvenile Marginality," 80–82; Konaté, *Prison Architecture*, 56.

8 Thiès Journaux, 1886–1900, entries from 20 July, 6 September 1888, Senegal 3i2.17, Archives Générales de la Congrégation du Saint-Esprit, Chevilly-Larue, France (hereafter AGCSE); Thioub, "Juvenile Marginality," 82–84; Thioub, "La gestion de la marginalité juvénile," 125–28; Faye, "Assister ou punir," 20–21.

9 Arrêté of 13 August 1888 in Sénégal et Dépendances, *Conseil général, session ordinaire de 1893* (Saint-Louis, Sénégal: Imprimerie du Gouvernement, 1894), 526–27; Projet de traité entre la Colonie du Senegal et le Préfet Apostolique pour l'entretien des jeunes détenus et condamnés confiés a l'École pénitentiare de Thiès, 11 October 1888, 3F26, ANS.

10 Projet de contrat, 13/22 January 1894, 3F26, ANS.

11 Fishman, *The Battle for Children*, 16–21; Jean-Jacques Yvorel, "L'enfermement des mineurs de justice au XIXème siècle, d'après le compte général de la justice criminelle," *Revue d'histoire de l'enfance «irrégulière»* 7 (2005): 82.

12 Thiès Journaux, 1886–1900, entries from 15 January, 19 May 1896; 19 May 1898; 6 April 1901, Senegal 3i2.17, AGCSE.
13 Bérenger-Féraud, *Les peuplades de la Sénégambie*, 40, 54, 278–79, 354.
14 Thioub, "La gestion de la marginalité juvénile," 128; Foster, *Faith in Empire*, chap. 3. In December 1904, the state opened an orphanage for "morally abandoned" boys in Sor, outside Saint-Louis, and it is likely that courts sent some young offenders there for a time, but this option vanished with the closure of the orphanage in November 1907. Note from Secrétaire Général, 8 December 1904, H142, ANS; Arrêté, 22 November 1907, H177, ANS.
15 Lieutenant Gouverneur to Procureur de la République, 10 November 1911, 3F25, ANS; Lieutenant Gouverneur to Chef du Service de l'Agriculture, nd December 1911, 3F25, ANS; Gouvernement général de l'Afrique Occidentale Française, *L'Afrique Occidentale Française en 1913: Rapport d'ensemble annuel* (Laval: Imprimerie L. Barnéoud, 1913), 259–60.
16 Colonie du Sénégal, *Conseil Général, session ordinaire de Juin 1911* (Saint-Louis: Imprimerie du Gouvernement, 1911), 165; Service de l'Agriculture, Note to Secrétaire Général, 28 October 1911, 3F25, ANS; Arrêté créant un orphelinat agricole à Richard-Toll (no. 396), in *Journal Officiel du Sénégal*, 14 March 1912, 225; *Journal Officiel du Sénégal*, 16 May 1912, 372; *Journal Officiel du Sénégal*, 29 August 1912, 647; *Journal Officiel du Sénégal*, 12 September 1912; *Journal Officiel du Sénégal*, 19 September 1912, 699; *Journal Officiel du Sénégal*, 28 November 1912, 922; *Journal Officiel du Sénégal*, 12 December 1912, 951–92. Also in December 1912, a twelfth "pupil," an orphan, arrived at Richard-Toll.
17 *Bulletin de l'enseignement de l'Afrique Occidentale Française* 1, no. 2 (February 1913): 58; Fishman, *The Battle for Children*, 22–26; Sara L. Kimble, "'For the Family,' France, and Humanity': Authority and Maternity in the *Tribunaux pour Enfants*," *Proceedings of the Western Society for French History* 31 (2003): 212–29.
18 Thioub, "Juvenile Marginality," 86–87. Many thanks to Abigail Warchol for sharing sources she collected on Makhana.
19 If closure was impossible, he was willing to compromise by allowing young offenders to continue working at the station, provided that the colony assumed full responsibility for running the reformatory and supervising and disciplining detainees. Directeur de la Station Expérimentale de l'Arachide to Inspecteur Général de l'Agriculture, de l'Élevage et des Forêts, 8 July 1922, 3F27, ANS.
20 Lieutenant Gouverneur Soudan to Lieutenant Gouverneur Senegal, 15 December 1925, 3F27, ANS; Administrateur Baol to Gouverneur, telegram-letter, 2 February 1926, 3F27, ANS; Administrateur Supérieur Casamance (E. Némos) to Gouverneur, Senegal, 25 February 1938, H284, ANS.
21 Décision portant réglement de l'École Professionnelle Spéciale de Carabane, Lieutenant Gouverneur Sénégal, 20 September 1927, 6M273, ANS; Internement de trois mineurs au Pénitencier de Carabane, Decision by Lieutenant Gouverneur, 23 December 1927, 3F27, ANS; Gouvernement Général de l'Afrique Occidentale Française, *Budget de la Colonie du Sénégal, exercise 1930* (Saint-Louis, Senegal: Imprimerie du Gouvernement, 1929), 152–53, 164–65; Modifications à la Décision no. 2409 du 20

Septembre 1927, École Professionnelle Spéciale de Carabane, 24 September 1936, H284, ANS; Thioub, "Juvenile Marginality," 91; Morag-Zamonski, "Being a Child in French West Africa," 104–17.

22 Fishman, *The Battle for Children*, 35–40. Occasional linguistic slips in which officials referred to the Special Professional School as the "Carabane penitentiary" suggest that older approaches and values remained relevant. See, for example, document transmission page to directeur de l'enseignement, n.d. [1929], 6M273, ANS.

23 See, for example, Coutume des Ouolof musulmans (Cercle du Baol), par M. J. C. Fayet, administrateur-adjoint des Colonies, 1937, in *Coutumiers juridiques*, 169–70.

24 Modifications à la Décision no. 2409 du 20 Septembre 1927, École Professionnelle Spéciale de Carabane, 24 September 1936, H284, ANS. The 1927 metropolitan law did not go into effect in Senegal, but it informed discussion and ultimately reform proposals in 1937 and 1938. These were passed and implemented only in 1952.

25 One observer commented in 1931 that there were forty-seven young people in the main Dakar prison. Thioub interprets this to mean that all forty-seven were serving sentences there, but it seems more likely to me that at least some of them were awaiting trial and, if necessary, transfer to Carabane. F. Cazanove, "L'enfance criminelle indigène," *Bulletin de la Societé de pathologie exotique et de filiales de l'Ouest-Africain et de Madagascar* 25 (1932): 826; Thioub, "Juvenile Marginality," 91.

26 Minor Detainees Database. Note that this total includes two young people (Léonie Guèye and one Samba Tène) who served their time in adult prisons, Léonie because she was a girl, and Samba due to confusion about his age and status.

27 Minor Detainees Database. These data are more fully analyzed in chapter 4, on public spaces and legal frameworks, in light of what they tell us about the ways that colonial courts constructed childhood, imposed concepts of chronological age, and inserted the state into family relationships. I include them here to provide some insight into the detainee populations in the institutions.

28 Procureur de la République to Lieutenant Gouverneur, 27 October 1911, 3F25, ANS.

29 Konaté, *Prison Architecture*, 194–97; Ibra Sene, "Crime, Punishment, and Colonization: A History of the Prison of Saint-Louis and the Development of the Penitentiary System in Senegal, c. 1830–c. 1940" (PhD diss., Michigan State University, 2010), 151–53. In a compelling analysis of juvenile sentencing in France, Jean-Jacques Yvorel identifies similar trends, suggesting that even as courts became less likely under the Third Republic to send minors to institutions (preferring instead to remand them to their families), those who were sentenced tended to spend five or more years in a facility. Yvorel suggests that this trend reflected the belief that rehabilitative education required significant time to succeed. See Yvorel, "L'enfermement des mineurs," 77–109.

30 Procureur de la République to Gouverneur Sénégal, 29 July 1927, 3F27, ANS; Décision prononçant l'internement au pénitencier de Bambey du jeune Alioune Kamara, 2 September 1927, 3F27, ANS; Schafer, *Children in Moral Danger*, chap. 1; Fishman, *The Battle for Children*.

31 Thioub, "Juvenile Marginality," 86–91; Konaté, *Prison Architecture*, 205–8. Dior Konaté, Ibrahima Thioub, and others have suggested that the labor demanded of minor detainees as part of the rehabilitative process veered quickly into labor extraction and exploitation. Whether or not this was the case, my reading of the evidence suggests that in designing these reformatories, officials in Senegal followed late

nineteenth-century French thinking, which suggested that hard work, along with education and vocational training, would help bring about moral reform.
32 Sénégal et Dépendances, *Conseil Général, session ordinaire de 1899* (Saint-Louis, Senegal: Imprimerie du Gouvernement, 1899), 244–45.
33 The youngest defendants, those under the age of about nine, were typically returned to their families for supervision and reform.
34 Denise Savineau, Rapport no. 17: La Casamance, n.d. [1938], 17G/381/126, ANS, https://www.francophoneafricaarchive.org; Administrateur Supérieur Casamance (E. Némos) to Gouverneur Sénégal, 25 February 1938, H284, ANS.
35 Commission de surveillance, 12 December 1889, in Sénégal et Dépendances, *Conseil Général, session ordinaire de 1899*, 339; Mission de Thiès, *Rapport du Comité de Surveillance du Pénitencier du Thiès 1893 et autres documents importants* (Saint-Louis, Senegal: Imprimerie du Gouvernement, 1893), 9, Senegal 3i1.22a3, AGCSE; Sénégal et Dépendances, *Conseil Général, session ordinaire de 1893*, 517; Thiès Journaux, 1886–1900, entry from 1 May 1899, Senegal 3i2.17, AGCSE; Sénégal et Dépendances, *Conseil Général, session ordinaire de 1899*, 246; Administrateur Baol to Gouverneur Sénégal, telegram-letter, 2 February 1926, 3F27, ANS; Décision portant réglement de l'École Professionnelle Spéciale de Carabane, Lieutenant Gouverneur Sénégal, 20 September 1927, 6M273, ANS; École Professionnelle Spéciale de Casamance, Rapport annuel de 1933, 2G33/60, ANS; Administrateur Supérieur Casamance (E. Némos) to Gouverneur Sénégal, 25 February 1938, H284, ANS; Savineau, Rapport no. 17: La Casamance, 20. At least during the early Thiès period, detainees could also earn "sweets" by exhibiting good behavior; at the same time, however, the 1892 surveillance commission called attention to the lack of "disciplinary rules" at the institution, which, members believed, led to leniency. Records indicate that detainee rations included millet or rice, meat, salt, and oil in 1926 and a mix of millet, rice, beans, meat, fish, cooking oil, and salt starting in 1927.
36 Commission de surveillance, 12 December 1889, in Sénégal et Dépendances, *Conseil Général, session ordinaire de 1899*, 338; Mission de Thiès, *Rapport du Comité de Surveillance du Pénitencier du Thiès 1893*, 2, 8–9, 22; Thiès Journaux, 1886–1900, entries from 1 January, 25 August 1896, 19 May 1898, Senegal 3i2.17, AGCSE; Sénégal et Dépendances, *Conseil Général, session ordinaire de 1892* (Saint-Louis, Senegal: Imprimerie du Gouvernement, 1892), 414–19; Sénégal et Dépendances, *Conseil Général, session ordinaire de 1899*, 244, 246.
37 Gouvernement général de l'Afrique Occidentale Française, *L'Afrique Occidentale Française en 1913*, 260; Colonie du Sénégal, *Budget des pays de protectorat: Exercise 1914* (Saint-Louis, Senegal: Imprimerie du Gouvernement, 1914), 91, 96. The decision to call the facility an orphanage hints at officials' tendency to place minor detainees and orphans in the same category of children needing "protection."
38 Directeur de la Station Expérimentale de l'Arachide to Inspecteur Général de l'Agriculture, de l'Élevage et des Forêts, 8 July 1922, 3F27, ANS; Rapport succinct sur les travaux effectués pendant le mois de juin 1922, 1R83, ANS; Rapport succinct des travaux executés pendant le mois de juillet 1922, 1R83, ANS; Rapport sur les travaux executés pendant le mois de février 1923, 1R83, ANS; Rapport sur les travaux executés pendant le mois d'avril 1923, 1R83, ANS; Rapport sur les travaux executés pendant le mois de mai 1923, 1R83, ANS. At Bambey, detainees received small monetary rewards

each day in recognition of their work, though these payments were withheld when the "beneficiary does not show himself to be worthy," adding another disciplinary tool. Directeur de la Station Expérimentale de l'arachide to Inspecteur Général de l'Agriculture et des Forêts, 14 January 1922, 1R83, ANS.

39 École professionnelle Spéciale de Carabane, rapport annuel 1932, 2G32/84, ANS; École Professionnelle Spéciale de Casamance, Rapport annuel de 1933, 2G33/60, ANS; Administrateur Supérieur Casamance (E. Némos) to Gouverneur Sénégal, 25 February 1938, H284, ANS. In 1932, the director noted that moral lessons discussed the "principles of uprightness, integrity, honesty." As of 1938, eleven of twenty-four detainees had apprenticeships.

40 Instituteur Supérieur (for Chef du Service de l'enseignement primaire) to Lieutenant Gouverneur Senegal, 31 August 1936, H284, ANS; Secretariat General, 1er Bureau, to Chef du Service de l'enseignement primaire, 15 September 1936, H284, ANS; Administrateur Supérieur Casamance (E. Némos) to Gouverneur Sénégal, 25 February 1938, H284, ANS; Savineau, Rapport no. 17: La Casamance, 20–24.

41 In the late nineteenth and early twentieth centuries, officials consistently emphasized the importance of agricultural training in colonial schools, even those situated in urban areas, which were supposed to maintain school gardens.

42 Andrew Burton and Hélène Charton-Bigot, eds., *Generations Past: Youth in East African History* (Athens: Ohio University Press, 2010); Argenti and Durham, "Youth"; Stacey Hynd, "Pickpockets, Pilot Boys, and Prostitutes: The Construction of Juvenile Delinquency in the Gold Coast [Colonial Ghana], c. 1929–57," *Journal of West African History* 4, no. 2 (2018): 47–74. For commentary on the tendency of historians to replicate this gendered understanding of youth, see Duff, "Childhood and Youth in African History."

43 Commissaire de Police to Secrétaire Général, 10 July 1922, 3F64, ANS; Décision, n.d. [July 1922], 3F64, ANS; Lieutenant Gouverneur to Directeur du Pénitentiaire de Bambey, 1 August 1922, 3F64, ANS; Directeur de la Station Expérimentale de l'Arachide to Gouverneur du Sénégal, 5 August 1922, 3F64, ANS; Procureur de la République to Lieutenant Gouverneur Sénégal, 8 May 1924, 3F64, ANS; Didelot to Procureur de la République, 23 June 1924, 3F64, ANS.

44 Commission de surveillance, 12 December 1889, in Sénégal et Dépendances, *Conseil Général, session ordinaire de 1899*, 337.

45 Thiès Journaux, 1886–1900, entry from 15 March 1897, Senegal 3i2.17, AGCSE.

46 Directeur de la Station Expérimentale de l'Arachide to Inspecteur Général de l'Agriculture, de l'Élevage et des Forêts, 8 July 1922, 3F27, ANS.

47 Savineau, Rapport no. 17: La Casamance, 20–21.

48 Minor Detainees Database; Thioub, "Juvenile Marginality," 88; Konaté, *Prison Architecture*, 223–29.

49 Projet de traité entre la Colonie du Sénégal et le Préfet Apostolique pour l'entretien des jeunes détenus et condamnés confiés a l'École Pénitentiaire de Thiès, 11 October 1888, 3F26, ANS. Missionaries failed in their attempts to secure sufficient funds to build a wall around the site, making flight a real risk. Richard-Toll and Bambey, connected to agricultural stations, also lacked this security feature. Carabane was a remote island, making true escape more difficult and additional security measures less crucial.

50 Procureur Général to Directeur de l'Intérieur, 12 September 1892, 3F26, ANS; A. Sébire to Directeur de l'Intérieur, 14 December 1895, 3F26, ANS; Directeur du Pénitentiaire de Thiès to Secrétaire Général, 2 March 1901, 3F26, ANS; Thiès Journaux, 1886–1900, entries from 16 April 1893, 10 October 1894, Senegal 3i2.17, AGCSE.

51 Procureur Général to Directeur de l'Intérieur, 12 September 1892, 3F26, ANS; Thiès Journaux, 1886–1900, entry from 2 October 1895, Senegal 3i2.17, AGCSE; A. Sébire to Directeur de l'Intérieur, 14 December 1895, 3F26, ANS.

52 Directeur de Pénitentiaire to Directeur de l'Intérieur, 23 January 1896, 3F26, ANS. On flight to Gambia, see Pénitentiaire to Intérieur, telegram, 26 April 1894, 3F26, ANS.

53 The evidence discussed here is in tension with Denise Savineau's observation in 1938, based on conversations with several young people at Carabane, that detainees had lost touch with their parents and other family members. The responses she received may have reflected relatives' limited literacy or access to public letter-writers rather than their desire to maintain connection to their detained children. Savineau, Rapport no. 17: La Casamance, 22–23.

54 Procureur Général to Directeur de l'Intérieur, 12 September 1892, 3F26, ANS.

55 Directeur du Pénitentiaire de Thies to Secrétaire Général, 2 March 1901, 3F26, ANS; Directeur du Pénitentiaire to Secrétaire Général, 4 March 1901, 3F26, ANS; Directeur du Pénitentiaire de Thiès to Secrétaire Général, 1 April 1901, 3F26, ANS.

56 Chef du Service de l'Agriculture to Lieutenant Gouverneur, p.i., 17 July 1915, 1R118, ANS. The other example consisted of a brief mention in a 1932 report on Carabane, which noted that Ibrahima N'Daw had received "two punishments for attempted escapes" during the third quarter of the year. See École Professionnelle Spéciale de Carabane, rapport annuel 1932, 2G32/84, ANS.

57 Extrait des Minutes du Greffe du Tribunal de première instance de Saint-Louis (Sénégal), 28 October 1925, 3F27, ANS; Fara Diallo to Gouverneur Sénégal, 3F27, ANS; Internement à Bambey du nommé Fara Diallo dit François, 14 November 1925, 3F27, ANS. Court documents list his parents as "unknown."

58 Konaté, Prison Architecture, 176–82.

59 Extrait des contrôles de la prison civile de St. Louis for Léonie Guèye, 17 February 1925, 3F64, ANS; Jore to Administrateur Podor, telegram, 13 August 1927, 3F27, ANS; Administrateur Podor to Gouverneur, telegram-letter, 30 August 1927, 3F27, ANS; Décision portant réglement de l'École Professionnelle Spéciale de Carabane, Lieutenant Gouverneur Sénégal, 20 September 1927, 6M273, ANS.

60 Sénégal et Dépendances, Conseil Général, session ordinaire de 1899, 245; Administrateur Baol to Gouverneur Sénégal, telegram-letter, 17 September 1926, 3F27, ANS; Administrateur Baol to Gouverneur Sénégal, telegram-letter, 6 October 1926, 3F27, ANS.

61 Directeur de l'Intérieur to Gouverneur Général, 10 July 1897, 3F26, ANS; Directeur de l'Intérieur to Directeur du Pénitentiaire, Thiès, 10 September 1897, 3F26, ANS.

62 Gouvernement Général de l'Afrique Occidentale Française, *Budget de la Colonie du Sénégal, exercise 1930*, 152–53, 164–65; Gouvernement Général de l'Afrique Occidentale Française, *Budget de la Colonie du Sénégal, exercise 1931* (Saint-Louis, Senegal: Imprimerie du Gouvernement, 1930), 152–53, 164–65.

63 Konaté, *Prison Architecture*, 87.

64 I have located evidence of this practice from the 1910s through the 1930s so far. See, for example, *Journal Officiel du Sénégal*, 8 April 1915, 287, and *Journal Officiel du Sénégal*, 10 June 1937, 401.
65 Administrateur commandant le cercle de Dagana to Lieutenant Gouverneur Sénégal, 22 October 1915, 2G15/28, ANS.
66 Directeur de la Station Expérimentale de l'Arachide to M. l'Inspecteur Général de l'Agriculture de l'élevage et des Forêts, 8 July 1922, 3F27, ANS; Savineau, Rapport no. 17: La Casamance, 20.
67 Savineau, Rapport no. 17: La Casamance, 19–21. Konaté describes well-developed networks and significant social connections between inmates in colonial (adult) prisons and residents of the surrounding communities in Senegal. Konaté, *Prison Architecture*, 176–81.

Chapter 3

1 Directeur de la Médersa to Administrateur en Chef, chef du Bureau Politique, 24 April 1914, 1G53, ANS; Seydou N'Diaye to Directeur de la Médersa, 24 April 1914, 1G53, ANS; N'Diaye to Chef du Bureau Politique, 24 April 1914, 1G53, ANS; Lieutenant Gouverneur, draft decision, n.d., 1G53, ANS. For more on the médersas, see Samuel D. Anderson, *The French Médersa: Islamic Education and Empire in Northwest Africa* (Ithaca, NY: Cornell University Press, forthcoming).
2 I began to explore some of these questions in a 2014 article, which examines student misbehavior in the School for Sons of Chiefs and Interpreters through the lens of challenges to state authority. This chapter asks broader questions about the meaning of childhood, documentation, and state power. See Kelly Duke Bryant, "Clothing and Community: Children's Agency in Senegal's School for Sons of Chiefs and Interpreters, 1892–1910," *International Journal of African Historical Studies* 47, no. 2 (2014): 239–58.
3 Abdou Moumouni, *Education in Africa*, trans. Phyllis Nauts Ott (New York: Praeger, 1968); Papa Ibrahima Seck, *La stratégie culturelle de la France en Afrique: L'enseignement colonial (1817–1960)* (Paris: Éditions l'Harmattan, 1993); R. J. Zvobgo, *Colonialism and Education in Zimbabwe* (Harare, Zimbabwe: Sapes, 1994); Carol Summers, *Colonial Lessons: Africans' Education in Southern Rhodesia, 1918–1940* (Portsmouth, NH: Heinemann, 2002); Gail Paradise Kelly, "Learning to Be Marginal: Schooling in Interwar French West Africa," in *French Colonial Education: Essays on Vietnam and West Africa*, ed. David H. Kelly (New York: AMS Press, 2000), 189–208; Tony Chafer, "'Teaching Africans to Be French?' France's 'Civilising Mission' and the Establishment of a Public Education System in French West Africa, 1903–1930," *Africa* 56, no. 2 (2001): 190–209; Carol Summers, "Education and Literacy," in Parker and Reid, eds., *The Oxford Handbook of Modern African History*, 319–37; Gamble, *Contesting French West Africa*; Kelly Duke Bryant, "Colonial Education," in Shanguhyia and Falola, eds., *Palgrave Handbook of African Colonial and Postcolonial History*, 1:281–302; Duff, *Children and Youth in African History*, chap. 5.
4 Pierre Foncin, *Les écoles françaises du Sénégal et du Soudan* (Paris: Armand Colin, 1890), 3–8; Georges Deherme, *L'Afrique Occidentale Française: Action politique, action*

économique, action sociale (Paris: Librairie Bloud, 1908), 107–10; Duke Bryant, *Education as Politics*, 12–18.
5 Sadji, *Education africaine et civilisation*, 67–87; Denise Bouche, "L'enseignement dans les territoires français de l'Afrique Occidentale de 1817 à 1920" (PhD diss., Université de Paris I, 1974), 1:chaps. 1–3.
6 See, for example, M. Le Bègue de Germiny, speech in Gorée, 30 July 1895, J6, ANS.
7 Arrêté, 24 November 1903, 1G4, ANS; René Lemé, *L'Enseignement en Afrique Occidentale Française* (Corbeil, France: Imprimerie Typographique, 1906), 32–34, 38–44.
8 Roux, *Manuel à l'usage*, 513–17; Seck, *La stratégie culturelle de la France*, 75–77; Chafer, "'Teaching Africans to be French?'" 196–206.
9 W. Bryant Mumford, *Africans Learn to Be French: A Review of Educational Activities in the Seven Federated Colonies of French West Africa, Based upon a Tour of French West Africa and Algiers Undertaken in 1935* (1937; repr., New York: Negro Universities Press, 1970), 28–43; B. Olatunji Oloruntimehin, "Education for Colonial Dominance in French West Africa from 1900 to the Second World War," *Journal of the Historical Society of Nigeria* 7, no. 2 (1974): 353–55; Seck, *La stratégie culturelle de la France*, 80–92; Chafer, "'Teaching Africans to be French?'" 206–7; Harry Gamble, "Peasants of the Empire: Rural Schools and the Colonial Imaginary in 1930s French West Africa," *Cahiers d'études africaines* 49, no. 195 (2009): 780–86; Gamble, *Contesting French West Africa*, 68–69, 77–87; Kelly M. Duke Bryant, "Education and Politics in Colonial French West Africa," in *Oxford Research Encyclopedia of African History*, 31 March 2020, https://doi.org/10.1093/acrefore/9780190277734.013.679.
10 Gouverneur Général AOF to Ministre des Colonies, 30 March 1934, 2H13(26), ANS.
11 Gouverneur Général AOF to Ministre des Colonies, 30 March 1934, 2H13(26), ANS. The number of boys enrolled may have been 10,617—the digit in the hundreds place is not totally clear.
12 For an example of this perspective, see Georges Hardy, *Une conquête morale: l'enseignement en A.O.F.* (Paris: Librairie Armand Colin, 1917), 3. Hardy viewed schooling as the center of a new "moral conquest" in French West Africa that would lead to economic development and the "native's reasoned attachment to our endeavors."
13 Rapport Annuel pour 1912 sur le Service de l'Enseignement du Sénégal, 2G12/8, ANS. In 1912, the colony employed thirty-two European teachers (twelve men, twenty women), sixty-eight African teachers (all men), and fifteen African monitors (fourteen men, one woman). Monitors, who had received some training in pedagogy but who lacked more advanced teaching credentials, normally taught beginner classes or served as school aids, though they sometimes ended up with more responsibilities in rural schools.
14 Benjamin N. Lawrance, Emily Lynn Osborn, and Richard Roberts, "Introduction: African Intermediaries and the 'Bargain of Collaboration,'" in *Intermediaries, Interpreters, and Clerks: African Employees in the Making of Colonial Africa*, ed. Benjamin N. Lawrance, Emily Lynn Osborn, and Richard Roberts (Madison: University of Wisconsin Press, 2006), 3–34.
15 Roux, *Manuel à l'usage*, 522–3; Unknown to Chef du service de l'enseignement, 31 July 1909, 1G19, ANS.
16 Roux, *Manuel à l'usage*, 517–18.
17 Cours d'Enseignement Secondaire de Dakar, Assemblée des Professeurs, Réunion du 21 Novembre 1925, O224/31, ANS; Cours Secondaire de Dakar, Procès-verbal

de la réunion des professeurs, la séance du 29 Avril 1932, O224/31, ANS. In true French style, this course, and many other schools in Senegal, did not hold lessons on Thursday afternoons.
18 To analyze these trends, I compiled data from 137 school inspection reports on schools in several administrative districts (Podor, Tambacounda, Louga, Thiès, Sine-Saloum, Ziguinchor, and the Rufisque commune) produced from 1931 to 1938. All of the reports used are found in file O527/31, ANS.
19 H. d'Erneville to Chef du bureau de l'Intérieur, 13 September, 7 October 1865, 1G1, ANS.
20 Negative comments in the same set of grade reports described students as "careless," lacking seriousness, or "fickle," among other things. École secondaire spéciale de Saint-Louis, État nominative de tous les jeunes gens admis à l'École depuis sa foundation et qui sont sortis de ladite École, 30 October 1889, J6, ANS.
21 Certificat de scolarité for Fara Diaw, École de Garçons de Rufisque, June 1904, 1G28, ANS. See also Director of École des Garçons de Rufisque to M. le Chef du Service de l'Enseignement, 15 June 1906, 1G28, ANS; Certificat de scolarité for Magathe Niang, École de Mouit, 31 January 1907, J61, ANS; and Certificat de scolarité for Magathe Niang, Louga administrator, 21 February 1907, J61, ANS.
22 Amadou Sylla to Monsieur le Délégué du Gouvernement du Sénégal à Dakar, and margin note, 23 September 1920, 1G53, ANS; Certificat de scolarité for Mamadou Sylla, École de garçons de Dakar, 3 October 1920, 1G53, ANS; Délégué du Gouvernement du Sénégal in Dakar to Lieutenant Gouverneur Sénégal, 5 October 1920, 1G53, ANS.
23 Bulletin d'Inspection, École Régionale de Kaolack—M. Ly Mamadou Hadramé, 19 January 1933, O440/31, ANS; Rapport d'inspection sur l'école régionale de Kaolack—cercle du Sine-Saloum—Visitée le 31 janvier 1935—M. TOURE Tamsir, O440/31, ANS.
24 École de Rufisque, Inspecteur des Écoles Chaigneau, 17 December 1934, O527/31, ANS.
25 Directeur Domenge, Rapport sur le cours complémentaire, année scolaire 1907–8, J28, ANS.
26 Rapport sur le fonctionnement de l'École en 1911–1912, J54, ANS.
27 Gouvernement Général de l'Afrique Occidentale Française, *Bulletin d'Information et de Renseignements*, 18 January 1937. Although the author of this short article seemed to want to move past this particular stereotype, he still advanced the notion that "the Black" had certain deficits along with certain positive attributes, all of them linked to a particular racial character.
28 Statistique Scolaire de l'école de filles de Dakar, 1906, J28, ANS; Statistique scolaire de l'école de filles de Saint Louis, 30 June 1911, J32, ANS.
29 Visite d'inspection du 30 June 1933, École Regionale de Kaolack—Mme. Cros, O440/31, ANS.
30 See, for example, École Normale de Saint-Louis, Bulletins trimestriels de notes for 3rd trimester of 1903–4, for Samba Laobé Diop, Hamidou Kane, M'Baba N'Gaye, Abdoulaye Yoro, Racine Elimane Kane, Alioune Sylla, Alioune Fall, Ely Semba, Coumba N'Doffène, and Lati Diop, J59, ANS.
31 Statistique scolaire de l'école de Garçons de Dakar (Rue de Thiong), 1914–15, J28, ANS.

32 Speeches for distribution des prix, n.d., J49, ANS.
33 Boubakar Diop to Inspecteur des Écoles Indigènes, 16 June 1893, J5, ANS; Massouba Diack to Inspecteur des Écoles Indigènes, 6 August 1893, J5, ANS; Instituteur U. Diarlé to Inspecteur des Écoles des Pays de Protectorat, 13 July 1895, J5, ANS. The official newspaper was known first as the *Moniteur du Sénégal et Dépendances* and later as the *Journal Officiel du Sénégal et Dépendances* or the *Journal Officiel du Sénégal*.
34 Letter [from Portes?] to Director, 28 July 1892, J7, ANS; Directeur Calvayrac to Chef du Service de l'Enseignement, 12 May 1905, 1G3, ANS; Instituteur chargé de la 2me classe, Louis Levistre, to Directeur de l'École de la rue de Lanneau, 30 May 1906, 1G3, ANS.
35 Gouverneur Général to Lieutenant Gouverneur Sénégal, 11 December 1912, J55, ANS.
36 Proviseur Morel, Rapport du Proviseur sur la fonctionnement du Lycée Faidherbe pendant l'année scolaire 1920–1921, 1G84, ANS. Indeed, the proviseur seemed especially keen to make the point that indecent gestures were fairly common in all sorts of schools, were not the same as "actions," and thus one should not "distort or exaggerate them."
37 Lycée Faidherbe, Rapport du Proviseur sur la situation au 12 Avril 1922, 1G84, ANS; Proviseur du Lycée Faidherbe to Lieutenant Gouverneur, 29 November 1922, 1G84, ANS.
38 Copie du Procès-verbal de l'Assemblée des professeurs, séance du 29 Janvier 1930, O224/31, ANS; Cours Secondaire de Dakar, Procès-verbal de la réunion du Conseil de discipline du 6 février 1932, O224/31, ANS. For another example, this time from the Lycée Faidherbe, of a school's disciplinary process showing extra leniency for a non-Black student, see Proviseur de Lycée Faidherbe, Situation au 1er Janvier 1927, 1G84, ANS. In this 1927 report, the school's headmaster noted that he had met with the father of young Beccaria five or six times already that year over the boy's misconduct, which had included mistreating young girls at the school and punching a fellow student in the eye. As in the example of Alfred Jaouiche, this report considered the possibility that Beccaria suffered from a mental issue of some kind. Ultimately, the father withdrew his son from the school and arranged to send him to the École de la Marine in Dakar.
39 Serigne Fall Seck, Mémoire de Vacances: Formation Morale de l'Enfant, 1949, XV-Se-12, CP, IFAN.
40 Moctar Bâ, Mémoire de fin d'études: Le Savoir vivre chez l'enfant, 1949, XV-Se-560, CP, IFAN; Souleyman Wane, Mémoire de vacances, n.d., XV-Se-13, CP, IFAN.
41 Conseil des Professeurs de l'École Normale de Saint-Louis, Séance du 22 Juin 1904, O732, ANS.
42 On navigating such "tensions" in colonial contexts, see Ann Laura Stoler and Frederick Cooper, "Between Metropole and Colony: Rethinking a Research Agenda," in *Tensions of Empire: Colonial Cultures in a Bourgeois World*, ed. Ann Laura Stoler and Frederick Cooper (Berkeley: University of California Press, 1997), 6–10.
43 Ibrahima N'Diaye to Directeur de l'Enseignement, 28 December 1903, 1G3, ANS.
44 Chef de Service de l'Enseignement to Garrigues/Response from Garrigues/Marginalia from Chef de Service de l'Enseignement, 28 December 1903, 1G3, ANS.
45 Rapport de fin d'année scolaire sur la 1ère classe de l'École de Garçons de Dakar dirigée par Monsieur Niénat, Dakar, 10 July 1907, J28, ANS; Note et réponse aux observations de M. Niénat sur ma direction, 14 July 1907, J28, ANS.

46 Domenge, Rapport sur le cours complémentaire, année scolaire 1907–8, J28, ANS; Georges Hardy (Inspecteur) to Gouverneur Général, 17 January 1914, 1G9, ANS.
47 Statistique scolaire de l'École de Garçons de Dakar (Rue de Thiong), 1908, J28, ANS; Rapport sur la 3e classe, École de la Rue de Thiong, 30 June 1908, J28, ANS. Domenge accused Abdoulaye M'Bengue of having no "authority" over his class.
48 Statistique Scolaire de l'École de Garçons de Saint-Louis (École Brière de l'Isle), 1911, J32, ANS.
49 Inspecteur de l'Enseignement musulman chargé, p.i., du Service de l'Enseignement to Gouverneur Général, 27 July [sic, should be June] 1907, J50, ANS.
50 Statistique scolaire de l'école de filles de Dakar, Deuxième classe, 6 July 1907, J28, ANS. This teacher wondered if the school could provide dresses that would be left onsite, to avoid this kind of problem in the future.
51 Director of École Laique to Chef de l'Enseignement, 2 March 1904, 1G3, ANS.
52 Mamoudou Djigo to Chef du Bureau Politique, 20 May 1914, 1G53, ANS; Directeur de la Médersa to Administrateur Chef/Chef du Bureau Politique, 20 May 1914, 1G53, ANS; Decision by Lieutenant Gouverneur Antonetti, 27 May 1914, 1G53, ANS.
53 Louis C. D. Joos, "General Trends in French-Speaking West Africa," in *The Educated African: A Country-by-Country Survey of Educational Development in Africa*, ed. Helen Kitchen (New York: Praeger, 1962), 442.

Chapter 4

1 The relevant police reports for Kaolack are all found in dossier 1F135 at ANS, and they form the basis for a dataset I created to analyze patterns of crime and policing (hereafter 1F135 dataset). I have examined police reports for many jurisdictions in the 1920s and 1930s, but none is as detailed as these. For this reason, I did not collect comprehensive arrest and ticketing data from other places (Saint-Louis, Dakar, Rufisque, Louga, Diourbel, Tivaouane, or Ziguinchor) but chose to focus more selectively on the police reports that mentioned minors, either as victims or as alleged perpetrators. I can therefore draw conclusions about overall crime patterns only for Kaolack, but I can make some comparisons to other towns for which I have more information. And for all jurisdictions, I have traced minors' encounters with the police and am confident in my conclusions about them.
2 1F135 dataset.
3 Datasets derived from 1F135, 1F138, 1F154, ANS.
4 Roger Villamur, *Les Attributions judiciaires des administrateurs et chefs de poste en service à la côte d'Afrique* (Paris: A. Pedone, 1902), 14–19; Gregory Mann, "What Was the Indigénat? The 'Empire of Law' in French West Africa," *Journal of African History* 50, no. 3 (2009): 331–53; Francis G. Snyder, "Colonialism and Legal Form: The Creation of 'Customary Law' in Senegal," *Journal of Legal Pluralism and Unofficial Law* 13, no. 19 (1981): 49–90; Richard Roberts, *Litigants and Households: African Disputes and Colonial Courts in the French Soudan, 1895–1912* (Portsmouth, NH: Heinemann, 2005), chaps. 2–3. African leaders could exercise a judicial function only over civil issues and minor criminal offenses involving African parties or defendants.
5 Recall that *originaires* were Africans who were born in Saint-Louis, Gorée, Rufisque, or Dakar, or who were born in any location to *originaire* parents. Granted certain French

citizenship rights, *originaires* also retained Muslim personal status. Dominique Sarr and Richard Roberts, "The Jurisdiction of Muslim Tribunals in Colonial Senegal, 1857–1932," in *Law in Colonial Africa*, ed. Kristin Mann and Richard Roberts (Portsmouth, NH: Heinemann, 1991), 131–45; Rebecca Shereikis, "From Law to Custom: The Shifting Legal Status of Muslim Originaires in Kayes and Medine, 1903–13," *Journal of African History* 42 (2001): 261–83; Mamadou Diouf, "The French Colonial Policy of Assimilation and the Civility of the Originaires of the Four Communes (Senegal): A Nineteenth Century Globalization Project," *Development and Change* 29 (1998): 671–96.

6 This difference also had an impact on civil society and political participation, since *originaires* could vote not only for local councils and mayors but also for a representative to the French National Assembly.

7 The 1924 Decree on Native Justice held that a young person who was or *who appeared to be* under age sixteen could be found to lack criminal capacity. Superseding any customary practice that treated younger children as adults in criminal proceedings, the 1924 decree reflected the principle, embedded in the civilizing mission, that customary law should be changed when morally repugnant to the French. But in practice, age was malleable, making these requirements anything but straightforward in their implementation, as I explore later on.

8 Art. 66, Penal Code of 1810, France, transcribed by Tom Holmburg, The Napoleon Series Archive, https://www.napoleon-series.org; "Décret du 22 mars 1924 réorganisant la Justice indigène en Afrique Occidentale Français," in *Journal Officiel de la République Française, Lois et Décrets*, no. 93, 3 April 1924, https://www.legifrance.gouv.fr. A 1931 reform decreased to age eighteen the threshold for adulthood for colonial subjects in French West Africa. As they negotiated and drafted child-protection policies in the late 1930s, officials revisited the issue of the ages of penal and criminal majority that had been applied differently to "subjects," *originaires, métis,* and Europeans. Chapter 6 explores this debate over age in the courtroom in some detail.

9 Decree on Sanitation and Public Order in Nianing, 1889, 1F150, ANS.

10 Kalala Ngalamulume, *Colonial Pathologies, Environment, and Western Medicine in Saint-Louis-du-Senegal, 1867–1920* (New York: Peter Lang, 2012), 175–76. An April 1904 *arrêté*, enacted by the governor general for all of French West Africa, required the governor general, lieutenant governors, and local administrators or mayors to enact and ensure enforcement of public health measures. This *arrêté* focused in particular on the need to improve sanitation, control disease vectors like mosquitoes, protect the water supply, and make new buildings safer, but it was light on details, leaving these to the lieutenant governors and local officials. See "Décret relatif à la protection de la Santé publique en Afrique Occidentale Française (Off. du 17 avril 1904)," *Recueil Général de Jurisprudence de Doctrine et de Législation Coloniales: La Tribune, Colonies et des Protectorats* 14, no. 3 (1904): 181–85.

11 Décret sur le Vagabondage du 29 Mars 1923, 6M273, ANS; "Décret du 29 mars 1923 Portant répression du vagabondage en Afrique Occidentale," *Recueil de législation, de doctrine et de jurisprudence coloniales* 26, no. 2 (April–June 1923): 313–14; Smith, "Assistance and Repression."

12 Police de St Louis, Rapport trimestriel, 3me trimestre 1909, Commissaire de Police, n.d. [October 1909], 10D4/10, ANS.

13 Datasets derived from 1F135, 1F138, 1F154, ANS.

14 These changes followed a similar shift in thinking about unruly children and problematic youth in France, prompted by new research on adolescence (and the emergence of this concept); growing international concern for children's well-being, evidenced by the establishment of child welfare organizations like Save the Children (1919); and other trends. See Fishman, *The Battle for Children*, 31, and Baughan, *Saving the Children*.
15 Ngalamulume, *Colonial Pathologies*, 105–15, 175–81.
16 Procès-verbal de contravention, Commissariat de Police, Saint-Louis, no. 732, 1F154, ANS; Procès-Verbal contre Ousmane Kayeré, no. 819, 2 August 1924, 1F154, ANS; Procès-Verbal contre Aïssa N'Diaye, no. 1026, 15 October 1924, 1F154, ANS.
17 Dataset derived from 1F154, ANS. This data comes from a set of documents found in a subfolder within 1F154, ANS, labeled "Saint-Louis, Procès-verbaux de contravention, Juillet à Novembre 1924, Juin 1925."
18 Procès-Verbal contre Maymouna Sy, no. 1026, 15 October 1924, 1F154, ANS.
19 Procès-Verbal contre Fama Niang, no. 493, 1F154, ANS.
20 For another example of resistance, from a fifty-eight-year-old woman, see Procès-Verbal contre la nommée Tioro Diagne, no. 541, 18 June 1925, 1F154, ANS.
21 This resulted as much from a lack of state capacity as it did from a dearth of public cooperation among Africans, especially those who were "subjects" in the colony and/or who lived in remote areas without ready access to representatives of the government.
22 See, for example, Procès-verbal de contravention, Commissariat de Police, Saint-Louis, no. 707, 1F154, ANS, and Procès-Verbal contre la nommée Tioro Diagne, no. 541, 18 June 1925, 1F154, ANS.
23 For a study of the politics surrounding trash collection and urban sanitation in late twentieth-century Senegal that highlights the roles of youth, see Rosalind Fredericks, *Garbage Citizenship: Vital Infrastructures of Labor in Dakar, Senegal* (Durham, NC: Duke University Press, 2018).
24 Mamadou Ndiaye, *L'Enseignement Arabo-Islamique au Sénégal* (Istanbul: Centre de Recherches sur l'Histoire, l'Art et la Culture Islamiques, 1985), 76–79; Duke Bryant, *Education as Politics*, 56–60.
25 As Rudolph T. Ware III demonstrates, many of the child-rights-/child-exploitation-oriented colonial critiques of Qur'an schooling were taken up by French-educated and France-oriented African elites and, since independence, by international human rights organizations. Ware, "Njàngaan: The Daily Regime of Qur'ânic Students in Twentieth-Century Senegal," *International Journal of African Historical Studies* 37, no. 3 (2004): 518–21, 537–38; Ware, *The Walking Qur'an: Islamic Education, Embodied Knowledge, and History in West Africa* (Chapel Hill: University of North Carolina Press, 2014), 39–48.
26 Ware, "Njàngaan," 523–24; Ware, *Walking Qur'an*, 1–9.
27 Zanettacci to Gouverneur, Sénégal, 11 May 1911, 1G47, ANS; Lieutenant Gouverneur to Gouverneur Général, 6 June 1911, 1G42, ANS; Gouverneur Général AOF to Lieutenant Gouverneur Sénégal, 9 July 1911, 1G42, ANS. Similar language of victimization can be found in other correspondence from the early twentieth century, including Jean Peuvergne to Gouverneur Général AOF, June 1910, 1G47, ANS. Na'ama Morag-Zamonski also describes French distaste for the child-begging associated with Qur'an schools. See Morag-Zamonski, "Being a Child in French West Africa," 62–65.

28 Commissaire de Police, Rapport à Monsieur le Lieutenant Gouverneur du Sénégal, 23 April 1909, 10D4/10, ANS.
29 Police de St Louis, Rapport trimestriel, 3me trimestre 1909, n.d. [October 1909], 10D4/10, ANS.
30 As Miranda Sachs explores, the French state's attempts to address child-begging in France at the turn of the twentieth century similarly portrayed them as both threats and victims. Officials deployed similar language in Senegal, and the emphasis on "protection" increased significantly during the 1930s. See Sachs, "'A Sad and ... Odious Industry.'"
31 On girl hawkers in colonial Lagos, see George, *Making Modern Girls*. Gouverneur Général AOF to Lieutenant Gouverneurs des Colonies du Groupe et M. l'Administrateur de la Circonscription de Dakar, 4 November 1936, H282, ANS; Lieutenant Gouverneur, p.i., du Sénégal to M. l'Administrateur Supérieur de la Casamance et M. les Administrateurs, Commandant les Cercles du Sénégal, 23 November 1936, H282, ANS. Cercles were territorial and administrative units, the smallest ones to be overseen by French officials. Cercles brought together even smaller units, called cantons, which were led by Africans appointed as canton chiefs, and which included multiple villages. See Jean Suret-Canale, *French Colonialism in Tropical Africa, 1900–1945*, trans. Till Gottheiner (New York: Pica Press, 1971), chap. 3.
32 Administrateur Cercle Kolda to Administrateur Supérieur Casamance, telegram-letter, 14 December 1936, H282, ANS; Administrateur Cercle Matam to Gouverneur Sénégal, telegram-letter, 11 December 1936, H282, ANS; Administrateur Commandant le Cercle de Ziguinchor to Lieutenant Gouverneur Sénégal, s/c M. l'Administrateur Supérieur de la Casamance, 4 February 1937, H282, ANS; Commandant Cercle de Thiès to Lieutenant Gouverneur Sénégal, telegram-letter, 8 January 1937, H282, ANS; Administrateur des Colonies, André, Commandant le Cercle de Tambacounda, to Gouverneur Sénégal, 15 December 1936, H282, ANS; Administrateur Commandant le Cercle de Louga to M. Gouverneur Sénégal, 17 December 1936, H282, ANS; Commandant de Cercle de la Haute Gambie to M. Gouverneur, 15 December 1936, H282, ANS; Commandant Cercle Bignona to Lieutenant Gouverneur, s/c M. l'Administrateur Supérieur de la Casamance, 11 December 1936, H282. Some administrators, including the commandants of Tambacounda and Kédougou, attributed the purported lack of child beggars to the tradition of "hospitality" and care for children among their local populations.
33 Administrateur Commandant le cercle du Bas-Sénégal to Gouverneur Sénégal, 8 January 1937, H282, ANS; Administrateur en Chef des Colonies Commandant le Cercle du Sine-Saloum to Gouverneur Sénégal, 9 January 1937, H282, ANS.
34 Administrateur Commandant le cercle du Bas-Sénégal to Gouverneur Sénégal, 8 January 1937, H282, ANS.
35 Na'ama Morag-Zamonski makes a similar point. See Morag-Zamonski, "Being a Child in French West Africa," 65–70.
36 Ware, *Walking Qur'an*, 46–48.
37 Ware analyzed many of these William Ponty notebooks, and my reading of them supports his argument about the longstanding importance of alms-seeking and hardship in Islamic education. I build on this point by exploring alms-seeking as such a central component of Muslim African childhood that the practice continued despite French efforts to turn *talibés* into victims in need of their intervention. Ware, *Walking Qur'an*, 10–12.

38 Serigne Fall Seck, Mémoire de Vacances: Formation Morale de l'Enfant, 1949, XV-Se-12, CP, IFAN; Baba Ndiaye, L'Islam au Sénégal: L'École Coranique, VII-Se-259, CP, IFAN; Almamy, Mémoire.

39 Over the ensuing decades, this critique would grow into much more widespread concern about Qur'an schools among many French-educated Senegalese people and child-rights advocates in Senegal and abroad. Ware, "Njàngaan"; Ware, *Walking Qur'an*, 212–27.

40 Duke Bryant, *Education as Politics*, 56–60.

41 Administrateur Circonscription Dakar to Gouverneur Général, AOF, 28 February 19__, 21G21/17, ANS; Claire S. Griffiths, "Colonial Subjects: Race and Gender in French West Africa: An Annotated Translation and Presentation of Denise Savineau's Report on Women and the Family in French West Africa, 1938," *International Journal of Sociology and Social Policy* 26, nos. 11–12 (2006): 486, 549.

42 Paul Ocobock, "Vagrancy and Homelessness in Global and Historical Perspective," in *Cast Out: Vagrancy and Homelessness in Global and Historical Perspective*, ed. A. L. Beier and Paul Ocobock (Athens: Ohio University Press, 2008), 1–2, 20–24; Andrew Burton and Paul Ocobock, "The 'Travelling Native': Vagrancy and Colonial Control in British East Africa," in Burton and Ocobock, eds., *Cast Out*, 270–301.

43 Chef du Service de l'Enseignement to Lieutenant Gouverneur, 21 January 1907, 1F150, ANS.

44 The colony's first juvenile reformatory, the Thiès penitentiary-school, had closed in 1903, leaving the colony without an institution to rehabilitate minors.

45 Thioub, "La gestion de la marginalité juvénile"; Thioub, "Juvenile Marginality."

46 "Décret du 29 mars 1923," 313–14. While the governor general correctly identified vagabondage as a new (colonial) phenomenon, his attempt to explain why it had become a problem missed the mark. This official blamed the mobility that had become possible thanks to the "peace and security" French rule had achieved, rather than the fact that colonialism made illegal a practice that Africans had long engaged in prior to colonial rule, effectively restricting their freedom of mobility.

47 Administrateur Thiès to Lieutenant Gouverneur Sénégal, telegram-letter, 29 September 1923, 3F27, ANS; Lieutenant Gouverneur, p.i., to Administrateur Thiès, 11 October 1923, 3F27, ANS; Copie du Jugement rendu par le Tribunal de Cercle de Thiès, 13 October 1923, 3F27, ANS.

48 Tribunal premier degré, Dakar, 6 August 1936, case no. 278, 6M279, ANS; Tribunal premier degré, Dakar, 13 August 1936, case no. 289, 6M279, ANS; Tribunal premier degré, Dakar, 27 August 1936, case no. 303, 6M279, ANS; Décision: Internement d'un Mineur à Carabane, 31 December 1936, 6M279, ANS.

49 Thioub, "La gestion de la marginalité juvénile"; Thioub, "Juvenile Marginality."

50 African children, of course, attended school, but their school day often included manual or agricultural labor, and they often worked outside of school hours.

51 *Journal Officiel de la République française*, 29 June 1938, 2H13, ANS; Ministre des Colonies and gardes des sceaux, Ministre de la Justice to Président, Réorganisation de la justice indigène à Madagascar, 13 April 1939, 2H13, ANS; *Journal Officiel de la République française*, 18 April 1939, 4968, Documentation AP-1, Tribunaux pour enfants, assistance vagabondage à Madagascar, 2H13, ANS. In France, a 1938 ordinance protected poor orphans, morally abandoned children, foundlings, and other so-called

assisted children from prosecution for vagabondage; instead, these children were to be provided for by the state and sent to a shelter. Authorities in Madagascar followed a similar approach.
52 Étude préliminaire sur l'organisation d'un centre de rééducation des enfants se livrant à la mendicité (aveugles et non aveugles), n.d. [1937], H282, ANS; Lieutenant Gouverneur Sénégal to Administrateur Circonscription Dakar et Dépendances, 10 March 1937, H282, ANS; Administrateur Circonscription de Dakar et Dépendances to Lieutenant Gouverneur Sénégal, 26 March 1937, H282, ANS.
53 Correspondence from 1945 shows that the state remained concerned about child vagabonds and *talibés* in the city and had attempted to return them to their villages of origin with little success. Directeur Général des Affaires Politiques, Administratives, et Sociales, Note pour M. le Gouverneur Général s/c de M. le Gouverneur Secrétaire Général [confidential], 2 June 1945, 2H13, ANS.
54 Kane, "Coutume civile et pénale toucouleur," 104–9.
55 On the history of prisons in Africa, see Konaté, *Prison Architecture*, and Bernault, ed., *A History of Prison and Confinement in Africa*.
56 Senegal, Rapports d'Ensemble, 1913, 2G13/7, ANS.
57 Rapport sur le fonctionnement de le Justice Indigène en 1936, 2G36/122, ANS.
58 Datasets for 1F135 and 1F138, ANS. Some minors allegedly committed multiple offenses. In the total number of "minors," I included all arrested individuals with (estimated) ages of nineteen or younger, plus two individuals described as "young" (*jeune*), a term French records usually, but not always, used for minors. The data are drawn from police records for Kaolack (1934, 1935, 1938), Thiès (1934, 1935), Louga (1934, 1935, 1936), and Tivaouane (1936).
59 Copie du Jugement rendu par le Tribunal de Subdivision de Tivaouane, 12 July 1923, 3F27, ANS.
60 Copie du Jugement rendu par le Tribunal de Subdivision de Tivaouane, 12 July 1923, 3F27, ANS. The age of majority fluctuated during this period, and it is unclear if it was eighteen or twenty years old in 1923.
61 Tribunal de Premier degré de Kébémer, decision no. 51, 8 August 1927, 3F27, ANS.
62 Tribunal de Premier degré de Kébémer, decision no. 51, 8 August 1927, 3F27, ANS.
63 Administrateur Supérieur Casamance to Lieutenant Gouverneur Sénégal, 9 June 1929, 2M281, ANS.
64 Administrateur Supérieur Casamance (E. Némos) to Gouverneur Sénégal, 25 February 1938, H284, ANS.
65 Projet de Décret tendant à modifier les articles 66, 67, 68, et 69 du Code Pénal et rétablissant l'article 340 du Code d'Instruction Criminelle en Afrique Occidentale Française, n.d., 2H13(26), ANS; [Draft] Décret instituant des juridictions spéciales et le régime de la liberté surveillée pour les enfants et adolescents justiciables des Tribunaux français en Afrique Occidentale Française, 2H13(26), ANS; Lieutenant Gouverneur Sénégal to Procureur Général, Chef du Service Judiciaire de l'Afrique Occidentale Française, 20 August 1938, H284, ANS; "Décret du 30 novembre 1928, complété par celui no. 52–662 du 3 juin 1952," *Recueil Jurisprudence AOF* 2 (October–December 1952): 66–76.

Chapter 5

1. Draft report, "La Protection de l'Enfance en AOF," n.d. [March 1934], 2H13(26), ANS.
2. On these tensions in another context, see Faye, "Assister ou punir."
3. Service Local de la Colonie, *Le Sénégal: Organisation politique, administration, finances, travaux publics* (Paris: Augustin Challamel, 1900), 132–34; Marcel Olivier, *Le Sénégal: Notices publiées par le Gouvernement Général à l'occasion de l'Exposition Coloniale de Marseille* (Paris: Émile Larose, 1907), 201–7; Gustave Reynaud, *Hygiène des établissements coloniaux* (Paris: Librairie J.-B. Baillière et Fils, 1903), 171–72; Georges François, *Notices publiées par le Gouvernement Général à l'occasion de l'Exposition Coloniale de Marseille: L'Afrique Occidentale Française* (Paris: Emile Larose, 1907), 170–72; L. Rigollet, *Evolution de l'Assistance médicale en Afrique Occidentale Française* (Paris: Agence Économique de l'Afrique Occidentale Française, 1922), 19–20; Griffiths, "Colonial Subjects," 550–52; Conklin, *A Mission to Civilize*, 48–50, 68–70, 220–22; Ngalamulume, *Colonial Pathologies*, 36–8, 61, 122; Kalala Ngalamulume, "Smallpox and Social Control in Colonial Saint-Louis-du-Sénégal, 1850–1916," in *HIV/AIDS, Illness, and African Well-Being*, ed. Toyin Falola and Matthew M. Heaton (Rochester, NY: University of Rochester Press, 2007), 72–73; Mor Ndao, "Colonisation et politique de santé maternelle et infantile au Sénégal (1905–1960)," *French Colonial History* 9 (2008): 194–95.
4. Alfred Bollet and Alfred Jay, *Plagues and Poxes: The Impact of Human History on Epidemic Disease* (New York: Springer, 2004), 75–81; Stefan Riedel, "Edward Jenner and the History of Smallpox and Vaccination," *Baylor University Medical Center Proceedings* 18, no. 1 (2005): 21–25; Alphonse Houillon, "Variole et vaccine en Afrique Occidentale Française pour l'année 1903," *Annales d'hygiène et de médecine coloniales* 8, no. 4 (1905): 546, 549; Ngalamulume, "Smallpox and Social Control," 65. The target of a coordinated global health campaign led by the World Health Organization from the mid-twentieth century, smallpox was declared eradicated in 1980, but during the period under study in this book, it remained a significant health threat that occupied the colonial administration in French West Africa.
5. In Sahelian West Africa, evidence suggests that people preferred to introduce smallpox matter into an incision in the recipient's arm. William H. Schneider, "The Long History of Smallpox Eradication: Lessons for Global Health in Africa," in *Global Health in Africa: Historical Perspectives on Disease Control*, ed. Tamara Giles-Vernick and James L. A. Webb Jr. (Athens: Ohio University Press, 2013), 34–36; Eugenia W. Herbert, "Smallpox Inoculation in Africa," *Journal of African History* 16, no. 4 (1975): 543–44. For an excellent analysis of Yoruba understandings of smallpox in nineteenth- and early twentieth-century Nigeria, see Oluwatoyin Babatunde Oduntan, "Culture and Colonial Medicine: Smallpox in Abeokuta, Western Nigeria," *Social History of Medicine* 30, no. 1 (2016): 48–70.
6. Houillon, "Variole et vaccine," 550–52; Dr. Henry Girard, "Variole et Vaccine au Sénégal," in *Rapport Général présenté à M. le Ministre de l'intérieur par l'Académie de Médecine sur les vaccinations et revaccinations pratiquées en France et dans les colonies françaises pendant l'année 1888* (Melun, France: Imprimerie Administrative, 1890), 62–65; "Mémoire de M. le Dr. Carpot, médecin du service local à Saint-Louis (Sénégal):

La variole au Sénégal," in *Rapport Général présenté à M. le Ministre de l'intérieur sur les vaccinations et revaccinations pratiquées en France et dans les colonies pendant l'année 1898* (Melun, France: Imprimerie Administrative, 1899), 46; William H. Schneider, "Smallpox in Africa during Colonial Rule," *Medical History* 53, no. 2 (2009): 198–200; Ngalamulume, "Smallpox and Social Control," 63–64, 73–74; Herbert, "Smallpox Inoculation in Africa," 542. The view that marabouts endangered public health by promoting a supernatural understanding of disease shaped French policies and plans in the twentieth century as well. French concerns were not limited to marabouts and smallpox but encompassed all traditional healers and health issues. Indeed, the concern about supernatural approaches to health and healing was one reason schools emphasized hygiene and rudimentary natural science instruction through most of the colonial period. See, for example, Hardy, *Une conquête morale*, 219–20, and Myron Echenberg, *Black Death, White Medicine: Bubonic Plague and the Politics of Public Health in Colonial Senegal, 1914–1945* (Portsmouth, NH: Heinemann, 2002), 24–26.

7 Commisssaire de police to Directeur de l'Intérieur, __ January 1889 [received 16 January 1889], H44, ANS; Doctor Duval, médecin du service local, to Director, 1 March 1889, H44, ANS; Administrateur Cayor to Gouverneur Général, telegram, 20 January 1898, H48, ANS.

8 Médecin en Chef Doué to Directeur de l'Intérieur, 23 March 1888, H39, ANS; Médecin en Chef to Directeur de l'Intérieur, 24 March 1888, H39, ANS; Commissaire de police to Directeur de l'Intérieur, 24 March 1888, H39, ANS; Médecin en Chef to Directeur de l'Intérieur, 18 April 1888, H39, ANS.

9 Rapport à Monsieur le Directeur de l'Intérieur à Saint-Louis, 17 January 1895, H39, ANS.

10 Administrateur Cayor to Gouverneur Général, telegram, 20 January 1898, H48, ANS. See also Administrateur Cercle Dakar-Thiès to Directeur des Affaires Indigènes, 12 March 1897, H48, ANS, and Extrait du rapport du Resident de Yang Yang du mois de Février 1903, H12, ANS.

11 Commissaire de Police to Directeur de l'Intérieur, 25 June 1888, H39, ANS.

12 Administrateur Cayor to Gouverneur Général, telegram, 20 January 1898, H48, ANS; Echenberg, *Black Death, White Medicine*, chaps. 4–5.

13 Mohamed Mâle, Mémoire de Fin d'Etudes Normales: L'Enfant dans le milieu familial, 1949, XV-Se-9, CP, IFAN. Barbara Cooper describes a similar reluctance to count children in Niger, and the cultural taboo persists in certain situations in contemporary Senegal. See Cooper, *Countless Blessings*, 113–22.

14 Avis, Service Sanitaire, n.d. [January or February 1889], H44, ANS; Rapport en conseil d'administration pour la séance du 28 février 1870, Directeur de l'Intérieur to Gouverneur, 26 February 1870, H39, ANS; Ngalamulume, "Smallpox and Social Control," 64–65.

15 Draft letter to Médecin en Chef, 24 May 1870, H39, ANS. This state of affairs also reflects the fact that the climate and other conditions often rendered the vaccine ineffective.

16 Médecin en chef de la marine to Ordonnateur, 14 May 1877, H39, ANS.

17 Commissaire de Police adjoint to Directeur de l'Intérieur and response, 3 March 1895, H39, ANS; Direction des Affaires Indigènes du Sénégal, draft letter, n.d. [1897 or 1898], H48, ANS; Note, 6 March 1897, H48, ANS; Directeur des Affaires Indigènes

to Gouverneur Général, 23 March 1897, H48, ANS; Médecin en Chef, Chef du Service de Santé to Directeur des Affaires Indigènes, 4 February 1898, H48, ANS.

18 Lydia Murdoch, "Carrying the Pox: The Use of Children and Ideals of Childhood in Early British and Imperial Campaigns against Smallpox," *Journal of Social History* 48, no. 3 (2015): 511–35. Murdoch argues that child vaccine producers in the British Empire "helped mark—and extend—the medical as well as the political and economic boundaries of empire" (527), thanks to their role in imperial medicine. She also suggests that the reliance on certain categories of children—poor British children, orphans, colonial subjects—showed that despite emerging universalist conceptions of childhood, the emotion-laden, domestic ideal of childhood did not extend to everyone.

19 Médecin en Chef to Directeur de l'Intérieur, 22 February 1871, H39, ANS; Commissaire de Police, Note pour M le Chef du 2e bureau de la Direction de l'Intérieur, 23 May 1870, H39, ANS.

20 Médecin en chef de la Marine Doué to Gouverneur Sénégal, 28 May 1888, H39, ANS. In contrast, the doctor posted to Podor wrote in 1877 that during an epidemic, numerous African parents asked him to vaccinate their children. See Médecin du poste de Podor to Médecin en Chef, 4 May 1877, H39, ANS.

21 Houillon, "Variole et vaccine," 549; Dr. Judet de la Combe, "L'épidémie de variole 1895–96—La variolization," in *Rapport Général présenté à M. le Ministre de l'intérieur par l'Académie de Médecine sur les vaccinations et revaccinations pratiquées en France et dans les colonies en 1896* (Melun, France: Imprimerie Administrative, 1897), 79–81; Dr. Porquier, "La variole au Sénégal," in *Rapport Général présenté à M. le Ministre de l'intérieur par l'Académie de Médecine sur les vaccinations et revaccinations pratiquées en France et dans les colonies pendant l'année 1897* (Melun, France: Imprimerie Administrative, 1898), 77–78.

22 Porquier, "La variole," 78.

23 Médecin en chef de la Marine Doué (Pierre-Adolphe) to Gouverneur Sénégal, 16 February 1888, H39, ANS; Dr. Rigollet, "Historique sommaire de la variole et de la vaccine au Sénégal," in *Rapport Général présenté à M. le Ministre de l'intérieur par l'Académie de Médecine sur les vaccinations et revaccinations pratiquées en France et dans les colonies en 1893* (Melun, France: Imprimerie Administrative, 1895), 94–95; Houillon, "Variole et vaccine," 559–60.

24 Rigollet, *Evolution de l'Assistance médicale*, 95; Houillon, "Variole et vaccine," 557–68; Olivier, *Le Sénégal*, 203. Much of colonial Africa followed a similar trend toward local production of vaccine matter. See Schneider, "Smallpox in Africa," 205, 209–12.

25 Roux, *Manuel à l'usage*, 492–93.

26 Service de Santé, rapport annuel sur l'assistance médicale indigène année 1913, 10 April 1914, 2G13/7, ANS; Lucien Camus, *Rapport Général présenté à M. le Ministre du Travail, de l'Hygiène, de l'Assistance, et de la Prévoyance Sociales par l'Académie de Médecine sur les Vaccinations et Revaccinations pratiquées en France, et aux colonies pendant les années 1924–1925* (Paris: Masson, 1926), 56–57; Lucien Camus, *Rapport Général présenté à M. le Ministre du Travail, de l'Hygiène, de l'Assistance, et de la Prévoyance Sociales par l'Académie de Médecine sur les Vaccinations et Revaccinations pratiquées en France, en Algérie et dans les Pays de Protectorat pendant l'année 1927 et aux colonies pendant l'année 1926* (Paris: Masson, 1928), 61–62; M. Lereboullet, *Rapport*

Général présenté à M. le Ministre de la Santé publique par l'Académie de Médecine sur les vaccinations et revaccinations pratiquées en France, en Algérie, et dans les pays de protectorat pendant l'année 1937 et aux colonies pendant l'année 1936 (Paris: Masson, 1938), 152–53, 161. In 1936, officials were able to check the effectiveness of only 9,606 first-time vaccines and found that 54.2 percent of them had been successful; of the 1,818 revaccinations they checked, only 24.5 percent had succeeded.

27 These percentages are in line with William Schneider's analysis of statistics related to colonial smallpox vaccination campaigns across Africa, which leads him to claim that these campaigns were the most wide-reaching and impactful public health interventions in colonial Africa. He also suggests that they used most of the same techniques and tools deployed by the World Health Organization in the 1960s and 1970s in its ultimately successful effort to eradicate smallpox. See Schneider, "The Long History of Smallpox Eradication," 34–36, and Schneider, "Smallpox in Africa," 201–3.

28 Service de Santé, rapport annuel sur l'assistance médicale indigène année 1913, 10 April 1914, 2G13/7, ANS.

29 Administrateur Circonscription Dakar to Gouverneur Général AOF, 28 February ___, 21G21/17, ANS. To be clear, this document does not specify that the hygiene service administered smallpox vaccines—it just says the children were vaccinated. However, given that there were ongoing annual efforts to vaccinate thousands of people against smallpox, I think it is likely that this is what they were doing. Yellow fever and tuberculosis vaccines were also available by this time, however.

30 Gouvernement Général de l'Afrique Occidentale Française, *Bulletin hebdomadaire d'information et de renseignements*, 1 January 1935, 12.

31 David Arnold, "Introduction: Disease, Medicine, and Empire," in *Imperial Medicine and Indigenous Societies*, ed. David Arnold (Manchester, UK: Manchester University Press, 1988), 1–26; Vaughan, *Curing Their Ills*; David Arnold, *Colonizing the Body: State Medicine and Epidemic Disease in Nineteenth-Century India* (Berkeley: University of California Press, 1993); Pratik Chakrabarti, *Medicine and Empire, 1600–1960* (New York: Palgrave Macmillan, 2013).

32 Hardy, *Une conquête morale*, 220–21.

33 In 1937, Denise Savineau observed that in places where Africans responded positively to French schools, "the acceptance of a local clinic" would not be far behind. Griffiths, "Colonial Subjects," 549.

34 The visits stopped after a few months, and the school director requested that they continue due to his concerns about student hygiene. R. J. Portes to Directeur des Affaires Politiques, Rapport sur le fonctionnement du Collège des fils de chefs et des interprètes, 26 May 1892, J7, ANS; Portes to Directeur des Affaires Politiques, 20 January 1893, J7, ANS.

35 Roux, *Manuel à l'usage*, 492–93, 520; Draft of arrêté portant règlement intérieur des écoles publiques urbaines de l'AOF, n.d. [1904], 1G18, ANS; Echenberg, *Black Death, White Medicine*, 32, 103. Those sick with smallpox also suffered the "destruction of their books and notebooks." Other illnesses prompted the removal of the sick person for specific lengths of time—forty days for scarlet fever and sixteen days for measles—and tuberculosis and leprosy cases were never allowed back at school. Smallpox was the only disease with a vaccination requirement at the time, and thus it generated the largest paper trail and most significant contact with the state.

36 François, *Notices publiées par le Gouvernement Général*, 171–72; Colonie du Sénégal, Service municipal d'hygiène de St Louis et du 1er arrondissement, Rapport annuel 1907, 7 March 1908, H32, ANS; Médecin chargé des services local et sanitaire du Gouvernement du Senegal à Dakar et des Services municipaux d'Hygiène du 2me Arrondissement to Chef du Service de Santé, rapport annuel de 1907 sur le fonctionnement des services municipaux d'hygiène du deuxième arrondissement, H32, ANS.

37 Decision by Administrateur en Chef, 21 January 1908, J51, ANS; Decision by Joost van Vollenhoven, 31 March 1908, J51, ANS; Chef du Service de Santé to Gouverneur, 8 January 1908, J51, ANS; Chef du Service de l'Enseignement to Gouverneur/response, 10 May 1906, H6, ANS; Draft note to Monsieur le Chef du Service de Santé, n.d. [May 1906], H6, ANS.

38 Marie Léonie Duhaumont, Directrice de l'école, to Administrateur, chargé du transit, 14 November 1904, 1G18, ANS; Beaufond, chargé du transit, to Secrétaire Général, 14 November 1904, 1G18, ANS; Marie Léonie Duhaumont, Directrice to Directeur de l'Enseignement primaire du Sénégal, 16 November 1904, 1G18, ANS.

39 Rapport de fin d'année scolaire sur la 1ère classe de l'École de Garçons de Dakar dirigée par Monsieur Niénat, 10 July 1907, J28, ANS.

40 Hardy, *Une conquête morale*, 217–21.

41 Public Advisory re: scholarship competition on 13 June 1874, 1G26, ANS; Arrêté no. 1487, 1907, 1G26, ANS.

42 Suzanne Loppy to Directeur de l'Enseignement au Sénégal, 21 June 1904, 1G28, ANS; Service de L'Enseignement, Demandes ou Réclamations, n.d. [1905], 1G28, ANS.

43 Certificate for Ibrahima [François] Niang, 11 July 1905, 1G28, ANS; Medical certificate for Ibrahima Niang, 8 July 1905, 1G28, ANS; Bagnick Niang to Directeur de l'Enseignement, 11 July 1905, 1G28, ANS; Certificate for Amadou Guèye from Director of Dakar boys' school, 11 July 1905, 1G28, ANS; Medical certificate for Amadou Guèye, 11, 16 July 1905, 1G28, ANS; M'Diombasse N'Diaye to Directeur de l'enseignement, 11 July 1905, 1G28, ANS; Certificate for Jean Diop from Director of Dakar boys' school, 11 July 1905, 1G28, ANS; Medical certificate for John Diop, 11 July 1905, 1G28, ANS; Alexandre Diop to Directeur de l'Enseignement, 11 July 1905, 1G28, ANS. Ibrahima Niang was not successful in obtaining a scholarship, despite protests about unfairness from his father. I am unsure about the outcomes of the other two requests. Bagnick Niang to M. Guy, Gouverneur Général [*sic*, Guy was lieutenant governor], 24 October 1906, 1G28, ANS.

44 Louis Vallier to Administrator, 17 July 1911, 1G32, ANS; Medical certificate for Madjighen N'Daw, 24 July 1911, 1G32, ANS. For additional discussion of this family, see Duke Bryant, "French Fathers and Their 'Indigenous Children.'"

45 "La Protection de l'Enfance en AOF," n.d. [likely March 1934], 2H13(26), ANS.

46 Compte rendu de la conférence faite à l'école normale de St Louis le 19 février 1906 par Monsieur Mairol, inspecteur de l'enseignement en AOF, O372, ANS. The director of the Normal School gave similar weight to hygiene instruction in his annual report for the 1907–8 year. See Rapport sur la situation de l'école normale pendant l'année scolaire 1907–1908, Directeur A. Morel, 7 February 1909, J52, ANS.

47 Rapport d'Inspection sur l'École préparatoire de Diakhao, visitée le 5 février 1935, Inspecteur des Écoles, chef du service de l'Enseignement primaire, O527(31), ANS.

48 Bulletin d'Inspection, École rurale de N'Dioum, Visite d'inspection du 11 Mars 1938, Chef du service de l'enseignement primaire, O527(31), ANS. On vaccinations, see also Bulletin d'Inspection, École préparatoire de Coki, Cercle de Louga, Visite d'Inspection du 20 Avril 1933, O527(31), ANS, and Bulletin d'Inspection, Visite de l'école rurale de Nioro-Rip, 30 March 1936, O527 (31), ANS.

49 On health interventions within colonial schools—and African responses—elsewhere in Africa, see Chau Johnsen Kelly, "Cattle Dip and Shark Liver Oil in a Technochemical Colonial State: The Poisoning at Malangali School, Tanganyika, 1934," *Journal of African History* 57, no. 3 (2016): 437–63, and Corrie Decker, *Mobilizing Zanzibari Women: The Struggle for Respectability and Self-Reliance in Colonial East Africa* (New York: Palgrave Macmillan, 2014), 57–61.

50 Gouverneur Général AOF to Ministre des Colonies, 30 March 1934, 2H13(26), ANS. Documents like these became important not only as records of past illnesses, vaccinations, and medical encounters but also as an early form of identification that could affect mobility. In the context of the plague outbreaks of the 1910s, Kalala Ngalamulume writes, the ability of Africans and "foreign minorities" to move about freely hinged on whether they could present a "health passport or medical certificate." This built on earlier procedures that required ship passengers to obtain sanitary passports as part of the effort to stop the spread of cholera and yellow fever. Ngalamulume, *Colonial Pathologies*, 131, 184–89. See also Echenberg, *Black Death, White Medicine*, 169.

51 Draft report, "La Protection de l'Enfance en AOF," n.d. [March 1934], 2H13(26), ANS.

52 See, for example, Bulletin d'Inspection, École régionale de Podor, Visite d'Inspection du 8 Fevrier 1933, O527(31), ANS; Rapport d'Inspection sur l'école élémentaire de N'Dioum, visitée le 28 Fevrier 1934, O527(31), ANS; Rapport de l'Inspection sur l'École préparatoire de N'Dande, visitée le 18 décembre 1934, O527(31), ANS; Bulletin d'Inspection, Visite de l'École préparatoire de N'Gohe, Cercle du Sine-Saloum, Circonscription Scolaire de Kaolack, le 1 Avril 1936, O527(31), ANS; Rapport d'Inspection sur l'École Régionale de Podor, cercle de Podor, visitée le 26 février 1935, O527(31), ANS; Rapport d'Inspection, École Régionale de Kaolack, Inspection des 18 et 19 Janvier 1933, Inspecteur de l'Enseignement Primaire, O440(31), ANS; and Rapport d'Inspection sur l'École Regionale de Kaolack, visitée les 30 & 31 janvier et le 2 Février 1935, O440(31), ANS.

53 Bulletin d'Inspection, École Régionale de Podor, Visite d'Inspection des 6, 7, et 8 Février 1933, O527(31), ANS.

54 Ndao, "Colonisation et politique," 191–211.

55 Rapport sur la protection de l'enfance malheureuse et déficiente en Afrique Occidentale Française, 4, 13 April 1940, 2H13(26), ANS.

Chapter 6

1 Colonie du Sénégal, *Conseil Général, session ordinaire de Juin 1911*, 158–59. Galandou Diouf would go on to serve as Senegal's representative in the French National Assembly from 1934 until his death in 1941.

2 Colonie du Sénégal, *Conseil Général, session ordinaire d'Octobre 1912* (Saint-Louis, Senegal: Imprimerie du Gouvernement, 1912), 184.
3 Field and Syrett, "Introduction: Chronological Age," 378.
4 On identity documentation, see, for example, Dalberto and Banégas, eds., *Identification and Citizenship in Africa*; Breckenridge and Szreter, eds., *Registration and Recognition*; and Caplan and Torpey, eds., *Documenting Individual Identity*.
5 For explorations of similar dynamics in East Africa, see Decker, "A Feminist Methodology of Age-Grading and History in Africa"; Decker, *The Age of Sex*, especially chap. 4; and Walters, "'Child! Now You Are.'"
6 Régistre-Tutelle, 10 July 1849 entry (for example), M3, ANS; emphasis added.
7 Marriage and childbirth were considered signs of majority and could trump age in determining whether a liberated minor should be emancipated. But because of significant shortcomings in the state's efforts to keep track of these minors, officials often did not know about such life events and therefore could not determine that guardianship had ended.
8 État des mineurs confiés à la tutelle de l'Administration de 1895 à 1904, February 1907, H174, ANS; Circular to all cercle administrators from Lieutenant Gouverneur, 27 October 1908, H174, ANS.
9 For example, Procès-Verbal contre Abdoulaye Diallo, no. 856, 19 August 1924, 1F154, ANS.
10 Recall that *originaires* were those Africans who had been born in Saint-Louis, Dakar, Rufisque, or Gorée, colonial towns administered as communes, as well as those who were descended from *originaires*. For a translation of article 66, see Tom Holberg, trans., "France: Penal Code of 1810," The Napoleon Series Archive. At least since the 1903 ordinance that organized the justice system across the new French West Africa federation, colonial law had distinguished between *originaires*—who could access French courts and French law—on the one hand, and subjects—justiciable in "native" or customary courts—on the other, though judges and officials regularly questioned this distinction and a short-lived 1912 decree gave Native Tribunals jurisdiction over all Africans. See Sarr and Roberts, "The Jurisdiction of Muslim Tribunals in Colonial Senegal"; Conklin, *A Mission to Civilize*, 86–92; and Shereikis, "From Law to Custom." Article 67 of the penal code allowed courts to determine that minors under sixteen had committed certain serious crimes *"avec discernement,"* meaning that they understood the criminal implications of their conduct. These minors were to be punished, but they received lighter sentences than adults found guilty of the same crimes, in recognition of their young age.
11 Article 54, Décret du 22 mars 1924 réorganisant la Justice indigène en Afrique Occidentale Française, *Journal Officiel de la République Française, Lois et Décrets* 93 (3 April 1924): 3179–80.
12 Gouverneur Général AOF to Ministre des Colonies, 11 July 1937, 2H13(26), ANS.
13 The proposed reform also would have shielded children under thirteen from internment, created a separate set of rules and procedures governing juvenile justice, and implemented a variety of other changes reflecting metropolitan reforms and increased concern with child welfare. Projet de Décret tendant à modifier les articles 66, 67, 68 et 69 du Code Pénal et rétablissant l'article 340 du Code d'Instruction Criminelle en Afrique Occidentale Française, n.d., 2H13(26), ANS; [Draft] Décret instituant des

juridictions spéciales et le régime de la liberté surveillée pour les enfants et adolescents justiciables des Tribunaux français en Afrique Occidentale Française, n.d. [1937?], 2H13(26), ANS.
14 Administrateur Supérieur Casamance (E. Némos) to Gouverneur Sénégal, 25 February 1938, H284, ANS.
15 Circulaire 267, Procureur Général to M. les Procureurs de la Republique de: Dakar-Saint-Louis-Kaolack-Conakry-Grand-Bassam-Lomé-Cotonou-Bamako, 23 September 1938, H284, ANS.
16 Directeur to Inspecteur, 25 November 1905, 1G3, ANS.
17 Rapport au Directeur sur le fonctionnement de l'École Secondaire pendant l'année scolaire 1911–12, 1G71, ANS; Sénégal, Rapport d'ensemble (enseignement), 1917, 2G17/18, ANS.
18 Institutrice adjointe E. Degrave to Chef du Service de l'Enseignement, 19 March 1906, 1G3, ANS; E. Mutterer, Commis des Affaires Indigènes au Gouvernement Général, to Directeur de l'Enseignement, 20 March 1906, 1G3, ANS; E. Degrave to Chef du Service de l'Enseignement, 24 March 1906, 1G3, ANS.
19 See, for example, Administrateur du Cercle (Podor) to Gouverneur Sénégal, 20 August 1909, J32, ANS.
20 Sénégal et Dépendances, *Conseil Général, session ordinaire de 1893*, 380–83, 399; Directeur Principal des Frères to Directeur de l'Intérieur, 20 April 1895, 13G39, ANS; V. Duval, directeur de l'école laïque, Rapport sur la situation de l'École laïque, 8 May 1895, 13G39, ANS; Directeur de l'Intérieur, L. Mouttet, to Gouverneur Sénégal, 10 May 1895, 13G39, ANS.
21 A decree issued in 1874 indicated that primary schools were for children ages five through sixteen, but I have not found references to this being enforced. To the contrary, numerous lists of enrolled students from the 1880s and 1890s indicate that primary schools frequently included students over age sixteen. Sixteen had been the upper limit at urban schools at least since 1904. See Drafts of Règlement pour les écoles urbaines, 1904, 1G18, ANS.
22 Sénégal, Rapports d'Ensemble, 1912, Rapport Annuel Pour 1912 sur le Service de l'Enseignement du Senegal, 2G12/8, ANS; *Bulletin de l'enseignement de l'Afrique Occidentale Française* 1, no. 4 (April 1913): 119–25; *Bulletin de l'enseignement de l'Afrique Occidentale Française* 1, no. 7 (July 1913): 233–34.
23 Gouverneur Général AOF to Ministre des Colonies, 25 June 1935, 2H13(26), ANS. The report indicates that there were 59,837 pupils, 51,309 of them boys, attending 453 primary schools. Senegal had the longest history of education and the most well-developed network of schools and therefore would have had the largest portion of these students.
24 Secrétaire Général for Lieutenant Gouverneur Sénégal to Gouverneur Général AOF, 1 January 1940, 2H13(26), ANS.
25 Pierre Cantrelle, "L'état civil en Afrique Occidentale: Un long malentendu," in *AOF: Réalités et héritages: Sociétés ouest-africaines et ordre colonial, 1895–1960* (Dakar: Direction des Archives du Sénégal, 1997), 2:981–83.
26 Even in 1955, magistrate André P. Robert complained that since civil records remained "embryonic" in French West Africa, courts still had to rely on defendants' "physical attributes" to determine whether they should be tried as minors under age sixteen.

Robert, *L'Évolution des coutumes de l'ouest Africain et la legislation française* (Paris: Librairie Autonome, 1955), 100–101.
27. See, for example, liberty certificates for Diénaba (24 September 1888) or for Awa Diara (30 September 1901), 1F1, ANS.
28. Lieutenant Gouverneur, Internement d'un mineur au pénitencier de Carabane, Decision, 26 March 1928, 3F25, ANS. For other examples, see Fiche de renseignements concernant le jeune Galbou N'Dao, candidat à la Médersa de Saint-Louis, 14 October 1916, 1G53, ANS, and Procès-Verbal contre Fa Seck Fall, 10 June 1925, 1F154, ANS.
29. Although age sometimes corresponded to measurable bodily features—height, pubescence, presence or absence of modifications like tattooing or circumcision, for example—it could not be precisely determined using these means.
30. Secrétaire Général, for Lieutenant Gouverneur du Sénégal, to Lieutenant Gouverneur du Soudan Français, 20 October 1926, 3F27, ANS.
31. Extrait des Minutes du Greffe du Tribunal de première instance de Saint-Louis (Senegal), 28 October 1925, 3F27, ANS; Internement à Bambey du nommé Fara Diallo dit François, 14 November 1925, 3F27, ANS.
32. Officier du Ministère public to M. l'Administrateur Supérieur de la Casamance, 11 June 1923, 3F27, ANS; Decision, Camille Maillet—Lieutenant Gouverneur, p.i., du Sénégal, 4 July 1923, 3F27, ANS. This was akin to the "feedback loop" in U.S. Pension Bureau records described by Corinne T. Field and Nicholas L. Syrett. See Field and Syrett, "Age and the Construction of Gendered and Raced Citizenship in the United States," AHR Roundtable, *American Historical Review* 125, no. 2 (2020): 445.
33. Internement du jeune Abdoulaye Lome au pénitencier de Bambey, Decision, 6 [?] September 1927, 3F27, ANS.
34. For example: Décision prononcant l'internement d'un mineur a Carabane, 26 March 1928, 3F25, ANS; Décision, 18 October 1928, 6M273, ANS. See also Décision prononçant l'internement de quatre détenus à l'E.P.S. de Carabane, 22 October 1931, 6M269, ANS.
35. Entries for Vacla Arba in Liste des mineurs délivrés de la captivité et confiés à la tutelle de M. le Procureur Général, Chef du Service Judiciaire depuis l'année 1895, H173, ANS; État de mineurs affranchis confiés à Saint-Louis ... Janvier 1906, H173, ANS; and État de mineurs délivrés de la condition de captivité, confiés à des personnes de Saint-Louis ... Novembre 1906, H177, ANS. See also Liberated Minors Database data for Vacla Arba, Gnia, and Moukhère Diagne.
36. Entries for Tienouma Diara in État de mineurs affranchis confiés à Saint-Louis ... Juillet 1905, H173, ANS, and État de mineurs affranchis confiés à Saint-Louis ... Septembre 1906, H173, ANS. See also Liberated Minors Database data for Tienouma Diara.
37. E. Degrave to Chef du Service de l'Enseignement, n.d., 1G3, ANS.
38. Similarly, Corrie Decker argues that girls and women in East Africa could use the gap between colonial emphasis on chronological age, on one hand, and officials' lack of records and minimal understanding of African age categories, on the other, to their benefit. Yet she makes a rather different point than I make here, suggesting that girls could go to a colonial court to claim majority based on chronological age, thereby circumventing traditional hierarchies of age and gender and asserting autonomy. Decker, "A Feminist Methodology of Age-Grading," 418–26.

39 Lieutenant Gouverneur to Abdoulaye Seck, commis principal des postes et télégraphes, 28 April 1919, 1G32, ANS.
40 Ibra Abdoul Azis to Administrateur du cercle de Podor, 3 October 1904, J60, ANS; Untitled notes, n.d. [1904], J60, ANS.
41 Ibra Abdoul Azis to Administrateur du cercle de Podor, 3 October 1904, J60, ANS; Ibra Abdoul to Gouverneur Général, 17 October 1904, J60, ANS; Ibra Abdoul to Martial Merlin, Secrétaire Général du Gouvernement Général, 22 October 1904, J60, ANS; Ibra Abdoul, fils de Abdoul Azis in Lao Boumba, 3 November 1904, J60, ANS; Ibra Abdoul Azis to directeur de l'enseignement, 14 November 1904, J60, ANS.
42 Rapport d'Inspection sur l'École rurale de l'Avenue Faidherbe (Dakar) visitée les 3 et 9 Décembre 1913 par M. E. Courcelle, Inspecteur de l'Enseignement du Senegal, J28, ANS.
43 Alpha Diol to M. le Délégué du Gouvernement du Sénégal, 16 September 1906, 1G28, ANS; Lieutenant Gouverneur to Délégué, Dakar, 28 September 1906, 1G28, ANS.
44 Délégué to Lieutenant Gouverneur, 10 October 1906, 1G28, ANS. For another example of a clear attempt to redefine a person's age with a specific strategic goal in mind—in this case, to remake a sixteen-year-old boy into a twenty-one-year-old man for the purpose of job eligibility—see Malick Gaye to Gouverneur, 10 December 1906, J61, ANS, and Letter from Chef du service [de l'enseignement], 24 October 1906, 1G28, ANS.
45 Tribunal Musulman de Dakar, 5 October 1906, 1G28, ANS.
46 Decision, n.d. [1907], J61, ANS; Directeur de l'École Normale to Gouverneur Général, 31 May 1907, J50, ANS.
47 For an East African counterexample, see Decker, *The Age of Sex*, chap. 6.
48 Droit commun, Colonie du Senegal, cercle de Podor, Extrait du Registre d'écrou du Cercle, 11 October 1926, 3F27, ANS.
49 Droit commun, Colonie du Senegal, cercle de Podor, Extrait du Registre d'écrou du Cercle, 11 October 1926, 3F27, ANS; Administrateur Podor to Gouverneur Senegal, telegram-letter, 16 October 1926, 3F27, ANS; emphasis added.
50 Gouvernement du Sénégal, Bureau Politique to Administrateur Podor, telegram-letter, 29 October 1926, ANS 3F27.
51 For a similar analysis of colonial India, see Pande, "Power, Knowledge, and the Epistemic Contract on Age."
52 Amadou Sall to Lieutenant Gouverneur Sénégal, 8 February 1925, 3F64, ANS.
53 Lieutenant Gouverneur Sénégal to Procureur de la République, 13 February 1925, 3F64, ANS; Lieutenant Gouverneur to Commissaire Police, telegram-letter, 13 February 1925, 3F64, ANS; Régisseur de la Prison de Saint-Louis to Lieutenant Gouverneur Sénégal, 16 February 1925, 3F64, ANS; Commissaire de Police de Saint-Louis to Procureur de la République, 19 February 1925, 3F64, ANS; Administrateur du Cercle de Louga to Lieutenant Gouverneur Sénégal, telegram-letter, 2 March 1925, 3F64, ANS; Commissaire de police de Louga to Procureur de la République, 30 March 1925, 3F64, ANS; Commissaire de police de Louga to Procureur de la République, 4 April 1925, 3F64, ANS.
54 Amadou Sall to M. le Lieutenant-Gouverneur du Sénégal, 12 April 1925, 3F64, ANS; Arrêté portant mise en liberté provisoire de la jeune Léonie Gueye, condamnée à l'internement dans un établissement pénitentiaire, n.d. [April 1925], 3F64, ANS.

55 This might also be an example of "age pluralism," in which older ideas about age remained relevant even as the colonial state sought to naturalize chronological age. Premo, "Meticulous Imprecision," 402.
56 Corinne T. Field and Nicholas L. Syrett suggest that modernizing states commonly implemented statutes and laws that involved knowledge of chronological age before they had the capacity to track and record vital statistics. I think colonial Senegal, like other places under colonial rule, offers a particularly compelling example of this phenomenon, since not only did the state lack knowledge and capacity of people's ages but age meant very different things and was measured differently in the region's cultures as compared to France. Field and Syrett, "Introduction: Chronological Age," 377; Field and Syrett, "Age and the Construction of Gendered and Raced Citizenship," 439–40.
57 Lamine Gueye, *Itinéraire Africain* (Paris: Présence Africaine, 1966), 13–16.

Conclusion

1 African Charter on the Rights and Welfare of the Child, adopted by the 26th Ordinary Session of the Assembly of Heads of State and Government of the Organization of African Unity, July 1990, entered into force on 29 November 1999, https://au.int; African Union, List of Countries Which Have Signed, Ratified/Acceded to the African Charter on the Rights and Welfare of the Child, 14 February 2023, https://au.int.
2 UN General Assembly, Resolution 45/25, Convention on the Rights of the Child RES/45/25, adopted 20 November 1989, entered into force 2 September 1990, https://www.unicef.org; UN Human Rights Treaty Bodies, Database, Ratification Status for the Convention on the Rights of the Child, https://tbinternet.ohchr.org. Earlier international agreements, including the 1924 Geneva Declaration of the Rights of the Child and the 1959 Declaration of the Rights of the Child, had not defined childhood and had not given upper age limits. League of Nations, Geneva Declaration of the Rights of the Child, 26 September 1924, http://www.un-documents.net; UN General Assembly, Resolution 1386(XIV), Declaration on the Rights of the Child, RES/1386/XIV, 20 November 1959, https://digitallibrary.un.org.
3 Code de la famille Sénégalais, 1972, https://www.equalrightstrust.org; République du Sénégal, Direction des Relations avec les Institutions, "Loi sénégalaise no. 1961/55 du 23 juin 1961," https://www.dri.gouv.sn.
4 Caplan and Torpey, "Introduction," 10–11; Wendy Hunter and Robert Brill, "'Documents, Please': Advances in Social Protection and Birth Certification in the Developing World," *World Politics* 68, no. 2 (2016): 191–228.
5 Fouquet, "L'état civil sénégalais aujourd'hui"; Yacob Sewoldi, "Snapshot of Civil Registration and Vital Statistics Systems of Senegal," report for the Centre of Excellence, International Development Research Centre, 2019, https://apai-crvs.uneca.org.
6 Séverine Awenengo Dalberto, Richard Banégas, and Armando Cutolo, "African Citizenships—A Biometric Turn?" trans. Rachel Robertson, in Dalberto and Banégas, eds., *Identification and Citizenship in Africa*, 29–35.
7 Premo, "Meticulous Imprecision," 399.
8 Dalberto, "The French West African Identity Card in Senegal."

Index

Note: Page numbers in italics indicate figures; page numbers followed by "t" indicate tables.

Abdoul, Ibra (Aziz), 151, 156, 157
Abdoulaye, 33–34
Abile, 25–26
Abou Diop, 33
abuse, 177n40
academic instruction, 58, 59
Achebe, Chinua, 167n3
administration officials, 78, 80, 85, 127, 193n31
adult prisons, 43, 46, 49, 56, 60, 68, 109, 154, 155, 182n25; escapees from, 63; minors in, 44, 49, 182n26; print media and, 68; rations in, 56; registers of, 66
African Charter of the Rights and Welfare of the Child, 159
African chiefs, 94–95
African childhood, particularity of, 170n23. *See also* childhood
age; "age pluralism," 206n55; "bureaucratic age," 140; chronological, 139–57; defining childhood and, 159; documentation of, 144, 146–50; justice system and, 191n8; of majority, 7–8, 149, 191n8, 202n7; malleability of, 191n7; of "penal majority," 143
agency, 17; "as argument," 10; children's actions and, 10–12
aggregates, 134–35
agricultural education, 74
agricultural labor, 54, 59; juvenile reform and, 46–47
"agricultural orphanages," 46–47, 57, 64
agricultural penitential colonies, 45, 49, 53; escapees from, 62–63

agricultural training, 74; in colonial schools, 184n41
Aïssatou, 31
Alcagny, 36
Almamy of Lao, 151
alms-seeking, 101–7, 128, 193n37
apprenticeships, 19, 24, 30, 39, 45, 58, 175n16, 184n39
Arba, Vacla, 148–49
arrêté of 14 April 1904, 118, 126, 191n10
artisans, 24, 25
assaults, 93, 116
assimilation, 74, 88
Assistance Médicale africaine (AMI), 118–19, 127, 130–31
attendance lists, 157
autoethnographic essays, 6–7
autonomy, 61
Awa, 38
awards, 82

Bâ, Moctar, 86
Bacari, 19
background, 9
Bakayoro, Dramané, 147–48
Bakel, 8
Bakily, Amady, 41–42, 67
Balla, 33
Bambara, 23
Bambey, Senegal, 47, 65, 67; agricultural penitentiary in, 53, 57–58, 60–63, 65, 67; juvenile reformatories in, 49, 113, 147–48, 154, 183–84n38; security at, 184n49;

207

Bambey, Senegal (*continued*)
  tensions between community and reformatory in, 69
Bancal, Mme. H., 31
Banégas, Richard, 160
Baol, Senegal, 67
Barthet, Monseigneur, 56–57
Basse, Gorgui, 148
Bas-Sénégal, 105
Baudin, Auguste, 14, 19–20, 23, 24, 142, 174–75n10
Bayérika, 33
Beccaria, 189n38
begging, 115, 128
behavior; behavioral norms, 44, 66; morality and, 35–39. *See also* misbehavior
Besnes, Doctor, 137
Béziat, Alexis, 31
Bilale, 24, 25, 26
Binta Sar, 19
biometric identification systems, 160
birth certificates, 144, 151–52. *See also* birth registration
birth registration, 171n35; lack of, 5, 6, 8, 13, 116, 137, 140, 144, 146, 147, 150, 151–52, 156, 203–4n26; as norm, 159
boarding schools, 15
the body, 117–38
Boulanger, 63
boyhood, 59; colonial, 42; ideal of, 45; remaking, 44, 53–54, 59; remaking of, 59; Senegalese vs. French, 44
boys, in domestic service, 177n35
boys' schools, 81, 88–89, 132, 133
Brévié, Jules, 3, 74, 117, 136
Brian, Madame, 84
British colonial Africa, 5, 42. *See also* specific countries
British Gambia, 63–64
Bulletin de l'enseignement de l'Afrique Occidentale Française, 2, 145
"bureaucratic age," 140

Calvayrac, Madame, 70
Calvayrac, Monsieur, 79
Caminade, Madame, 23
Caminade, Monsieur, 23

Carabane, Senegal, 55; École Professionnelle Spéciale (Special Professional School) in, 48, 49, 55, 56, 58–59, 61, 66, 68, 69, 143–44, 182n22, 184n49, 185n53, 185n56; isolation of, 184n49, 185n53; juvenile reformatories in, 47–48, 115; tensions between community and reformatory and, 69
carceral spaces, 41–69. *See also specific institutions and types of institutions*
Carde, Jules, 74
Carrère, Frédéric, 23, 24
Casamance, Senegal, 7, 143
cash crop production, 16
Catholic boys' schools, 73
Catholic Church, baptisms recorded in, 146
Catholic missionaries, 14, 16, 175–76n21
Catholicism, 45, 73
Cayor, Senegal, 86, 105, 106, 122
Cécilé, 36–37
cercles, 193n31
charity, 115
Charton, Albert, 74
"child," category of, 3, 17, 161; mapping onto chronological ages, 4
child labor, 2, 24
child mortality, 2, 17, 119
child protection, 12–13, 40, 48, 55, 72, 74, 77, 94, 98, 135–36, 173n49, 183n37, 192n14; child begging and, 193n30; child "protection" interventions, 138, 149, 191n8; chronological age and, 140; vs. control, 56; discipline and, 105; discourses around, 2–4, 59, 107, 110–11, 115–16, 141; programs for, 12–13, 16–17; schooling and, 145; shifts in thinking about, 59, 116
child reform, 45–46, 54–61
child welfare, 2, 55, 202–3n13. *See also* child protection; child welfare organizations, 192n14; child welfare policy, 75–76
child-begging, 103–5, 193n30. *See also* religious mendicancy
childbirth, majority and, 202n7
child-focused policies and programs, 17
childhood; age-based definitions of, 159; categories of, 42; changing understandings of, 4, 6, 59, 192n14; childhood

norms, 4–9, 66; defined by domestic or manual labor, 39, 61–66; defining, 4–9, 17, 126, 159, 168n14; discourses about, 71; documentation of, 75, 97–98, 107, 116, 117–38, 139–57; guardianship and, 19–40; language of, 168n14, 169n15; medicalization of, 117–38; notions of, 23; particularity of African, 170n23; public spaces, 93–116; resistance to notions of, 23; reworking of, 4–9, 61, 68, 72; terminology applied to African societies, 168n14

children, 5, 42. *See also* detainees, minor; liberated minors; actions and agency of, 10–12, 17, 40; age of, 141–46; defining, 126; defining "disciplined," 71, 75–81; documentation of, 90, 123, 157; effort to influence own circumstances, 25–26; fear of counting, 123; health of, 117–38; legal status of, 95; medicalization of, 135–36; *métis*, 3, 9, 17; perception of, 65–66; perspectives of, 11–12, 40; state dependence on, 11; tried as adults, 191n7; unruly, 44–49; vagabond, 107–11

children's history, 10–11
children's institutions, 6
children's voices, sources of, 11–12
child-rights language, 105
Christian mission, 71
Christianity, 57, 71
chronological age, 5–6, 139–57; African vs. French understandings of, 6; claims-making and, 150–56; colonial legal apparatus and, 142–43, 191n7; determining and documenting, 2, 4–9, 13, 17, 20, 146–50, 203–4n26, 204n29, 204n38, 205n44, 206n55, 206n56; inventing, 146–50; as matter of negotiation, 5; racism in determining, 8–9; surveillance and, 141; trumped by marriage or childbirth, 202n7

circumcision, 7, 8, 169n20
Cissé, Ibrahima Ben Mady, 7
citizenship rights, 114, 190–91n5, 191n6
citizenship status, 95, 114, 137, 190–91n5, 191n6
civil law, 8

civil registration, 160–61. *See also* birth registration
civil status, bifurcation in, 95
class; class rules, 75–81; discourses about, 71
cleanliness, 132. *See also* hygiene
clemency, 60
clerks, 5
codes, 141–46
colonial administration, importance of age to, 150–57
Colonial Council, 68
colonial courts, 60
colonial economy, production of workers for, 53
colonial legal apparatus, 94–95, 112, 142–43, 144
Colonial Ministry, 74
colonial rule, "humanitarian," 72
colonial schooling, 5, 70–92; agricultural training in, 184n41; culture of, 71; documentation and, 129–37; expansion of, 110; funding of, 177n39; health interventions and, 118; history of, 73–75; impact of, 1–2; medical visits and, 129–37; vaccinations and, 118, 129–37
colonial schools, 1–2
colonial spaces, vagabond children in, 107–11
colonial state, 12–14; administrative and judicial structures of, 67; health priorities of, 118; interests of, 44; limitations of, 43; lists kept by, 141–42; power of, 43; reformatories and, 42–43
colonial subjects, model, 66
colonialism, 44, 194n46; benevolent, 3; education and, 15–17; language and, 87; portrayed as humanitarian, 4, 74, 119; schools and, 73–75
commissions, 27–28
communes, 15, 16, 30–31, 73, 96, 127, 134, 137, 146, 202n10
connection, resistance and, 61–66
control, 20, 56
Cooper, Barbara, 3
Cooper, Frederick, 171n35
Cor, Henri, 46, 103
Couly, 19
Cours Secondaire, 84

courts system, 16, 94, 96, 97, 141, 146, 149, 153; chronological age and, 144; court documents, 147, 157; court officials, 144; court transcripts, 11; wardship courts, 4
Crespin, J.-J., 31, 33, 139, 177n43
crime, 93–94, 111–15, 116, 190n1, 191n7
criminal responsibility, age of, 143
cultural alienation, 2
cultural assimilation, 71
cultural superiority, 17
customary courts, 202n10
customary law, 95, 143, 191n7
Cutolo, Armando, 160

Daffa, Nouba, 34
Dagana, Senegal, 78
Dahomey, colony of, 83
Dakar, Senegal, 17, 26–27, 30, 51, 53, 84–85, 136, 152–53, 189n38, 202n10; adult prisons in, 182n25; juvenile delinquency in, 109–12; plague in, 123; policing in, 97; schools in, 72, 75, 79, 80, 88–89, 131, 132, 133, 144, 151; vaccinations in, 127, 128
Dakar boys' school (Rue de Thiong), 80, 88–89
Dakar School of Medicine, 117
Dalberto, Séverine Awenengo, 160, 161
De Coppet, Marcel, 17
Decker, Corrie, 204n38
Decree on Native Justice of 1924, 191n7
defendants, tried as adults or considered minors, 143
deference, 79
deficit thinking, 81
Demba, 63
demographic information, lists of, 141–42
Deproge, Paul, 35, 36
déracinés, 73
d'Erneville, Edouard, 36
detainees, minor, 44, 143, 182n27, 183n33, 183n35, 183n37, 195n58; in adult prisons, 182n26; age of, 148; contact with family members, 185n53; database of, 51t, 52t, 62–63; discipline and, 55–56, 69; escaped from penitentiary schools, 62–64, 153; experience of, 54–61; experiences of internment, 42; families of, 54–55, 64; female, 42–43, 49, 54, 59, 60–61, 69, 155, 182n26; fleeing reformatories for families, 64; offenses of, 51; overview of detainee populations, 49–54; records of, 49–51, 50t, 51t; in reformatories, 61–66; rehabilitation of, 182–83n31, 182n29; sentences of, 52–53, 52t, 115, 141, 143–44, 148–49, 154, 182n29, 202–3n13, 202n10; social connections of, 64–66
Diagne, Soukeyna, 34
Diakhao Preparatory School, 135
Diallo, Fara, 65, 148
Dialo, Ibrahima, 63, 64
Dialo, Sadio, 63
Diara, Niélé, 33
Diaw, Fara, 79, 133
Diol, Alpha, 152, 156
Diol, Matar, 152, 153, 156
Diop, Abdoulaye, 151–52, 156
Diop, Alioune, 1–2, 3
Diop, Amadou, 113
Diop, Babakar, 150
Diop, Jean, 133
Diop, Maïssa, 113–14
Diop, N'Doye Fall, 98
Diouf, Amadou, 83
Diouf, Galandou, 139, 140, 201n1
Diouf, Yacine, 35
Diptee, Audra A., 170n23
discipline, 2–4, 15–16, 44, 45–46, 53, 54, 59, 69, 78–79, 116; child protection and, 105; children's responses to, 71; chronological age and, 140; detainees and, 55–56; disciplinary apparatus, 85–90; disciplinary proceedings, 11; juvenile reform and, 66–67; meanings of, 71–72; protection and, 94; pushback against, 61–66, 71, 85–87, 89–90; resistance to, 10, 85–87; sanitary, 128, 129; in schools, 70–92; teachers and, 71–72, 76–77
disease, 9, 118, 191n10, 196–97n6
doctors, 122–23, 126–27, 131, 134; marabout, 132; vaccinating, 124
documentation, 1, 3–4, 12–14, 20, 27–28, 40, 75, 90, 94, 98. *See also specific types of documentation*; of age, 139–57; of

citizenship status, 114; health and, 117–18; of identity, 160–62; impact on childhood, 123; increased emphasis on after 1903, 39, 40; juvenile reform and, 61–69, 66–67; lack of, 140; lost, 41–42; medical, 124–25, 132–33, 134, 136; at reformatories, 44; resistance to, 10; in schools, 90–92
Domenge, 88–89
domestic service, 30–31, 177n35
domestic skills, 73, 81
Dorine, 23
doubleness, 2
Dramé, Matar, 147
Duprat, Edouard, 36
Duval, Senegal, 87

Eastman, 33
École de la Marine, 189n38
École de la Rue de Thiong boys' school, 80
École Duval, Saint-Louis, 87–88
École Professionnelle Spéciale (Special Professional School), 48, 49, 55, 56, 58–59, 61, 66, 68, 69, 143–44, 182n22, 184n49, 185n53, 185n56
École Rurale de l'Avenue Faidherbe, 151
economic productivity, French expectations of, 19
education, 1–3, 6–7, 14–17, 48, 70–92. *See also* schools; training; vocational training; *specific schools and types of schools*; academic instruction, 58, 59; access to, 139, 144–45; age limits and, 139, 144–46; biomedical care and, 129–31, 134, 137; as center of new "moral conquest" in French West Africa, 187n12; child welfare policy and, 75–76, 145; French rhetoric valuing, 75; hygiene and, 129–35; Islamic, 108 (*see also* Qur'an schools); labor and, 194n50; medicalization and, 129–31; racism and, 9, 144–45; rehabilitative, 182n29; Roume's decree on, 73–74; sanitation and, 129–31; secularization of, 46; underfunding of, 75
education certificates, 79
education reforms, 73–74, 139

educational hierarchy, perceived authority of, 88
emancipation, law on, 14, 19
embezzlement, 112
"empathic inference," 22
enslavers, former, as guardians, 23
epidemics, 122, 123, 127. *See also* smallpox
escape, from penitentiary schools, 184n49
ethical questions, 11
ethnographic essays, 86
"ex-captives," 174–75n10, 175n16
expulsion, 70

Faidherbe, Louis Léon César, 15, 23–24, 73, 153
Fall, Balla, 31, 33, 177n43
Fall, Hama, 114
Fall, Niégui, 52
falsification, 112
families; of detainees, 54–55, 64; detainees fleeing to, 64; expectations of, 89–90; rehabilitation and, 45; removal of children from, 54–55, 61
Family Code of 1972, 159
Fathers of the Séminaire du Saint-Esprit, 173n44
Faye, Ousseynou, 22, 44
Field, Corinne T., 5, 140, 206n56
food, 68–69
Foucault, Michel, 13
Fouta Toro, Senegal, 128
France, 44; child protection regimes in, 12–13; "civilizing mission" and, 5, 72, 73, 77, 94, 191n7; juvenile reform in, 46; "moral conquest" of West Africa, 132
Franco-Muslim schools, 70, 74
fraud, 112
Fréau, Monsieur, 37
French colonialism, 14–18, 17; child protection and, 2–3; efforts to justify as humanitarian, 140–41, 173n49
French courts, 95, 116, 202n10
French culture, 5, 45
French emancipation law of 1848, 14, 19
French juridical infrastructure, 111–15
French language, 5, 56, 58, 59, 73, 74, 87, 139

French law, 14, 19, 43, 57, 95, 96, 111–15, 143, 202n10
French pronatalism, 173n49
French regulations, 6
French schooling, 1, 15–16, 139. *See also* colonial schools
French Soudan, 47, 51
French West Africa, 17
French West Africa Federation, 16
Frères de l'Instruction Chrétienne (Ploërmel Brothers), 15, 73, 173n44. *See also* Ploërmel school

Garrigues, Monsieur, 87–88
gendarmes, 62, 93, 94. *See also* police
gender, 9; domestic service and, 30–31; juvenile reform and, 42; vocational training and, 29–30
General Council session of 1911, 139, 140
General Council session of 1912, 140
George, Abosede A., 9, 43, 44, 170n23
germ theory, 118, 120
gestures, indecent, 189n36
Getz, Trevor R., 20–21
Girard, Dr., 125–26
girlhood, 42, 61, 69
girls; in adult prisons, 182n26; guardianship and, 174–75n10; hygiene ordinances and, 98–100; incarceration of, 42–43, 49, 54, 59, 60–61, 69, 155, 182n26; regulation of sexuality and, 37–39, 54, 60
girls' schools, 73, 81, 131
Gleason, Mona, 10, 22
Global South, 160
Godel, P., 31
Gorée, Senegal, 14, 15, 19–20, 26, 202n10; colonial schooling in, 73; girls' school in, 149
Goundou village, 33
Great Depression, 16, 49, 68
group homes, 3
guardianship, 8, 14, 15–16, 37, 146, 161, 162, 177n40, 177n42, 179n57, 179n62; abuses of, 16; acceptance of, 40; age determinations and, 148–49; as antidote to French emancipation law, 19–20; childhood and, 19–40; creation of, 24; database of, 22; database on, 22; decisions about, 141; girls and, 174–75n10; history of, 20–21; intention of, 22, 24; monitoring and, 40; in nineteenth century, 23–26; record-keeping and, 40; reform and, 26–28, 142, 176n26; resistance to, 23, 39–40; responsibility and, 142; state power and, 20–21; termination of, 38; transferred to penitentiary schools, 42
guardianship commissions, 148–49
guardianship councils, 11, 19, 23, 24–25, 174–75n10, 175n16
guardianship proceedings, 149
guardianship programs, transfers and, 180n3
guardianship records, 22–23
guardianship registers, 22, 147
guardianship system, 142, 153
Guet N'Dar, Senegal, 52, 98–99, 122, 125
Guèye, Amadou, 133
Guèye, Hamet, 34
Gueye, Lamine, 157
Guèye, Léonie, 49, 60–61, 155–56, 182n26
Guillabert, Louis, 139
Guy, Camille, 27, 96

Hardy, Georges, 2, 132, 187n12
Hassett, Dónal, 170n23
hawkers, 43
health infrastructure, 16, 130–31; expansion of, 118; school-based, 129–31, 134
health policy and interventions, 3, 4, 95–96, 117–37, 134–35, 162; colonial schooling and, 118; school inspection process and, 135–36; surveillance and, 119, 126
historical context, 14–18
"houses of correction," 96, 108, 111, 143
human rights organizations, 192n25
hygiene, 1–4, 17, 94–97, 98–101, 115–16, 117–38, 162, 196–97n6, 199n34; education and, 129–35; hygiene agents, 122, 134, 142; hygiene committees, 118; hygiene education, 132, 134–35, 200n46; hygiene initiatives, 118; hygiene policing,

129; hygiene services, 131; hygiene violations, 98–101, 141; municipal hygiene services, 130–31; racism and, 129

identification, medical records and, 201n50
identity, documentation of, 160–61
identity cards, 161
indigénat, 94–95
infant mortality, 2, 17, 119
institutionalization, deemphasized in France, 46
internment, 42, 143–44, 148. See also detainees, minor; *specific institutions*
interpreters, 5
Islam, 15, 101–7, 108
isolation, 54, 55, 65

Jaouiche, Alfred, 84, 189n38
Jenner, Edward, 120
Jolof Oriental, Senegal, 122
judges, 94
justice system, 94–95, 202n10; age of majority and, 143, 191n8; "native," 143
justification supplétif, 147
juvenile courts, 46
juvenile delinquency, 106, 110, 111–15, 143; discourses about, 59; responses to, 43–44
juvenile justice, 202–3n13
juvenile penitentiary registers, 147
juvenile reform, 41–69; agricultural labor and, 46–47; discipline and, 66–67; documentation and, 66–67; gender and, 42; limitations of, 42; shifts in French thinking about, 59
juvenile reformatories, 4, 41–69, 108–10, 162, 173n44, 175–76n21, 182–83n31; age limits and, 143–44, 147–48, 155; in Bambey, Senegal, 183–84n38; boys at, 42; in Carabane, Senegal, 47–48; colonial state and, 42–43; criticism of, 56–57; detainees in, 61–66; escape from, 184n49; escapees from, 62–64; guardianship transferred to, 42; lack of reformatories for girls, 49; minor detainees in, 50t, 51t; print media and, 68; rations in, 56, 69, 183n35;

recordkeeping at, 44; remote location of, 54; resistance to, 61–66; in Thiès, Senegal, 45, 46, 183n35, 194n44 (*see also* Thiès penitentiary-school)
juvenile sentencing, 182n29, 202–3n13, 202n10

Kaédi, Senegal, 65
Kamara, Bilaly, 53
Kaolack, Senegal, 81, 93, 97, 190n1, 195n58
Kaolack Tribunal, 147
Kayeré, Ousmane, 98–99
Kébémer, Senegal, 41, 113–14
Klein, Martin, 20–21
knowledge, creation of, 13
Kolda, Senegal, 104
Koli, 25
Konaté, Abdoulaye, 64–65
Konaté, Dior, 63, 68, 182–83n31

labor, 14, 74. See also labor expectations/requirements; after 1895, 28–35; forced, 16; schooling and, 194n50; unpaid, 16
labor camps, 46
labor expectations/requirements, 59; disagreement regarding, 34–35; similar to slavery, 24–25
labor training, 56, 58. See also training; vocational training
Lagos, Nigeria, 43
language, colonialism and, 87
larceny, 115
law, 94–95. See also colonial legal apparatus; civil, 8; customary, 95, 143, 191n7; French, 8, 19–20, 57, 95–96, 111–15, 143, 202n10; metropolitan, 144, 182n24; penal, 8, 95; rule of, 8, 141
lawyers, 94
Le Franc, Madame, 36
League of Nations, 3, 74
League of Nations Committee on Child Welfare, 3
Leahy, Carla Pascoe, 11
LeFranc, Madame, 32
legal procedures, chronological age and, 144
legal status, bifurcation in, 95

legibility, 12–14
letters, 11
Lezongar family, 122
liberated minors, 24, 26–30, 28–35, 29t, 39–40, 42, 142, 175n16, 176n26, 179n57, 179n62, 179n63; abuse of, 177n40; behavior of, 35–40; challenging expectations, 33–35, 39–40; complaints about, 36; complaints from, 33–35; database of, 29t; disagreements regarding treatment of, 34–35; disobedience of, 36–37; guardianship and, 141; inspections of, 26; "insubordinate," 53; morality, 35–40; pregnancy and childbearing and, 38–39; runaways, 33, 38, 40, 177n42; sexually targeted by guardians, 38; training for boys, 29–30
liberation certificate, 142
liberation register, 142
lists, 141–42
literacy, 69
loitering, 94, 107–11
Lome, Abdoulaye, 148
Loppy, Suzanne, 132–33
Louga, Senegal, 97, 134, 195n58
Ly, Mamadou Hadramé, 79
Lycée Faidherbe Saint-Louis, 1, 83, 133, 152, 153, 189n36, 189n38

magistrates, 54–55, 94–95, 144
majority, age of, 143, 149, 202n7; defining, 7–8; justice system and, 191n8
Makhana, Senegal, 47
malaria, 131
Mamadou, 63
marabouts, 1, 103–4, 105, 109, 126, 128, 132, 196–97n6
marriage, majority and, 7–8, 202n7
Matam, Senegal, 104
Maynes, Mary Jo, 10
Maza, Sarah, 11
M'Baye, Abibou, 34–35
M'Baye, Maissa, 37
M'Bengue, Abdoulaye, 88–89
M'Boup, Amadou, 37
Mbour, Senegal, 55
médersa, 70, 74

medical dispensaries, 16, 101, 117, 131, 134, 137
medical documentation, 129, 131, 134–37, 149; discourses around, 132–33; identification and, 201n50; vaccination certificates, 130, 132–34, 201n50
medical spaces, 4. *See also* medical dispensaries
medical visits, 129–37
medicalization, 129–31, 132, 134–37
medicine, 117–38; military, 129; racism and, 9
memoirs, 11–12
métis children, 3, 9, 78–79
metropolitan law, 144, 182n24
metropolitan-style education, 73, 74
minors. *See* children; detainees, minor; liberated minors
misbehavior, 36–37, 61–66, 70, 72, 84–85, 186n2, 189n38. *See also* juvenile delinquency
mise en valeur, 16, 72, 77
missionaries, 41, 45, 56–57, 63–64, 184n49
mistreatment, correcting, 40
mobility, 115; affected by medical records, 201n50; freedom of, 194n46; policing of, 37–38
Moitt, Bernard, 22, 174–75n10
monitoring. *See* policing; surveillance
monitors, 187n13
morality, 3, 5; instruction in, 58; (mis)behavior and, 35–39; moral development, 54–55; moral reform, 45, 182–83n31, 184n39
Morilhon, Monsieur, 177n43
Moruzi, Kristine, 11
mothers, prenatal consultations and, 138
Moussa, 41–42, 53, 67
Murdoch, Lydia, 198n18
Musgrove, Nell, 11
Muslim Tribunals, 95, 152, 153
Muslims, 73, 101–7, 123, 131; alms-seeking and, 193n37; variolation and, 120, 121

"native" justice system, 95, 143
native languages, punishment for speaking, 56
Native Medical Assistance (Assistance Médicale Indigène (AMI)), 118–19

"native minors," 143
Native Tribunals, 94–95, 112, 116, 143, 144, 202n10
N'Dao, Bara, 38
N'Dar Toute, Senegal, 125
N'Daw, Ibrahima, 185n56
N'Daw, Madjighen, 134
N'Diaye, Aïssa, 99
Ndiaye, Baba, 106
N'Diaye, Babacar, 79–80
N'Diaye, Bigué, 32–33
N'Diaye, Ibrahima, 87–88
N'Diaye, Katy, 34
N'Diaye, Papa, 87
N'Diaye, Seydou, 70
N'Dioum Rural School, 135
Némos, E., 55, 58–59, 104–5, 143–44
Ngalamulume, Kalala, 98, 118, 123, 201n50
Niang, Biram, 151–52, 156
Niang, Fama, 100–101
Niang, Ibrahima, 133, 200n43
Niang, Maty, 134
Nianing, Senegal, 96
Niellé, 37
Niénat, Monsieur, 88, 132
Niger, 3
Nigeria, 9, 42
njàngaan, 102
Normal School, 6–7, 11, 74–75, 80, 83, 86, 87, 106, 135, 151, 200n46
nuisance violations, 94

obedience, 78, 79, 85–87
officials, 5
oral histories, 11
order, 4, 8–9, 11–14, 18–19, 45–46, 53, 58–59, 141. *See also* discipline
Organization of African Unity, 159
originaires, 77, 95, 114, 140, 143–44, 146, 190–91n5, 191n6, 191n8, 202n10
orphanages, 16, 173n44, 175–76n21, 181n14, 183n37
orphans, 108, 174–75n10, 194–95n51

parents, 5, 16. *See also* families
paternal rights, state intervention in, 16
Patterson, A., 33–34

peanut cultivation, 47
Pearson, Susan J., 171n35
Pécarrère, M., 122
Peignet, V., 31
Pellegrin, Charles, 37
penal law, 8
penitentiary schools. *See* juvenile reformatories; Thiès penitentiary-school
personal narratives, 11–12
personhood, documented, 100, 111, 138
petty crime, 94
Peulh, 86
physical fights, 93
Pinet-Laprade vocational school, 30
Pire, Senegal, 112–13
Pire-Goureye, Senegal, 122
plague, 123
Ploë, 87
Ploërmel school, 73, 87, 88, 145
Podor, Senegal, 153–54
Podor Regional School, 136–37
police, 41–42, 63, 65, 93, 94, 97, 103, 141, 142, 149. *See also* policing; hygiene policing, 129; police records, 195n58; police reports, 11, 93, 190n1; sanitary police, 118, 121–22, 123, 124–25
policing, 93–94, 97, 98, 111–15, 116, 146, 162. *See also* surveillance
Political Bureau, 154
Ponty, William, 103
Popular Front government, 17, 49, 104
Poye, Ibra, 63, 64
praise, in schools, 81–85
prayer, 45
primary schools, 73–74, 152, 203n23; access to, 139, 144–45, 153, 203n21; age limits and, 139, 141, 203n21; in Dakar, Senegal, 144
print media, 68
prison escapes, 93
prison sentences, 154
prison wardens, 66
prisons, 94. *See also* adult prisons; juvenile reformatories
prizes, 82
pronatalism, French, 173n49
protection, 20, 44

puberty, 8
public health, 196–97n6. *See also* health policy and interventions; hygiene'
public health decree of 1904, 130–31, 132, 135; public health reform, 126–29
public spaces, control of, 4, 93–116
punishment, 44, 59, 84–85, 116, 153. *See also* discipline; corporal, 56; race and, 70–71, 85; racism and, 70–71; in schools, 72, 81–85

quarantines, 121, 122, 199n35
Qur'an, study of the, 45
Qur'an schools, 1, 7, 73, 94, 101–7, 108, 123, 128, 139, 144–45, 150, 157, 192n25

Race; punishment and, 70–71, 85; racial segregation, 118; racialization, 44; teachers' expectations and, 84
racism, 17, 80–81; chronological age determinations and, 8–9; education and, 9, 144–45; hygiene and, 129; medicine and, 9; punishment and, 70–71; sanitation and, 129; vaccination and, 126
rations, 69
Razy, Elodie, 11
recordkeeping. *See* documentation
redemption, 56–57
reeducation, 56
reformatories. *See* juvenile reformatories; Thiès penitentiary-school
regional schools, 74, 79–80, 81
registers, 66, 157. *See also specific types of registers*
regulatory system, 94–97, 98–101, 141–46
rehabilitation, 45, 48, 59, 143, 154, 182–83n31, 182n29
religious mendicancy, 94, 107, 110–11
religious practices, 6, 101–7. *See also* circumcision; religious mendicancy
religious schools, 15
religious training, 73
Renaud, Hélène, 23
resistance, 10, 23; (re-)connection and, 61–66; "everyday forms of," 36; to notions of childhood, 23; reformatory detainees and, 61–66; to vaccinations, 132

responsibility, 61
restraints, 56
Reuther, Jessica, 170–71n27
Richard-Toll agricultural station, 46–47, 49, 57, 58, 62; escapees from, 64–65; food at, 68–69; security at, 184n49; tensions between community and reformatory and, 69
Richard-Toll agricultural station ("agricultural orphanage"), 64
Rigollet, Dr., 125
rituals, 6
Robert, André P., 203–4n26
Rodet, Marie, 11
Roume, Ernest, 27, 35, 73; public health decree of 1904, 118, 126, 130–31, 132, 135; reforms of, 27–28, 30, 39
Roume commissions, 27
Roumégaux, Henri, 37
Roumégaux, Monsieur and Madame, 36
Roux, Émile, 76
Rufisque, Senegal, 26, 31, 51, 64, 83, 131, 132–33, 139, 202n10; boys' school in, 79; juvenile delinquency in, 111–12; schools in, 79–80; vaccinations in, 127
rules, 44–49, 75, 141–46. *See also* discipline; order
runaways, 26, 62–64
rural schools, 74

Sachs, Miranda, 193n30
Sahel, the, 3, 196n5
Saïdane, 37
Saint-Louis, Senegal, 14–15, 19–20, 30, 64, 65, 81, 202n10; colonial schooling in, 73; court cases in, 60–61; detainees from, 51, 52; guardianship councils in, 19, 23; guardianship in, 26, 27; hygiene service in, 131; juvenile delinquency in, 111–12; *originaires* from, 114; policing in, 97; regulatory system in, 98–99; sanitary police in, 121, 122; schools in, 70, 72, 79, 83, 133; vaccinations in, 123, 127; vagabondage in, 107
Sall, Amadou, 155–56
Samba, Mamadou, 63
Samba, Tiephi, 36
sanitary discipline, 128, 129

sanitary passports, 201n50
sanitary police, 118, 121–22, 123, 124–25
"sanitary status," 135
sanitation, 94, 95–96, 98–101, 115, 191n10; education and, 129–31; racism and, 129
Sar (N'Diaye), Baca, 34
Savineau, Denise, 17, 55, 56, 59, 62, 69, 185n53
Schneider, William, 199n27
scholarships, 200n43
school aids, 187n13
school assignments, 11
school attendance records, 162
school directors, 79, 85, 134–35, 199n34
school enrollment records, 147, 161
School for Sons of Chiefs and Interpreters, 83, 124, 130, 186n2
school gardens, 74, 184n41
school inspection process, health interventions and, 135–36
school inspection reports, 79–80, 136–37
school leavers, 74, 75–76
school officials, 88
school registration, 149
schooling. See education
schools, 1–2, 4, 11–12, 16, 70–92, 141, 144, 162. See also specific schools and types of schools; access to, 153; age limits and, 144–46; colonialism and, 73–75; culture of, 71; disciplinary apparatus and, 85–90; discipline in, 70–92; documentation in, 90–92; hygiene interventions and, 131, 134–37; praise in, 81–85; punishment in, 72, 81–85; secular public, 15
Scott, James C., 13, 36
Sébire, Père A., 64
Seck, Abdoulaye, 150
Seck, Momar, 108–9, 110
Seck, Serigne Fall, 86, 106, 110
Seck, Souleyman, 103
secondary schools, 79
secular public schools, 15
Séminaire du Saint-Esprit (Spiritans), 73
Senegalese, criticism of, 80
separation of church and state, 16
Sereer-Ndut people, 8
Sexuality; policing of, 37–38, 39, 60; regulation of, 54

Sèye, Amadou, 63
Sèye, Ousmane, 109, 110
Siga, Awa, 32
Sine-Saloum, Senegal, 104
Sisters of Saint-Joseph of Cluny, 15, 37, 73, 128, 173n44
Sisters of the Immaculate Conception, 128
slave liberation procedures, 23
slavery, 16; end of, 14; labor expectations echoing, 24–25
smallpox, 118, 119–26, 137–38, 196–97n6, 196n4, 196n5; health interventions and, 120–23; threat to rural areas, 124; vaccinations for, 117–18, 120–26, 131, 133, 135, 199n27, 199n29, 199n35
social relationships, 6, 7
social welfare, 2–3, 17, 49, 72, 77, 119
socialization, 72, 73
Sons of Chiefs Section of the Normal School, 151, 153
Sor, Senegal, 99, 107, 121, 123, 125, 126, 175–76n21, 181n14
Soudan, 51, 147–48
Soumaré, Benita, 122
sources, 11–12, 22, 39
South Africa, 42
Sow, Marième, 38
Spirit Mission, 45
Spiritan Fathers, 41
Spiritan Mission, 56–57, 63
state power, guardianship and, 20–21
status, 9. See also citizenship status; class
stigma, combatting, 40
students, disciplinary apparatus and, 85–90
Superior Council of Primary Instruction, 145
surveillance, 2–4, 12–13, 28, 42, 54, 75, 97, 98–101, 112, 115–16, 129–30; chronological age and, 141; health and, 119, 126; impact on childhood, 123; increased emphasis on after 1903, 39, 40; of public spaces, 94; resistance to, 10; sanitary, 136–37
surveillance commissions, 56–57, 67, 183n35
Sy, François, 84–85
Sy, Ismaël, 112–13, 114

Sy, Maymouna, 99–100
Sylla, Mamadou, 114
Syrett, Nicholas L., 5, 140, 206n56

talibés, 102–3, 106–7, 110, 128, 193n37, 195n53
Tall, Penda, 26
Tanganyika, 42
taxation, 16
teachers, 75–85, 88, 131, 134, 137, 145, 187n13; authority of, 78, 81, 83; discipline and, 71–72, 76–77; disease-reporting obligations and, 135; evaluation of, 71–72; evaluations of, 135; hygiene education and, 134–35; rebellion of, 83; training of, 74–75; vaccination and, 130
Tène, Samba, 153–54, 156, 182n26
theft, 97, 111–15, 116
Thiès, Senegal, 104. *See also* Thiès penitentiary-school; adult prison in, 109; closure of reformatories in, 64; escapees from, 62–63; escapees from reformatories in, 63–64, 67; juvenile delinquency in, 111–12; juvenile reformatories in, 41, 42, 45, 46, 49, 55, 56–57, 61–64, 67, 183n35, 194n44; police records for, 195n58
Thiès penitentiary-school, 45, 46, 53, 56–57, 61–64, 67, 194n44
Thioub, Ibrahima, 22, 44, 63, 108, 110, 182–83n31, 182n25
Thomas, Lynn M., 10
Tivaouane, Senegal, 112–13, 195n58
Toucouleur education, 86
Touré, Abdoulaye, 114
Touré, Tasmir, 79
Toute, N'Dar, 38
trades, 30, 45
trafficking, 14, 15–16
training, 45–46, 48, 53, 56, 58, 59, 86. *See also* vocational training; community-based, 73; training schools, 131
Trawalé, Sokhna, 33
Trawaré, Sokhna, 37
trials, 149

United Nations Convention on the Rights of the Child of 1989, 159
urban schools, 74

vaccination certificates, 124–25, 129, 130, 132–34, 161–62
vaccinations, 3–4, 16, 129–38, 198–99n26, 198n18, 201n50; documentation of, 124–25, 133 (*see also* vaccination certificates); racism and, 126; resistance to, 132; for smallpox, 117–18, 120–26, 131, 133, 135, 199n27, 199n29, 199n35
vagabondage, 94, 96, 97, 107–11, 112, 114–15, 194n46, 195n53; criminalization of, 108; protection of orphans for prosecution for, 194–95n51
Vallier, Louis, 134
variolation, 120–21, 126, 196n5
Vernochet, Monsieur, 87
Vigier, Madame, 33
village schools, 73–74
vocational training, 58, 59, 73, 74
Voltaire, 25

Waalo, Senegal, 105
Wane, Souleyman, 86
Ware, Rudolph T., III, 102, 106, 192n25, 193n37
whites, 17
William Ponty Normal School, 6–7, 11, 74–75, 86, 106. *See also* Normal School
"William Ponty Notebooks," 6–7, 11, 193n37
Wolof, 2, 6–7, 80, 87, 102, 113–14
women religious, 73. *See also specific religious orders*
work, 66
work requirements, 48
World War I, 127
World War II, 17

yalwaan, 102
Yang Yang, Senegal, 122
Yène, Senegal, 64
Yoro, 24, 25
Yvorel, Jean-Jacques, 182n29

Zanettacci, Monsieur, 103
Ziguinchor, Senegal, 104, 148

www.ingramcontent.com/pod-product-compliance
Lightning Source LLC
Chambersburg PA
CBHW030649230426
43665CB00011B/1013